A Fire On the Mountains

A
FIRE
ON THE

Oakland Ross

MOUNTAINS

Exploring the
Human Spirit
from Mexico to
Madagascar

Alfred A. Knopf Canada

PUBLISHED BY ALFRED A. KNOPF CANADA

Copyright © 1995 by Oakland Ross

All rights reserved under International and
Pan-American Copyright Conventions. Published in
1995 by Alfred A. Knopf Canada, Toronto. Distributed
by Random House of Canada Limited, Toronto.

Canadian Cataloguing in Publication Data

Ross, Oakland
    A fire on the mountains

ISBN 0-394-28061-X

1. Ross, Oakland, 1952–   . - Journeys.
2. Voyages and travels. I. Title

G465.R67 1995   910.4   C95-931293-5

Text design: Gordon Robertson
Maps: Jeff Meek & Associates

First Edition
Printed and bound in the United States of America

For Kathleen and Robert

Acknowledgments

I was able to write this book mainly because Richard Doyle and Roy Megarry sent me to Latin America to work as the correspondent in the region for the Toronto Globe and Mail and because Norman Webster and Geoffrey Stevens later posted me to Africa as the Globe's correspondent there. I owe them a huge debt of thanks. I also want to thank a succession of Globe foreign editors. They include Don Manley, John Gray, Gene Allen, Paul Knox, and Ann Rauhala.

Both in Latin America and in Africa, many people gave me their companionship or counsel or both; more than a few of them appear in these pages, and I'm grateful to them all. I especially want to thank Alma Guillermoprieto, who introduced me to Central America, and Ruby Lum, who helped to make the days in Zimbabwe such a fresh and constant pleasure.

Back in Canada, Jan Whitford, my agent, was indispensable. This project started with her, and she stuck by me as I struggled to organize my scattered ideas for the book; I'm grateful for her support and friendship from beginning to end. I want to thank Louise Dennys at Knopf Canada for her trust, enthusiasm, and encouragement. Finally, in Diane Martin at Knopf, I found a finer and more thoughtful editor than I had imagined possible. She made the task of revision seem like a dance across the earth.

Much of this book grew out of reporting I originally did for the Globe and Mail. The chapters on Madagascar were adapted and expanded from an article that appeared in Destinations magazine. Parts of the chapter on AIDS in Africa were drawn from a research project I undertook in southern Africa in 1993 on behalf of the Canadian International Development Agency.

Death is just a stone, oblivious.
I love you. Upon your lips I kiss joy.
Let us gather kindling. Let us build a fire on
the mountains.

– Pablo Neruda

Contents

Prologue:
Day of
the Dead

"THERE'S A FUNERAL this morning!" A voice burst over the telephone line, clamouring in Mexican Spanish. It belonged to a new acquaintance of mine, a priest who worked in a slum area of Mexico City, out near the international airport. "Hurry! Come! Come right now!"

I jotted the details down and hung up the phone. It was a Saturday morning and I'd only just got out of bed. I wasn't feeling exactly my best — I would discover, a few days later, that I'd been hit by a hepatitus infection. Still, there was a funeral, and it was a funeral that I wanted. So I grabbed a notebook and headed out onto the Paseo de la Reforma to hail myself a cab.

It was October, 1983. I was based in Mexico City as the correspondent in Latin America for the Toronto *Globe and Mail*. I spent a lot of my life in airplanes in those days, flying from one Latin American capital to another, to cover stories of regional or even global significance: the civil war in El Salvador, the Sandinista revolution in Nicaragua, the Falklands/Malvinas war in Argentina, life in Fidel Castro's Cuba. I attended formal press conferences or closeted myself in interviews with politicians, military officers, diplomats, or other People of Importance. When I headed out into the countryside, it was not just to admire the view or to get a handle on the local culture. It was for Some Newsworthy Purpose — in most cases, to cover a war.

Now, here I was, riding in a taxi out to a nondescript church in a vast slum on the southeastern edge of Mexico City to attend the funeral of an anonymous young man who had died of natural causes following a long illness. I had decided that I wanted to write an article for my newspaper about the Mexican Day of the Dead, a festival — part-Christian, part-pagan — that is celebrated each year on November 2. I wanted to add some human colour to the piece, and I had hit on the idea of attending a funeral to see how ordinary Mexicans confronted the harsh fact of death. I'd borrowed the idea from Oscar Lewis, who wrote a riveting book on the same theme — *A Death in the Sanchez Family*. Anyway, I made some inquiries and was soon put in touch with a priest who worked in a poor *barrio* of the city.

When I first told the priest what I wanted, I was half afraid that he would promptly evict me from his parish as some sort of ghoul. But he didn't. In fact, he thought my idea was perfectly reasonable. What better way to spend a morning or afternoon than by attending the funeral of someone you didn't know? He wrote down my phone number and said he'd call me as soon as the right kind of funeral came along. I had told him I wanted a straight-forward death — a humble person of lowly social rank, no suspicion of foul play.

And he'd proved to be as good as his word. Name of deceased: Jesús Molina Corona. Age: thirty-two. Occupation:

auto mechanic. Cause of death: rheumatic fever, following a lengthy illness. The dead man was survived by his mother, his wife, a brother, a sister, and four children under the age of twelve.

My taxi pulled up in front of the Santiaguito church in Ixtapalapa, one of the sprawling *ciudades perdidas* — the lost cities — that surround the Mexican capital, some of them home to literally millions of impoverished residents. I paid the driver and headed inside, to attend the funeral of some- one I thought of as an obscure and ephemeral man — which, to me, he was. In the normal course of events, no foreign journalist would have shown up to write about this man's death. But what I discovered, before that day was over, was that Jesús Molina Corona was neither obscure nor ephemeral.

In those days, I had a tendency — common to North Americans of an upper-middle-class sensibility — to think of "poor people" largely in the abstract. A couple of years spent living and working in Latin America had moderated but not entirely overcome this habit of the mind. I still tended to see the poor as a faceless mass, a kind of undifferentiated back- drop to some significant event or other. They might briefly be drawn on stage, as victims of famine or war or an earth- quake. Then they'd be pushed back into the wings. They were people to whom terrible things sometimes happened but who barely existed in the interim, or at least not as fully realized individuals. For me, in a sense, the poor were less than real. But, in time, that impression changed.

I think back to that Saturday morning in October, 1983, and the funeral service for Jesús Molina Corona. I don't believe that poverty blurred the day or muffled its meaning for the people who filed out of the Santiaguito church in Ixtapalapa at the end of the funeral service. In silence, they boarded a pair of Bluebird buses — both painted a discreet grey — to be carried to the sprawling San Lorenzo cemetery for the burial. The dead man's mother and his widow were in tears, and yet they seemed the embodiment of dignity and grace. They agreed that I could come along and invited me to ride with them in the front of the leading bus. Even at this moment — maybe especially at this moment — they maintained their sense of decorum. Meanwhile, the coffin was pushed into the back of a wood-panelled Ford station wagon, and our convoy set off. The Ford led the way, with a huge floral wreath on its roof rack.

When we got to the cemetery, the buses had to pull over at the entrance so that we could wait our turn. It was a busy day for funerals. While we waited, young boys clambered aboard to sell fruit-flavoured ices to the mourners. The children began to cry. After half an hour or so, the drivers fired the buses up again and rumbled into the cemetery. We got to an area where about fifty fresh graves had been dug in a long row, each separated from its neighbours by earthen walls no more than half a metre wide.

Now it was time to wait some more — another burial was still in progress just ahead of us. The mourners of Jesús Molina Corona climbed out of the buses and milled about, the children still howling, while the gravediggers tried to lower someone else's coffin into the first grave in the new row — but the damn thing wouldn't fit. The workers set the casket down, got themselves some pickaxes and shovels, and set about widening the grave.

Finally, the work was done. The coffin was lowered into

the ground and covered over with earth. A smattering of mourners decorated the grave mound with powdered-milk tins filled with bunches of marigolds. This was all done without much ceremony. One of the women in our group remarked on how few people had come to the just completed burial, and how none of them was crying.

Now the interment of Jesús Molina Corona could begin. The workers eased his simple metal coffin into the ground, suspended on a pair of ropes. Immediately, the women began to wail. Ermalinda, the dead man's widow, stood by the grave with her head and shoulders hidden in a navy-blue blanket. She heaved low painful sobs, and several other mourners held her by the arms to keep her from falling down.

Meanwhile, Molina's mother staggered over to a pile of earth by the graveside and abruptly collapsed, unconscious. Several mourners hurried over to her aid. They fanned her with pieces of cardboard or tried to revive her by blowing cigarette smoke onto her face or by dabbing her lips with rubbing alcohol. The cardboard, the cigarettes, and the rubbing alcohol had clearly been brought along for just this purpose.

The burial continued. The workers soon yanked their ropes out from beneath the settled coffin, and the mourners tossed clumps of earth and bunches of flower petals into the grave. Others shook out bottles of holy water. The diggers spaded the earth back into place. Still unconscious, Molina's mother was carried off a little distance and laid down beside a young friend of her son who also had collapsed. Nearby, the dead man's sister stood weeping by herself, and the widow Ermalinda wandered away, farther into the vast and treeless cemetery, clutching a toddling daughter by the hand.

The friends and relatives of Jesús Molina Corona would remain like this — in deepest mourning — for nine more days. In Mexico, this period is called *la novena*. At a certain time each day, they would gather in the Molina home to pray. On the final day, a large mass would be celebrated in his honour, probably followed by a procession through the streets, led by someone bearing a Cross.

This drama in Ixtapalapa got me thinking, even as it was being played out. Where does this notion come from, this suspicion that those who are very poor are somehow less than fully realized in their humanity? Why do some people think this way? I have an idea. There's an intriguing term some psychologists use to describe a related phenomenon — "pseudo-speciation." It's what we do when we pretend, consciously or not, that certain members of our own species are actually something else, that they are really "lower" forms of life. You see this sort of thing in gangster movies all the time. The villain draws his pistol and aims it at his cowering victim. He spits out the crucial words, or something like them: "Now you're going to get it, you dirty rat."

That's the pivotal phrase — *you dirty rat*. Those are the words that release some mechanism in his mind and allow him to pull the trigger. It may be an awkward thing to shoot a man, but how much easier does it become if, in a part of your brain, you believe that this creature before you is not entirely a man, that he is also in some sense a verminous rodent with poor personal hygiene? I'm not sure — I've never done it — but I imagine it's no great chore to shoot a dirty rat. Armies at war with each other engage in the same kind of self-deception. They don't quite believe they are killing fellow humans. Instead, at some level, they truly believe they are exterminating lower animals of some particularly despicable kind.

I wonder if, in a greatly subdued fashion, we don't commit a similar kind of perceptual sin when we walk along the streets of our cities, in North America or Europe, and ignore the derelicts on the sidewalks. We may give them money, but we certainly don't make eye contact. And God forbid that we should *talk* to them, treat them as fellow human beings. Instead, we treat them as something a bit less than human — we *think* of them as less than human — and maybe that makes it just a little bit easier to accept their state. How else would you expect "animals" to live?

I spoke to a man in Guatemala once, a wealthy plantation owner, who was explaining to me why he opposed any effort to redistribute his country's land. (Guatemala had probably the most inequitable pattern of land distribution in all of Latin America.) This man had a lot of reasons to support his position, none of them very persuasive, but one of his ideas seemed especially provocative. He told me that a land-reform programme would entail the migration of peasants from their villages to areas some distance away, where land was available, and he assured me that such a thing would never work. Peasants, he told me, were *como perros*. Like dogs. If you tried to move them, they would always go right back to the places they considered home.

Like dogs — such a memorable phrase. And what is perhaps most memorable about it is this: I don't think the man was speaking metaphorically. In part, he may have been, but I think that in some important way he meant the phrase literally. Peasants were *literally* like dogs. In a way, they *were* dogs. They were not as complex as were wealthier, better educated people. Not as rational. Not as subtle. Up to a point, you could teach them tricks — to fetch and sit and roll over — but that was about it. I doubt that this man would have admitted to thinking such things (or at least not in the presence of a foreign newspaperman with an open notebook), but I'm sure I haven't got him far wrong.

I suspect that we all share some of the same limits that constrained this man's imagination. It's in our interests — our selfish interests — to be as unimaginative as we can manage to be. Injustice is far easier to accept and much easier to defend if it can be made to seem the natural order of things, if it can be entrenched in our minds. A rose is a rose is a rose, and the poor are poor because they're poor. If it's preordained, the will of God, then why worry? Why fret about things that can't be changed?

In 1987, after having spent almost five years in Latin America, I moved to Africa to work as a foreign correspondent there. In Africa, things were different than in Latin America, but they were also in many ways the same.

I got to know a man named Danny Meyer in Zimbabwe, where I lived. He'd come up from South Africa following Zimbabwean independence in 1980 because he wanted to make a go as a white liberal in a black country — something that wasn't really possible in his country at the time. He launched a medical-supply company and, in only a few years, he'd built it into the largest such firm in Zimbabwe. Most of his managers were black — a rare thing in Zimbabwe — and almost all of his management trainees were also black. Meyer was as close to making a success of white liberalism as any man or woman I've encountered.

Meyer told me that racism in his view is fundamentally a

problem of imagination, a *lack* of imagination. To understand a man whose life is different from yours — to understand how he thinks and why he acts as he does — you have to try to imagine yourself *in his place*. Of course, that takes a lot of time and trouble, not to mention a considerable degree of curiosity. And not everybody has that much interest or is willing to take the time or the trouble. It's much easier to interpret others by your own lights, rather than by trying to understand theirs.

Even before I met Danny Meyer in Zimbabwe, I'd managed to stumble to a similar conclusion on my own, although I'd never articulated it quite as clearly as he did. I'd already decided that I wanted to avoid this trap, this tendency to present people who are different from myself — and especially poor people — as some kind of colourful but not entirely human collective, as people who are exotic perhaps, picturesque maybe, but certainly *not like me*. To the extent that I could manage it, I wanted to write about people as though we were members of the same species. Because we are. This may not seem like a revolutionary ambition, but neither is it the invariable norm of Western journalism.

This is what I have tried to do, both while I lived in Latin America and later in Africa and now in this book. Not all the people who will show up in these pages are poor, although the great majority of them certainly are, poverty being by a considerable margin the prevailing economic circumstance in the world. Still, there are exceptions. A Mexico City police chief will show up, for example, and he was anything but poor. At least one national president will make an appearance. A prosperous businessman or two. Even a small white elite in an African country. But I have tried to apply the same approach in all cases — to write about people *as* people, as characters in the foreground, and not as a backdrop to events.

For nearly a decade I lived abroad and was able to travel almost constantly to places that were very far away from the country where I was born and raised. It so happened that I turned up in Latin America at an extraordinary time. It was 1981, and there was a revolutionary government in Nicaragua; soon there would be a war. There was already a war in El Salvador, another in Guatemala. Argentina would shortly do battle with Britain over the Falkland, or Malvinas, Islands. A particularly eerie insurgency — the *Sendero Luminoso* — was emerging in Peru. The United States would invade Grenada. Ordinary Chileans would rise up against the dictatorship of General Augusto Pinochet. And the economies of most of the major countries of the region would just about collapse, producing what we now refer to as the Latin American debt crisis of the 1980s.

Those years kept me busy. But, more than that, they kept my heart racing in a way that I had never known before. Whatever stout Cortés may have felt (I know, I know: it was really Balboa), silent upon a peak in Darién, was what I seemed to feel nearly all the time. I lived a life of almost constant revelation and epiphany. I went out for a run most afternoons in whatever country I happened to be, and not only because I wanted the exercise. I jogged through the streets of San Salvador during much of the war — in this, I was by no means alone — and I did it mainly in order to deal with the overwhelming excitement I was feeling. I was like a jet airplane in those days, always having to burn off extra fuel before attempting another emergency landing.

I suppose that all people are suspended in a more or less uneasy balance between the forces of gravity and centrifuge, between home and horizon. It so happened, in those days, that I barely had a home and so felt little of that gravitational weight, that pressure to return. I was without an orbit, in a kind of free flight. And maybe that freedom, that voluntary homelessness, made it easier for me than it might be for others to work at imagining myself into realities that were very different from my own, to think of the people I met as being something more than bit players in someone else's play.

Whatever the reason, that afternoon in October, 1983, on the outskirts of Mexico City when I attended the funeral of Jesús Molina Corona, it was certainly clear to me that his mourners were far more than walk-on characters in a drama that was not their own. They were the central players here. This was their show. And I realized that my desire to write about them did not depend on their lives being "newsworthy" in the traditional sense, the sense of their being caught up in a drama that was somehow Larger Than Their Own.

As far as I could tell, the mourners of Jesús Molina Corona were important to no one but themselves. They were the cast, the crew, and the audience; this story was their own; and that was precisely what made it seem important to me. This was a lesson I was to learn and forget and then learn again, over and over, during a decade on the road in Latin America and Africa: just *tell the stories* and let the news take care of itself.

Eventually, on that October afternoon, the time came to leave the San Lorenzo cemetery. Everyone climbed back into the buses, to be borne back toward San Pedro Ixtacalco, an utterly wretched slum tucked out of the way not far from Mexico City's international airport. It had no running water and no drainage system. Local residents pirated their electricity by running makeshift cables from power lines located out along a main road.

On this occasion, the journey back to San Pedro took a little extra time because Molina's mother collapsed again along the way. The buses had to stop so that she could be dragged out onto the grass by the roadside. The women huddled around her once more, blowing cigarette smoke into her face and calling out for additional supplies of rubbing alcohol.

When we got to San Pedro, the mourners piled out of the vehicles and headed into the community on foot. They were all bound for the Molina home, to share the meal that traditionally follows a burial in Mexico. The house turned out to be a three-room shanty built of scrap wood with a tar-paper roof. Inside, the walls were covered with commercial wrapping paper. The structure and its neighbouring dwellings were separated from each other by a network of dirt walkways, each no more than a metre wide. Molina had lived here in this house for years, with his mother, his brother and sister, his wife, and their four children.

The women promptly busied themselves in the kitchen, preparing lemonade and putting the last touches on a lunch of boiled rice and *nopalitos* — bits of prickly-pear cactus in a green chile sauce. Meanwhile, the men lounged outside the house, smoking and talking in low voices. Death among these people was very much a communal affair. For example, the funeral that day had cost thirty-thousand pesos, or about two-hundred dollars, money that had been raised through donations from neighbouring slum-dwellers. This was the customary thing in such cases, for no family could afford to pay for a funeral on its own.

Already, the grieving had been going on for two days. During that time, Molina's body had been laid out in the family house, in a room that adjoined the kitchen. A makeshift altar still stood against one wall. On the dirt floor, there was a bowl of onions and vinegar, intended to absorb noxious fumes. Beside it, several mounds of white powder had been fashioned into the shape of the Cross.

As the women worked in the kitchen, Molina's sister remained by herself here in the room where her brother had been laid out. She was hunched in a chair, silent, and she stared without a break at the rough Cross on the floor. She did not look up, even as the women in the kitchen began to serve the midday meal and the men trooped in to eat.

1

EL SALVADOR

Johnnie
Walker,
Red Label

I MET José (Pepe) Dutríz because I talked to the person
seated next to me on an airplane. It was a good way to
meet people — sometimes quite surprising people —
and at least a few such encounters had resulted in articles for
my newspaper somewhere down the line. But I didn't sit
beside Pepe Dutríz on an airplane. I sat beside his wife.

It was the early 1980s, and I was on a flight from Mexico
City, where I was living at the time, down to El Salvador, a
country at war. It was a TACA flight — Transportes Aéreas
Centroamericanas, the Salvadoran airline. My seat-mate for
the trip was an animated woman with short brown hair done
up in a pert style. She caught my attention at once. She was
certainly pretty and proved to be highly articulate and intelligent as well. She had the air of a prosperous and sophisticated young housewife, dressed for a downtown shopping
spree. She wore a cream-coloured blouse and a dark, practical skirt. And she was a *gringa* — an American. She said she
was from California.

I was surprised; we were flying, after all, to El Salvador,
where ten thousand people died each year in fighting between

government forces and leftist rebels. There was a nightly curfew in the cities. After it fell, death squads roamed the streets at will. In the darkness, you heard gunshots, bomb blasts. Even by day, life in the capital wasn't exactly a stroll across the plaza. Government officials might be gunned down in their cars at any moment. Soldiers rumbled past in jeeps, trucks, or armour-plated *tanquetes*. Without warning, the power might suddenly go off — the rebels blowing up another pylon north of the capital.

East of the city, it got worse. It was a chancy business to drive any distance at all: the phone lines were down; most of the bridges were bombed; there were rebel roadblocks or army roadblocks; and the cicadas sang with an eerie, sinister roar. All in all, El Salvador was a twitchy country to live in or travel through in the 1980s. You didn't find a lot of foreigners going there, apart from diplomats and journalists — and this bright, chatty young woman from California didn't seem to be either of those. Yet here she was, jetting down to San Salvador from Mexico City, looking as if she were dressed for shopping in Manhattan or for a ladies' luncheon at the country club in New Jersey.

I asked her why.

"Because," she said, "I live in San Salvador." It was her home. She was the wife of José (Pepe) Dutríz.

I knew the name. Pepe Dutríz was the owner of *La Prensa Gráfica*, among other things. It was one of a pair of morning newspapers in the Salvadoran capital and was, if anything, the more conservative and reactionary of the two, its contents a jumble of anti-Communist screeds, effete society notes, and a dash of fairly straightforward but very selective foreign news. Plus, blanket coverage of beauty contests, of which there were a seemingly endless number in war-time El Salvador. In essence, *La Prensa* was the house organ of the Salvadoran oligarchy, or *Las Catorce* as they were known, the fabled Fourteen Families who ruled the country in league with the army.

Well, this was a stroke of luck, I thought — to find myself seated on an airplane beside the wife of the owner of *La Prensa Gráfica*. After all, it was not an easy thing to get on close terms with rich Salvadorans in those days. They were aloof, obsessed with security, and they didn't trust the press — the *foreign* press. The insularity of the Salvadoran elite had long been a frustration for me. The other players in the Salvadoran drama — the soldiers, rebels, peasants, and politicians — these were all people you could seek out and get to know. But the oligarchs who resided at the top were a much trickier proposition.

They lived in San Benito or Escalón, the posh residential districts of the capital, behind high walls of reinforced concrete topped by rolls of concertina wire. Private guards armed with submachine guns or automatic rifles patrolled the entrances to their houses, where the dark steel gates rolled back only by electronic command, and where video cameras monitored every movement on the streets outside. Even when they did venture beyond those forbidding walls, the Salvadoran rich travelled in bulletproof Jeep Wagoneers or Cherokee Chiefs with polarized windows.

It was a difficult thing to get to know wealthy Salvadorans. Still, sometimes you got lucky. You found yourself seated beside the wife of Pepe Dutríz on an airplane.

As our TACA flight winged south above the clouds over Mexico, we chatted about one thing and another until she mentioned, more or less in passing, that it would be a good thing if Pepe and I got together. Her husband was of the opinion that all foreign journalists were closet Communists bent on the dismemberment of his country. This didn't seem to be the case with me, she remarked. It would do Pepe good to talk to a foreign journalist. She said she would arrange it.

Several days later, I was standing beneath the flame trees, by the small circular drive at the entrance to the Hotel Camino Real, where most of the foreign press stayed in San Salvador. At one o'clock sharp, a Jeep Wagoneer swung off the Boulevard los Héroes and pulled up in front of the hotel, with José (Pepe) Dutríz seated in the back. He struggled out through the passenger door — a slim elderly gentleman in a lightweight tweed jacket and brown slacks. He had sleek white hair, a somewhat nasal voice, and a patrician's bearing. He was certainly a lot older than his wife.

We shook hands and exchanged greetings. Then Pepe Dutríz took a second look at me; he shook his head — it turned out that I wasn't dressed for the occasion. I looked down at myself. I thought I'd done okay. I'd ditched the standard blue jeans for a pair of dark cotton slacks, and I'd put on one of my new Mexican *guayaberas* (those loose, slightly frilly dress shirts that make a gathering of Latin American men look like a convention of sun-worshipping dentists). I thought I looked just fine.

But Dutríz took a different view. "*Hay que vestirse en chaqueta y corbata,*" he declared.

I took a breath — jackets and ties were not exactly standard fare among the Salvadoran press corps. Not even the president of El Salvador, His Excellency Alvaro Magaña, had managed to change that. One of a succession of war-time

Salvadoran leaders, Magaña had once attempted to impose his sartorial will on foreign journalists. He had dictated that henceforth there was to be a dress code in effect for all his press conferences. Jackets and ties to be worn by all men, and correspondingly proper garb for women.

"*Sí, su excelencia,*" his aides said. And a proclamation was issued forthwith. But not even a Latin American ruler, with the full backing of the army, could make a bunch of North American journalists look respectable. The code was completely ignored, and reporters and photographers went right on wearing what they had always worn — blue jeans and polo shirts. So what was I to do now? Wear a jacket and tie? In El Salvador, I didn't *have* a jacket and tie.

Nonetheless, I hurried back into the hotel and rode the elevator up to the second floor, where the international wire agencies had their offices. The Associated Press reporter was a friend of mine, and I thought he might be the sort of fellow who would have a jacket lurking somewhere in the depths of his closet. Plus, he was about my size. It turned out that I was right — a jacket *and* a tie. I carried them to my room, changed my clothes, descended to the lobby, brushed a trace of lint from my lapel, and strode out to the hotel entrance, where the sunlight dazzled and where the trials of Pepe Dutríz were only beginning.

Because the Wagoneer was just a two-door model, Dutríz and I both had to clamber into the back by climbing over the front seat. He kept grunting and huffing in irritation. I could tell what he was thinking — this was all so undignified. I thought, why don't we just ride in the front with the driver? But that was sure to be out. I didn't bother to suggest it.

When we were both more or less settled in the back, Dutríz gave instructions to the driver that we be borne to the Club Deportivo — the Sports Club. He snorted into his handkerchief, cleared his throat, and apologised at length for this appalling inconvenience, this infernal business of climbing over seats. He couldn't seem to get it out of his mind. He shook his head and then explained that there was a problem with his other four-wheel-drive vehicle, a four-door, armour-plated Cherokee Chief. It was down for repairs. And then, of course, his wife was out shopping in the Mercedes. The Mercedes, he noted, was also bulletproof.

All these trials had combined to put Dutríz severely out of temper. Still, there was nothing for it but to drive off in our humiliating two-door vehicle. We made our way through the twisting streets of San Salvador, bound for the Club Deportivo. We rolled passed the commercial jetsam of the city — the billboards for Marlboro cigarettes, the American-style fast-food outlets, and the shabby little rumshops and *pupuserías*. Cars blared and rattled past, even the traffic police carried automatic rifles, and the sidewalks swelled with vast legions of people in substandard footwear. You could never really forget that El Salvador was the most densely populated country on the mainland of the Americas, or that most of its people lacked for proper shoes. Overhead, the huge green volcano, el Boquerón, seemed to carry on its shoulders the sheer blue sky, and the spring-like sun poured down its endless gallons of light.

We reached the Sports Club, disengaged ourselves from our vehicle, and strolled inside. Once ensconced within the air-conditioned confines of the club's dining room, with its lime-green tablecloths and its astonishingly orange chairs, we decided to order a drink before our meal. Dutríz summoned the waiter. "What kind of scotch do you have?" he asked.

"Johnnie Walker," replied the waiter.

Dutríz nodded encouragingly, as if he expected the waiter to continue, but the poor man had apparently run the list of scotches right down to the ground. Dutríz frowned. "Johnnie *Walker* . . . ?" he repeated, as if he hadn't heard this right, or couldn't quite believe it, or there was some other brand of scotch that began with the word "Johnnie".

The waiter nodded.

Dutríz cocked one of his eyebrows, and his gaze betrayed a glint of hope. "Johnnie Walker, *Black* Label . . . ?" he said.

"No." The waiter shook his head. "Only Red Label."

"*Red* Label . . . ?"

The waiter nodded again.

"Oh." Dutríz glowered for several moments. He seemed engaged in a dreadful internal debate. "Oh, all right," he said at last. "Red Label then." He flicked his hand at the waiter. "*En las rocas.*"

I asked for a beer. Silently, the waiter withdrew.

We said little as we waited for our drinks. I gazed out the picture window at the flashing turquoise waters of an Olympic-size swimming pool, deserted now. I still had high hopes for the lunch. I was hoping that Pepe Dutríz might give me some new perspective on the horror of his country, another layer of insight, some glimmer of understanding. After all, for better or for worse, his was the class that had made the place what it was. Would he not have something interesting to say?

As it turned out, Dutríz did not really have a great deal to offer, certainly not in the way of complex social analysis. It seemed that he was not a highly reflective individual nor even very curious. He merely repeated the most predictable and familiar nostrums of his class. If the people were hungry, they should get off their duffs and find a job. If they were Communists, they should be killed. Before long, I put away my notebook and concentrated on lunch. As a sociological phenomenon, I still found the Salvadoran rich intensely interesting, but on an individual basis I was prepared to allow that there might be an exception or two.

On the other hand, José (Pepe) Dutríz did make one memorable comment that day, and it has remained in my mind ever since — just a few words, but they were worth the entire afternoon. We were still waiting for our drinks, and I'd been musing to myself about the uncomfortable irony of our position, his and mine. Here we were, in a country caught in the vice-grip of war. Tens of thousands of people had already been killed, most of them poor, most of them murdered or massacred, their bodies dumped by the dozen along the sides of roads, or scattered on the barren lava at a place not far from the capital called El Playón, or washed up on the shores of the Río Lempa out in the eastern rebel country.

The economy was a shambles. Hundreds of thousands of the rural poor scraped along living marginal lives, deprived of land or anything in the way of work, save back-breaking day labour for dirt wages in the coastal cane fields or on the coffee plantations of the highlands. Slums burgeoned on the edges of the cities or spilled through the garbage-strewn ravines. Already, countless peasants had fled the fighting, to crowd into refugee settlements across the border in Honduras.

Others now dwelt in camps for displaced people within El Salvador itself, where they were confined like prisoners, surrounded by tall wire fences.

And here we were, in this calm and pleasant room — albeit a room dotted with chairs that were a bit too orange for my taste — wearing jackets and ties and waiting for our drinks before lunch, and when lunch was done we would again be subjected to the ignominy of climbing over the front seats and into the back of our two-door, armourplated Jeep Wagoneer for the return trip to the Camino Real.

El Salvador, I was thinking: Land of Contrasts.

Then our drinks arrived and the waiter shuffled away. For some time José (Pepe) Dutríz simply glared at his glass. He ground his teeth, shook his tidy grey head, said not a word. He was brooding about this galling turn of events — the whisky before him was Red Label, a plebian bar scotch, rather than Black Label, the premium brand. At last, he took a gulp, swallowed, and scowled. He crunched down on a cube of ice and set his drink back on the table. He grimaced at me. "You *see* . . . ?" he said. He waved at his glass. "You *see* what's happening to this country?"

Massacre at
Palo Blanco

T HERE WAS A TIME IN MY LIFE when I did not
believe in the existence of evil. I thought it was a
hocus-pocus word. I believed that what people
called evil was really something else, something far less
gothic. People weren't evil, I thought. They just made mis-
takes. Or they were incompetent. They had misunderstand-
ings. They got drunk. They became over-excited. Maybe
they went temporarily insane. But evil as a thing in itself? I
didn't believe in it. It was too romantic-sounding, a fairy-
tale word. That was what I thought then.

I was the product of privileged circumstances in central
Canada, an exceptionally peaceful corner of this unruly
world. My early life had been a sort of North American idyll
— Pony Club meetings on Saturdays and riding lessons at
the Hunt Club on Sundays (from Buck Ishoy, the dashing,
bull-chested Dane). My summers were a swirl of horse
shows and tennis matches. There'd be fox-hunting in the
fall, skiing every weekend in winter, and annual pilgrimages
to Antigua or St. Lucia in the early spring, with my mother
and father and innumerable sisters. I'd been extremely
lucky in my choice of places to be born and in my selection of parents to bear me. I certainly hadn't encountered

much, if anything, in the way of evil during my early life.

That would change in El Salvador, where I soon learned that evil was not simply a menacing word, any more than cancer is just a concept, or good is only a whim. It was real, and it had come to a place called Palo Blanco.

Palo Blanco at the time consisted of a smattering of mud-brick houses covered with thatched grass or smoky clay tiles. The village crouched in the broad shade of a grove of *amate* trees, all folded into the pleated hills that rose above the northeastern edge of Lake Ilopango, an hour's drive east of the capital. It would be hard to imagine a more idyllic setting for a massacre.

A series of loamy terraces scaled the nearby slopes, strewn in mid-March with the yellowed hulls of corn stalks that rattled in the shrivelling breeze. The expanse of Lake Ilopango unfurled to the west far below, a royal-blue banner spread across the crater of an old and now dormant volcano. To the south, almost directly beneath the village, a fine sandy delta swam out into the lake, fringed by palm groves. Goats bleated in the distance, and the sun sang down.

You wouldn't think that terrible things could happen here, but such were the ironies of evil and of war that they most certainly did. Eighteen people perished in Palo Blanco one night late in the Salvadoran dry season. Five of them were women. Eleven of them were children. One of the children was just two years old. All but one of the women had been raped repeatedly before being killed, as had three of the children — two girls aged twelve, and another girl, Rufina Hernández, aged fourteen.

Eighteen people. It was a small affair, by Salvadoran standards in those grim days. But the massacre at Palo Blanco had several remarkable aspects that distinguished it from run-of-the-mill Salvadoran atrocities. And that was why we — two other foreign reporters and I — spent a lot of time out there in that quiet hamlet, turning over stones, both real and figurative, to see what lay beneath.

Two weeks after the killings, it was already difficult to imagine the events of that night — they seemed so out of place. The trip to Palo Blanco from the capital was a gorgeous drive. The Pan-American Highway threaded its way along a serpentine route of hilltops and ridges, the dry-season terrain unfolding on all sides — the baking cornfields, the sinewy hills. The roadsides burst with sprays of purple and orange bougainvillea, and the constant jumble of Central American rural life tumbled past: choking country buses; rickety market stalls crowded in the shade of *ceiba* trees; hordes of goats and chickens; flocks of school children.

I made that drive many times in the wake of the Palo Blanco killings. The three of us had stumbled onto the fact of this massacre, and now we were tracking down the details. We chain-smoked Marlboros, talked Salvadoran politics, and shared the latest gallows humour — a way to soothe rattled nerves among the Central American press corps. We drove fast and carelessly, the way you do in a rented car in a subtropical country bristling with guns. We had imbibed that strange sweaty recklessness, one of the many contagions of war. But we were reckless for just so long. As we drew closer to the vicinity of Palo Blanco, we would grow wary and less talkative. Whoever was driving would take more care. There'd be a firmer grip on the wheel, a lighter touch on the gas. I don't know if people have a sixth sense about death. I do know we had an acute sense of fear.

Eventually, we skirted north, above the broad blue flag of Lake Ilopango, and soon we wound up near the market town of Cojutepeque in the province of Cuscatlán. From there, it was a short detour off the Pan-American Highway, along a series of rutted tracks that led to Palo Blanco itself. And that would be a careful drive. As we edged past them, local people eyed us suspiciously, or we thought they did. We had begun to feel afraid, all three of us had, and that was odd. What did we think — that these people could be killers, too? It seems crazy, but it was so. Almost anyone could be a killer now. And we were strangers here.

I never met Rosa Amalia Beltrán Ulloa or the seventeen others who died with her one night in March at the height of the Salvadoran war, but I got to know some of the texture of their lives. I walked through Palo Blanco, climbed the surrounding hills, inspected the break in the stream where she and the others were killed. And I met the men responsible for the killing — sad-faced, unremarkable men for the most part, men evidently bewildered by what they'd done. If evil was a kind of virus, it had worked its way through their systems by the the time I spoke to them. They bore no special insignia upon their faces, no marks of Cain. They had no demonic glint in their eyes. You'd pass them on a country road without a second thought. Poor farmers, mainly. Simple folk. Husbands and fathers. Nothing out of the ordinary at all.

And yet they'd raped a bunch of little girls, not to mention the girls' mothers, hacked them all to death, and dumped them in a shallow grave.

When I spoke to these men, they knew what they had done, but they couldn't explain it. They couldn't understand it themselves. It seemed that there was this thing called evil, and it had come over them. Besides, they were poor; in the war between the rich and the poor, it was the poor who did the killing, and the poor who died. Of course, in Palo Blanco, there weren't a lot of class distinctions. In Palo Blanco, everybody was poor.

When we first got to the village, some days had passed since the massacre, and the only conspicuous evidence of the killings was the pervasive silence of the place. Already, Palo Blanco was on its way to becoming a ghost town. About half of the twenty families that once lived here had fled, fearing reprisals in the wake of what they called *el caso grave*. The serious case. An old man in a faded brown coat led the three of us down along a trail to the *quebrada* — the break in the stream — where the killings had occurred and where the bodies had later been buried in the soft, sandy earth. Gazing around in the vivid light of a late morning in March, you'd never think that this was that kind of place, a place where people had been put to death. But so it was.

In El Salvador, in war-time, this was not an unusual geographic feature. Similar atrocities were committed with dulling frequency, week after week, year after year. If you marked all such locations on a map of the country, you'd have produced a pointilist's portrait of hell — and most of these horrors never even got reported or investigated. Most of them never have been uncovered and probably never will be. And so, you might wonder: what was so dramatic or significant about the killings in Palo Blanco?

As I say, it certainly wasn't the scale of the thing; yet the massacre in Palo Blanco was unusual, even by the standards of El Salvador, a country where the wholesale murder of peasants had long constituted — how shall I put it? — the

Instrument of First Resort in the Resolution of Class Conflict. That may sound monstrous, and it was, but they weren't entirely mindless, these massacres. They had a crude intelligence to them, a kind of Cro-Magnon acuity. Whatever else they did or didn't do, they tended to exert a dampening influence on peasant support for the leftist rebels. For many people, that was justification enough. It was the logic of the war.

Palo Blanco, however, was not in a region where the rebels were strong — there was not a single guerrilla camp in the entire province of Cuscatlán. This was a part of El Salvador that had long been insulated from the main effects of the war. Besides, neither the police nor the army were involved in the killings at Palo Blanco, or not directly. Instead, the men who committed the killings were all local residents, a bunch of strutting, small-time bullies and goofs, members of a variety of slapdash, part-time counter-insurgency organizations — outfits that would have been a joke if only they didn't have access to guns. Or if only this hadn't been El Salvador. But they did. And this was.

I can think of at least one other factor that distinguished the killings at Palo Blanco from the normal run of Salvadoran carnage. It was this: the men responsible for the massacre at Palo Blanco made a stupid, almost unbelievable blunder. They killed the *wrong* people. Of all the thousands of Salvadorans they could have chosen to slaughter on that grim March night, they managed to make just about the worst choice possible. They killed eighteen innocent people — well, nothing unusual about that — but one of these innocents just happened to be a police officer's wife.

That was bad enough, but there was more. Another of

the victims was the police officer's sister. Three more were the same police officer's brothers. And even that wasn't all. A few nights earlier, there'd been an initial round of killings that had done away with this unfortunate police officer's brother-in-law, along with two of his nephews. Were these killers crazy? No — just stupid. Or unlucky. And in a police state it doesn't get much more stupid or more unlucky than this. Of course, the killers didn't know about these connections at the time of the killings, which meant — in El Salvador — that they didn't know anything at all.

The massacre at Palo Blanco took place at about ten p.m. on the night of March 4, 1982, less than three years into the war (with ten more years to go). But the events leading up to the killings actually began at least a couple of weeks earlier and about twenty kilometres away, in the village of San Pedro Segundo, near the town of San Martín. Here, the war was not so distant a reality. *Enfrentamientos*, or firefights, commonly occurred around San Pedro Segundo, between leftist rebels and government forces.

After a recent outbreak of fighting, a group of residents — almost all of them related to one another — decided they'd had enough. They left San Pedro Segundo and fled south. Eventually, they found themselves in Palo Blanco, where there was an abandoned house they thought they could fix up and live in for a time. This small party included a twenty-one-year-old woman named Rosa Amalia Beltrán Ulloa, as well as her two young sons, her infant daughter, and her husband, whose name was Antonio Montano Martínez. Also among the group was María Esperanza Alas, seventeen. She was the common-law wife of Rosa Amalia's brother. They came down to Palo Blanco because they wanted to find some peace.

But this was El Salvador. The group's arrival from San Pedro Segundo soon aroused suspicion among some of their new neighbours. And suspicion was not a thing you wanted to be tainted with, not in this country at this time, not even in a quiet pastoral community like Palo Blanco. There was a crude paramilitary presence even here — the local *patrulla cantonal*, a ragtag and bobtail outfit composed of several village men who were supposed to keep their eyes peeled for evidence of sedition, do a little foot-patrolling on the side, and think of themselves as bigshots. After all, did they not have access to guns?

In Palo Blanco, they did. In Palo Blanco, the local *patrulla cantonal* was led by a man named Emilio Rivas, a diligent fellow. He felt there was a prima facie case that these new arrivals, these strangers, were rebel sympathizers. You only had to look at the facts. They had fled from San Pedro Segundo, where there were occasional outbreaks of fighting between guerrillas and the army. So there you were. Case closed. This, too, was the logic of the war.

Rivas made his suspicions known to his superiors, and matters proceeded quickly. Acting on orders from the Treasury Police detachment in San Pedro Perulapán, a town about twenty-five kilometres to the north, he got together a few of his men. They picked up four of the new arrivals. The captives included Antonio Montano Martínez — the husband of Rosa Amalia — as well as the couple's two young sons and her husband's brother. Rivas had been told to conduct an interrogation, which, in El Salvador, was a euphemism for something rather different. In any case, the mission was accomplished quickly. Rivas and his men shot and killed their prisoners with twenty-two-calibre rifles.

They tied rocks to the feet of the two dead men and the two dead boys and rowed them out onto Lake Ilopango. They then dumped the bodies overboard in the deepest part of the lake. That was on February 27.

The following day, Rivas reported on the mission to another paramilitary officer, a certain Moises Montenegro Bolaños, forty-six, who was commander of the *escolta militar* in San Agustín, a village near Palo Blanco. The *escolta militar* was another element in the rural network of right-wing paramilitary forces. It was composed of discharged soldiers now on reserve. Like the *patrulla cantonal*, it operated under the aegis of El Salvador's ministry of defence and was part of the government's front-line arsenal against social unrest in rural areas. It sounds elaborate and sophisticated, but it wasn't. These were not precisely organized outfits, charged with discipline. These were gangs of weak-willed men led by a few local thugs.

But they had guns, or they knew how to get them, and that was important. Imagine what access to guns must have meant. Imagine the life of a poor farmer in El Salvador. He doesn't control his circumstances or his prospects. He is subject to the whims of the weather: if it rains, he will eat; if not, he will go hungry. He has not enough land and will never have more. When he goes into town to sell what little he can, the townspeople look down on him because he is so poor.

And then, one fine day, someone comes to him and gives him a gun. The weapon seems to tremble in his hands. Suddenly, he feels a sensation of power — different from any he has known before. It is like a drug, this feeling. It makes his head spin. It makes him ponder things he has never dared to imagine, has never been capable of imagining. And, in Palo Blanco, or near Palo Blanco, there were guns.

Following the first round of killing, Rivas made his report to Montenegro. He said it was certain the two dead men and two dead boys had been subversives. And he had more news. This business in Palo Blanco, he said, was not over yet. Some women and some other children had also come to the village, along with the four males who'd already been dealt with.

Rivas told Montenegro that these women had to be subversives, too. It was only logical. You just had to look at the facts. Rumours were going around that they had washed clothes and prepared food for revolutionary elements up around San Pedro Segundo. Besides, Rivas said, he'd heard that there was a priest living over in San Martín who was suspected of having ties to the guerrillas. In Rivas's mind, this somehow constituted yet more evidence against the women.

But Montenegro opted for caution. Rather than swing into action at once, he first took the matter up with his superior at the Treasury Police in San Pedro Perulapán. That officer recommended that the women be "investigated." This was another euphemism, apparently. It was now the morning of March 4.

By this time, Rosa Amalia Beltrán Ulloa had already fled Palo Blanco. Following the disappearance of her husband and two sons, she'd done exactly what any sensible person would do. She got the hell out of there. She went to stay with her mother in Soyapango, a community on the eastern outskirts of San Salvador. And that was where she should have stayed for good. She should never have returned to Palo Blanco.

Nevertheless, on March 3, Rosa Amalia made the journey back to the lovely village overlooking Lake Ilopango.
She was accompanied by eight other people, including her
sister-in-law, María Esperanza Alas, and four of her brothers
— José Alberto, José Julio, José Hector, and José Jesús
Beltrán Ulloa. She left her infant daughter with her mother
in Soyapango. The group planned to pack up Rosa Amalia's
possessions and to transport them back to her mother's. She
had decided to leave Palo Blanco for keeps, owing to the
disappearance of her husband and sons. This was obviously a
good decision, but her timing was poor.

The job of packing up Rosa Amalia's household belongings took longer than expected, so the party was forced to
stay in Palo Blanco overnight. Everyone spent the next
morning — the morning of March 4 — carrying Rosa
Amalia's things down from the house to pile them under a
large *amate* tree that stood on a path overlooking Lake
Ilopango. That done, Rosa Amalia and her sister-in-law,
María Esperanza, set off on foot towards a neighbouring
hamlet called San Agustín. They were looking for Nicolás
Montenegro, the owner of a pickup truck. They wanted to
arrange for him to drive the group and Rosa Amalia's
belongings to Soyapango.

Meanwhile, at about noon that day, a local peasant named
José Arturo Zavala Amaya was walking home from the fields
to his house in Buena Vista, another village not far from Palo
Blanco. Zavala was thirty-five years old, a peasant farmer
who hired himself out as an agricultural labourer for the
equivalent of $2.25 a day. During his walk, he encountered
several men under the command of Moises Montenegro.
Montenegro told Zavala there was a group of suspected

subversives in Palo Blanco, three kilometres away, preparing to leave the area. Montenegro said the group must be guarded and compelled to remain. Zavala protested that he knew some of these people. "They are not subversives," he insisted.

It was the wrong thing to say. Montenegro told Zavala he could wind up dead himself if he didn't watch his step or if he disobeyed orders. So Zavala got several of his friends together. Armed with machetes, they set off for Palo Blanco. Meanwhile, Montenegro and his men continued down the lakeside trail to San Agustín, in order to retrieve their firearms — a modest arsenal of twenty-two-calibre rifles, twelve-gauge shotguns, and bolt-action Czech rifles. On their way, they were overtaken by a pickup truck driven by Montenegro's brother, Nicolás.

And here was a coincidence — two of the suspected subversives were already riding in the back! These were the two women, Rosa Amalia and María Esperanza, who had headed off that morning in search of transport. The driver whom they had hired happened also to be the brother of the very man who at that moment was plotting their execution. It's a small world — and never any smaller, it seems, than on the day you are destined to die. When he saw Nicolás's truck, Moises Montenegro flagged the vehicle down and spoke to his brother briefly in a low voice. The two women in the back couldn't make out what was being said. Eventually Nicolás nodded, put the vehicle back in gear, and continued along the rough dirt track that led up to Palo Blanco. It was now a little after one p.m.

Back in Palo Blanco, Rosa Amalia's four brothers — one of them just a youngster — had carried the rest of her belongings down to the *amate* tree and were waiting in the shade. They began to worry. What was taking the two women so long? Twice during this period, the brothers were approached by a group of strangers, all carrying machetes — Zavala and his crew. Both times, the strangers withdrew without saying a word. Finally, at about one-thirty, the pickup truck arrived. The two women reported that they'd been stopped along the way by a group of men — evidently Moises Montenegro and his underlings.

It was now that things began to go seriously wrong. Nicolás Montenegro suddenly began to seem oddly evasive about making the planned trip to Soyapango. He kept finding reasons for delay. Finally, at about two p.m., the three older Beltrán Ulloa brothers lost patience with the driver and his endless excuses. This was ridiculous. What the hell was going on? They decided to leave their sister's possessions in a pile and go off on foot in search of someone else with a truck who would carry them to Soyapango without all this pointless delay. So they set out in the direction of San Agustín.

Before they got far, the three brothers ran into that same group of men — the ones with the machetes — who ordered them to turn around and go right back to Palo Blanco. They had no choice but to comply. An hour later, seven more men arrived. They were armed, and they were under the command of Moises Montenegro. The armed men proceeded to interrogate the two women. It was the younger woman, María Esperanza, who protested most vehemently. She kept insisting — of all the crazy things — that she was the wife of an officer in the National Police.

Of course, María's captors refused to believe her. "*Sí,*

señora," they likely replied. "Your husband's a police officer — and we're all the president of El Salvador!" None of the armed men was going to fall for this sort of nonsense.

In fact, María Esperanza was exactly who she said she was. She was the common-law wife of Agent 1898 of the Third Line Company, General Garrison, of El Salvador's National Police — one José Medardo Beltrán Ulloa. And that wasn't all. Not only was María Esperanza a police officer's wife, but her sister-in-law, Rosa Amalia, was the same policeman's sister. The three men and one boy who had come to help her move to Soyapango were the policeman's brothers. Rosa Amalia's husband, now dead, had been the policeman's brother-in-law. Her two sons, also now dead, had been his nephews.

Tot all these relatives up — a wife, a sister, four brothers, a brother-in-law, two nephews — and it was evident that what Moises Montenegro and his men were preparing to undertake on the afternoon of March 4 was nothing less than the extermination of almost the entire remaining family of a Salvadoran police officer, not exactly a stroke of genius.

Montenegro's only excuse was that he didn't know. And, of course, he did not. After all, he merely spent the better part of an afternoon with the truth being shouted right at him. All María Esperanza did was declare the truth, over and over again. But the more vehemently she protested, the more her captors disbelieved her. "Those are lies," they scoffed, and they kept their prisoners right were they were, under the *amate* tree on a hill overlooking Lake Ilopango.

It was to be a long wait. Montenegro, it seemed, was in no hurry to kill these people. For some reason, he wanted darkness. I don't know why. Was it some atavistic impulse? Or maybe something he'd been taught? Or did he know from experience that killings were better by night? Maybe he simply wished to make this rare March day last, to luxuriate in this welling of power.

The long sunlit afternoon crept by, with the Beltrán Ulloa family and a few other unfortunates crowded under the *amate* tree amid an assortment of bundles and belongings, the jumbled accumulation of a family's life — battered pots and fraying baskets, cheap suitcases knotted with twine, sticks of chipped furniture, hobbled chickens, a woman's Sunday hat.

In all, nineteen people were being detained under that tree — the Beltrán Ulloas plus several residents of Palo Blanco itself. These others were under suspicion because they'd been friendly to Rosa Amalia or had offered her help. This meant of course that they were subversives, too. They included three local women — Salvadora de Jesús Pichente Carpio, thirty, Paz Hernández, fifty-five, and María Amelia Romero, thirty-four years old and seven months pregnant.

Also among the detained were a total of eleven children — among them, the four children of Paz Hernández, plus the youngest Beltrán Ulloa brother, José Jesús, who was twelve. Seven of the children were not yet ten years of age. The youngest was just two. There were also three somewhat older girls — Rufina Hernández, fourteen, and two others, both twelve.

And so the hours passed with an aching slowness, punctuated by María Esperanza's protests, repeated over and over, until her captors probably thought, "Somebody slug that bitch." The air was dry as tinder, and the ebbing amber light glistened against the waxy leaves of the *amate* trees and glanced off the sheer blue surface of the lake far below. As the sun went down, its oblique rays caught the floating dust motes in the air, to cast a golden aura over this terrible day. Finally, the sun drifted below the hills west of the lake, and the light dissolved quickly, as it always does in El Salvador. Round about seven, darkness fell like a breaking wave.

With the coming of darkness, the mysterious internal clock of Moises Montenegro rang out some private alarm, and made him decide that now was the time, but this was not the place.

Montenegro and his men roused their prisoners and herded them down a hillside path toward a wooded area near the shores of Lake Ilopango. The trail was buried in darkness, and the captives tripped and stumbled on their way, their minds spinning. What do you focus on at such a time, when you're being guided down to your death?

They soon reached a narrow gulley, where the path crossed a stream called El Guayabo. Here, some of the men were dispatched to dig a grave in the loamy soil of the stream bank. Montenegro told the other men that they were free to have *relaciones sexuales* with the women. And so, just like that, they did. Yes, sir. Right away, sir. Six men proceeded to rape three of the women, plus the fourteen-year-old girl, and the two twelve-year-old girls.

Montenegro went off with a couple of his men to find a more private location some distance away. He wanted Rosa Amalia first and ordered his two men to bring her to him. This, they did. Later, he wanted María Esperanza. She, too, was delivered. Evidently a man of large appetites,

Montenegro later sent his men to bring him Rufina Hernández, the fourteen-year-old. And so they obeyed, did exactly as they were told. The child's sobs twisted back to the others through the darkness, loudly at first, then softly — as if stifled by a man's fist.

Shortly before ten p.m., the three older Beltrán Ulloa brothers were taken off a considerable distance from the others — about four hundred metres or so. José Alberto, eighteen years old and an evangelical Christian, railed against what was being done. He told his captors, "All right, as you are going to do something to me, I will give thanks to my Christ." He fell to his knees on the ground and began to pray.

One of Montenegro's men — Ulises Rosales, fifty-three — was having none of this. "Now you will respect the armed forces!" he shouted. He promptly fired off two rounds and killed the younger brother of Agent 1898 of the Third Line Company, General Garrison, of El Salvador's National Police. Just like that, a man was dead.

Now something went very wrong for the killers. Another of the captured brothers — José Hector Beltrán Ulloa — managed to work free of the cord that bound his thumbs behind his back. In an instant, he was off, scrambling up through the wooded hills and the darkness. He didn't stop running until he reached the village of Buena Vista. And so he survived, to tell what had happened and to identify his captors.

Meanwhile, Moises Montenegro's men went back to work. A third Beltrán Ulloa brother was hacked to death with machetes. Back at the *quebrada*, the five women and eleven children were being pushed down the banks of El

Guayabo and into the stream itself. They were surrounded by the men, who stood above them on the banks. Rosa Amalia Beltrán Ulloa, who had already been raped and beaten and terrified, now undertook what was to be her life's final act. She reached into the pocket of her dress to pull out a bunch of *colónes* — Salvadoran bank notes. She offered them to one of her captors, Miguel Angel Menjivar, whom she knew by name. "Do me the favor, Don Miguel," she said. "Take this money to Don José Amado so that he will go to my Mamá and give it to her to buy milk for my little girl. And tell her not to look for me . . ."

These were her final words. Within moments, Rosa Amalia was struck repeatedly with the blade of a curved machete and died from a gash in the back of her head that partly decapitated her.

Two-year-old Amalia Pichente Hernández was wrested from her mother's arms. She was first strangled, then had her skull crushed by a blow from a rifle stock.

Her mother, Paz Hernández, was chopped through the face until she died.

José Jesús Beltrán Ulloa, twelve, was strangled.

María Amelia Romero — seven months pregnant — was shot first, then mutilated with a machete.

In all, two men, five women, ten children, and a two-year-old girl, were killed. All of the women, except Paz Hernández, had been raped repeatedly. So had three of the girls, two aged twelve, and Rufina Hernández, aged fourteen. When it was over, the two older Beltrán Ulloa men were buried where they died. The women and children were piled into the common grave that had already been dug in the soft soil above the stream bank.

And so, the job was done. It was over. The massacre at Palo Blanco was now a thing of the past. And, in most other circumstances, this story would have ended right then and there. The camera would have pulled back above the trees and maybe panned across the moonlit surface of Lake Ilopango, where Rosa Amalia's husband, brother-in-law, and two sons already lay submerged, their fates never to be discovered. The surrounding volcanic hills would heave through the darkness. Fade to black. Let the credits roll.

Actually, in other circumstances, this story might never have been told at all. There'd have been no story to tell. This was El Salvador, a country where killers were almost never identified, and where their victims simply disappeared. In other circumstances, Moises Montenegro and his men would have gone home and proceeded with their lives. Twenty-two Salvadorans — the eighteen murdered by the stream plus the four who'd been killed several nights before — would have vanished from the face of the earth, never to be seen or heard from again. They'd have disappeared, just like that. Gone. And that would be all.

But it wasn't all, simply because the massacre at Palo Blanco was unlike so many other horrors of the Salvadoran war. The wrong people were killed — the relatives, after all, of a police officer — and one of the intended victims was allowed to escape. He survived to tell what had happened.

Two days later, the unthinkable occurred. A detachment of the National Police arrived in Palo Blanco to round up the twelve men believed to have committed the crimes. The men were required to unearth the bodies, which were identified in the presence of a Justice of the Peace and examined by medical personnel before being reburied not far away.

The suspected killers were then arrested and incarcerated in the central prison in Cojutepeque, fifteen kilometres to the west. Also arrested was Manuel de Jesús Bolaños Morales, an agent of the Treasury Police in San Pedro Perulapán.

So, for all its horror, the massacre at Palo Blanco had at least one redeeming aspect — its victims were discovered, their fates made known. And they got a decent burial. Thousands of others, tens of thousands, were not so lucky. They just disappeared.

Soon after the killings in Palo Blanco, a preliminary investigation was launched by the Court of the First Instance in Cojutepeque. Among the documents on file at the court were the sworn depositions of the arrested men — astonishing for their candor and their detail. Also on file were forty-seven black-and-white photographs of the dead, taken immediately upon their exhumation. Here, now, was that rare thing in El Salvador — precise documentary proof of an atrocity. There could never be any doubt that these acts really had been committed.

That was where matters stood when we left Palo Blanco for the final time. It was late on a Friday afternoon, one of those wonderful dry-season afternoons in El Salvador. The flowering trees glistened through the shimmering air, and everything had that special Central American clarity, that preternatural glow — as if some celestial housekeeper had gone at the entire landscape with an infinity of lemon wax and elbow grease. There were three of us in our rented car, and we crept along the hillside trail above Lake Ilopango, heading back towards the Cojutepeque road. It was late, and the local peasant farmers were trudging home from the fields. They straggled past us, heading back the way we'd come — lean men with dark bronze skin, each carrying a machete. They all wore wide-brimmed hats that cast shadows over their faces. You couldn't see their eyes.

In the car, we didn't say much, barely spoke at all. We just smoked our Marlboros and kept on moving. Nobody told any torture jokes for once, or moaned about what a disaster it was to light another cigarette just when you'd sworn you were going to quit. We wanted to get back to the capital I guess, away from this place — that was about all. We didn't think about anything or, if we did, it was maybe just to look out and wonder at the sparkling texture of the air.

'They'll Name a Road After Us'

"**Y**OU SEE . . . ?" said Pepe Dutríz that afternoon at the Club Deportivo in San Salvador. "You see what's happening to this country?"

At the time, I believed that I did, and I wasn't thinking of the shortage of premium scotch. What I had in mind were the killings at Palo Blanco — things like that, terrible things. There was a buyer's market for horror in El Salvador in those days. And I could imagine what some North Americans must have thought when they looked up from their newspapers or their TV screens. They must have rolled their eyes, shaken their heads, and muttered to themselves, "Those *people*! Those *Salvadorans*!" There they all were — raping, killing, and slaughtering each other, and falling down dead. I imagine this was the impression that a lot of people outside El Salvador were getting back in the days of the war.

And, in fact, that impression wasn't entirely wrong. There really was a flood tide of death in El Salvador. A lot of people *were* dying, helplessly, through no fault of their own. One day, a man helped a young girl down from a country bus. The next day, he raped her and then used a machete to chop off her head. Why? Who could say? Maybe someone told him to.

In El Salvador, the deaths piled up, higher and higher, year after year — a thousand more each month — and you certainly couldn't blame people who envisioned such countries as places gone mad, lands without hope, where the people were either killers or utterly helpless victims, and where normal human enterprises had been obliterated by the war. That was pretty much what I thought was happening to El Salvador. And I wasn't wrong. But I wasn't exactly right, either. Thousands were dying — no doubt about that. But the dying wasn't all.

Early one morning, for example, in the tinder-box of the late Salvadoran dry season, I headed out of the capital in a rented car. My companion was a photographer from California named Cindy Karp, and we were headed for rebel country, a guerrilla camp in the eastern province of Usulután. We had put in a good supply of American cigarettes, and that was about all we took, apart from Cindy's cameras and my notebooks. Soon, we had left the city behind us and now traced the giant ravines that tumbled down the dry, southern flank of El Salvador, toward the Pacific coastal plain at Comalapa.

When we reached the sweltering flats not far from the ocean, we bore east along the Carretera del Litoral, the coastal highway that runs the length of the country, all the way to the port city of La Unión on the Gulf of Fonseca. But we weren't planning to go that far. We were looking for a trail that snaked south off the highway, a short distance east of the garrison town of Usulután. Cindy had been there once before. She felt pretty sure she'd recognize the place when she saw it again.

It was a fine morning, and the sun shone down, glancing against the coastal mountains that swelled above us to the north. Soon we passed the broad pyramid of the San Vicente volcano where it pried its way into a pure blue sky. Rural El Salvador unfolded all around — the smoky, overburdened country buses, the women strolling past with basins or baskets on their heads, the dark-faced men clutching machetes as they roamed their fields of broken corn stalks, the boys cantering past on scrawny chestnut ponies. It was crackling hot, and we had our windows rolled down. The wind breezed through our hair.

At the Río Lempa — gateway to rebel country in eastern El Salvador — we had to line up with the other traffic to inch our way one vehicle at a time across an old railway bridge that ran above the river. It had been converted for use by automobiles after the massive suspension bridge — the Puente do Oro — was crumpled by guerrilla bombs a year earlier. Even now, that great wrecked bridge made an astonishing sight. It sprawled across the baking earth and the slow brown river, a rage of toppled towers, huge slabs of concrete, and tangled suspension cables, as if the very stairway to heaven had plummeted from the sky.

Not far east of the provincial capital of Usulután, Cindy told me to slow down. "There," she said and pointed off to the right. "I think that's the one."

I braked and swung the car off the road and onto a narrow dirt trail that stumbled south through low trees and burnt fields toward the coastal village of El Espino, about twenty-five kilometres away. The trail got narrower almost by the minute. Somehow — by luck rather than subterfuge — we managed to elude the army foot patrols that were pretty much a constant in the area, and we eventually reached El Espino. Above the town, a rough path twisted into the rounded coastal hills. I coaxed the car up that treacherous route, rocking and lurching over the rough, irregular terrain. After about fifteen minutes of slow ascent, it became clear that the car wasn't going any farther. We'd have to continue on foot.

I killed the engine and pulled on the handbrake; Cindy and I climbed out to look around and get our bearings. Almost immediately, I sensed some movement. I looked up and saw two men and a woman as they emerged from a thicket of gnarled trees on an overhanging ledge. They clambered down the steep earthen slope and advanced towards us. All three were young — just kids really, in their middle teens. Their clothing was unremarkable: the boys wore scuffed jeans and frayed nylon shirts; the girl was dressed in a faded yellow dress; and they all had on shoddy, black leather boots. The thing I noticed, though, was that all three were carrying M-1 semi-automatic rifles with wooden stocks. It was the sort of detail that caught your eye. Apart from that, they didn't look like much, in strict military terms, but they were guerrilla sentries all the same.

And so, it seemed that we had come to the right place. Just like that, without quite knowing it, we'd crossed an invisible barrier, passed from one world into another. We were in rebel country now. *Territorio libre.*

Within a few minutes, the three young sentries had agreed to guide us up into the camp, but first they helped us hide the car. We moved it beneath some trees and partly covered it with small branches. Then we resumed our climb. We marched up into a rebel camp in El Salvador at the height of the civil war, just as though it were the easiest thing in the world. While we lived with them, the rebels fed us, loaned us sleeping bags, took us out on training man-oeuvres, guided us through their bomb "factory" (really just an open-air workshop), and granted some pretty high-level interviews. I took notes, Cindy took pictures, and a young rebel named Salomán took us both in hand.

Now here was an interesting guy. Before the war, he'd been an architecture student in the capital, but now he'd traded in his drafting tools for a pair of hiking boots and an automatic rifle. He was bearded, with a broad brow and scruffy black hair. He had a reserved manner that seemed a bit cool at first, but he grew steadily warmer and friendlier as we got to know him. Like many of his *compañeros*, he seemed as fascinated by us, a pair of North American jour-nalists, as we were by him.

One night, Cindy and I gathered in a low adobe building with three rebels, including Salomán. We had just finished another dinner of beans, *tortillas*, and water. Several tin plates were scattered atop a battered wooden table, and a hurricane lantern shed a dull monochromatic glow. Salomán chal-lenged me to a game of chess, and we wound up playing two games on a crude, hand-painted board. Instead of pawns, we used old bottle caps or small stones. Salomán played in an aggressive, unorthodox style and easily beat me in the first game. He blundered badly in the second, though, and I managed to win without quite knowing how I'd done it.

After we put the chess pieces away, we sat up by the light of the hurricane lantern, talking about the war. At one point, Salomán eased himself forward on his bench. His manner changed. It seemed he was getting down to serious business now, preparing to discuss the things that were fore-most on his mind. He asked us if we were ever afraid for our safety, covering the fighting in his country.

We nodded — yes. This pretty much seemed to go with-out saying.

Salomán drew closer. He asked if our families at home ever worried about us, about our security down here in El Salvador. We replied that we thought so. In fact, we were sure that they did. Salomán frowned, then tilted his head. He asked if we had . . . *seguro de vida.*

I stared at him. "You want to know if we have *life insurance?*" Salomán nodded.

I shook my head. I couldn't believe this. "Never mind about us," I said. "What about you? Do *you* have life insur-ance?"

And Salomán drew himself up on his wooden bench. It was as if we were a comedy team; I was the straight man, and he was the guy who got all the best lines. My question — did *he* have life insurance? — was evidently his cue. His face was half-lit by the lantern's glow, and now he cleared his throat. "A guerrilla has two forms of life insurance," he intoned. "One is tomorrow. And the other is the knowl-edge that — if we should die — after the triumph of the rev-olution, they'll name a road after us."

I suppose we talked on for a time after that, but I don't remember what else was said, not on that night anyway. I do remember that line, though. Those words have remained with me ever since. I've never quite managed to get them out of my mind. *They'll name a road after us.*

I don't know if Salomán is alive now or dead. A fair number of years have rattled by since that night atop a remote hill in eastern El Salvador when we played chess together and talked of war. Tens of thousands of Salomán's compatriots have been killed. Maybe he was among them. Or maybe not. I don't know. I do know that there is no road in El Salvador named after Salomán now. The war in his country finally ended, but the revolution did not triumph. The old roads kept their old names, and any new ones that have been built aren't likely to become monuments to fallen revolutionaries — not now and not anytime soon.

Of course, Salomán wasn't speaking only for himself that night. He said that he was speaking for all rebels, and maybe that was so, but it struck me that he also could have been speaking for just about anybody in this world who isn't in a position to insure himself with The Prudential Insurance Company of America or its local equivalent. When it comes to security of life, most people in this world have to get by on a pretty bare minimum: the promise of tomorrow maybe, plus some faint glimmer of immortality.

Yet most people seem to get by — even those, like Solomán, who test their luck right to the limit, who take up arms, say, against what they believe to be an unjust regime. Even they find a way to hold off death for a good long while, or a lot of them do. Of course, most people don't push their chances quite that far. Most people merely struggle to attach one more tomorrow to one more today, to raise their children, plant their fields, and stave off the huge weight of oblivion. This is no small feat either, but most people manage it.

Once I travelled into the mountains of the Central American continental divide, on the Honduran side of the border between El Salvador and Honduras. I spent some

time with Salvadoran refugees there, people who were living in truly miserable conditions. These were peasants
who'd fled their villages to escape the fighting, and now they
huddled in the shadow of the war, living in scrap-wood hovels, surviving mainly on the generosity of Honduran farmers
who were not much better off themselves. At the time,
Salvadoran soldiers were marauding across the border. They
were seizing younger refugees and dragging them back to El
Salvador or simply killing them on the spot. By night, as I
tried to sleep in a hammock under the trees, I could hear
mortar blasts and small-arms fire just over the next ridge.

This was a terrible time to be a Salvadoran refugee. And
yet, one evening in those mountains, as I was having dinner
on the verandah of a small adobe house, my Honduran hosts
— a pair of peasant farmers and their wives — suddenly told
me to turn around. I did, and realized that I had become the
centre of attention for about two dozen Salvadoran children,
all dark faces, torn clothes, huge eyes, and tangled hair. They
wanted to find out about this strange gringo who'd shown
up in their midst. They wouldn't go away, and I didn't want
them to. I wanted to talk to them, teach them some English
phrases, and the first one I hit on was "I love you." They
picked it up in a flash. For the rest of that evening, and that
night, all I had to do was call those three words out, and
immediately I'd be rewarded with a throaty chorus wailing
in reply, "*Ai lobe chooo . . . !*"

After dark that same night, I hiked up onto a small plateau
with several dozen of the Salvadorans — men, women, and
children. The men had built a bonfire. Now the fire roared,
and the adults arranged themselves on piles of logs to talk of
home, while their children joined hands and danced around

the blaze. That was all. There was nothing to eat or to drink. No one had dressed up, for no one had extra clothing. At night, at the edge of war, a celebration consisted only of this — a fire, some friends, a turmoil of dancing children. Barefoot and wild-haired, the children sang at the tops of their voices and swayed through the firelight, throwing long, intertwining shadows against the trees. And, around them, their parents talked and laughed and shook their heads and huddled close — all these dispossessed and homeless people, riding upon a mountainside into the night.

This was the larger truth, I thought. This was the really remarkable thing about human beings in the dwindling years of the twentieth century — not how spineless they can be or how meek. But how resilient. This was what impressed me that night, and it was what struck me a year or so later, after the chess games with Salomán in the rebel camp in Usulután. *They'll name a road after us.*

The morning after that night of chess and lantern-lit conversation on a hilltop in eastern El Salvador, Cindy Karp and I climbed down to our car, along with Salomán and a couple of other rebels. It was time for us to be heading back to the capital. We exchanged long goodbyes, got the car turned around, and Cindy and I bounced back down the rutted track to El Espino and headed north until we reached the Carretera del Litoral. Later, we took a detour farther north, to the Pan-American Highway, and headed back to the capital through the heart of El Salvador at war.

We had a spot or so of trouble along the way — a couple of army road blocks and a small matter of two transport trucks that had been torched by the rebels and now blocked the highway. But we got back to the capital in time to have a beer in the lobby bar at the Camino Real and then dinner at a Mexican restaurant on the Calle Lamatepec not far from the hotel. And that should have been the end of the story. But it wasn't, quite.

Some years later, a friend of mine, a Canadian photo-journalist named Derek Debono, happened to be out in the eastern regions of El Salvador, near a beach not far from the village of El Espino, and he stumbled upon a party of guerrillas out there. Debono got to talking with one rebel in particular and mentioned in passing that he was a Canadian. The rebel suddenly grew more interested. It turned out that he had struck up an acquaintance with another Canadian a few years earlier, a newspaper reporter. The rebel mentioned the reporter's name — mine — and asked Debono if he happened to know me. Debono said that he did.

The guerrilla was Salomán, of course. He had lost almost all of his hair by this time — some subtropical infection, I suppose. Other than that, though, he seemed in pretty good health. His spirits were fine. He even mentioned something to Debono about those chess games he and I had played together, that night in Usulután. He asked Debono to tell me hello.

And that was how I knew that Salomán managed to survive at least a few more years of the war, while others surely did not. Who knows how he did it? Some combination of luck and skill, I suppose. A determined spirit. A stout heart. That day with Debono, out on the beach near El Espino, Salomán didn't say anything about the nomenclature of streets. He didn't muse about life insurance, rebel-style. He didn't say, "They'll name a road after us." And so I guess he was still investing his faith in tomorrow, and tomorrow was seeing him through.

The
Crazy
Years

O NE MORNING in San Salvador, I was up early at my hotel and rode the elevator down to the lobby. As I did every morning, I strolled out to the front where another brilliant day was inventing itself — a sky of Marian blue yawning above the green volcanos and the distant undulating hills that surround the capital. A gang of grimy boys in tattered pants came by each morning to sell local newspapers to the hotel residents, and now I bought mine. I headed back inside to the coffee shop, where maybe a dozen other members of the Salvador Press Corps Association (SPCA for short) were already having breakfast.

I slumped down at a table, flipped open one of the newspapers — it was *El Diario de Hoy*, I think — and was promptly confronted with a brief official-looking communiqué boldly printed in a box. It went straight to the point.

"This is to inform the journalists of radio, television, and the written press that all those who collaborate with the enemies of our Republic will be executed, whether for sending cables that distort reality or for repeating false news that comes from abroad, because all that these things do is confuse our people and make them pawns for the terrorist bands and for the bands of journalists, whose salaries are paid by International Communism."

The communiqué was signed, "The Salvadoran Anti-Communist Command" and concluded with the slogan "For a victory against Communism!"

I swallowed a couple of times and read the communiqué again — just the thing to perk up the press corps at breakfast. Already, at the other tables, this unexpected greeting from a Salvadoran death squad seemed to be causing a bit of a stir — a sudden commotion, a rustling of newspaper pages, and much nervous laughter. Eventually, the old insouciance kicked in, and people started making jokes about it. "'Repeating false news,'" someone said. "What does that mean? Does that mean they kill you for plagiarism around here?" As usual, everyone started putting on masks to cover their fear.

Still, the communiqué was real. And, no matter how hard you tried to deny the fact or to disguise it, you couldn't help but be unsettled when confronted at breakfast by a death threat, even one as vaguely worded as this.

As far as I know, no one ended up being killed as a result of that communiqué. But, if nothing else, it was another reminder that foreign journalists were not universally loved in El Salvador. The same was true in Guatemala, or in Nicaragua, or in any of the other Central American countries where journalists would show up in those years, singly or in groups, to cover another coup attempt, another election, another round of fruitless peace talks, another peasant massacre.

In El Salvador the foreign journalists at the Camino Real

inevitably became a kind of community, with a community's similarities — and a community's differences. The press corps had its leftist sympathizers, its right-wingers, its stars, its veterans, its rookies. It had its pecking order, of course, its disputes and rivalries, but it also was a group of people held together by common threads of circumstance, self-interest, and fear.

In those days, the Camino Real in San Salvador was a kind of journalistic epicentre for a larger story that included all of Latin America. A diverse array of reporters, photographers, and TV crews ranged over one and a half continents, now dispersing, now converging. The faces you saw over breakfast at the Camino Real in San Salvador one Monday morning might well be the same faces you would encounter at dinner at Los Ranchos in Managua on Tuesday the following week, or in the Indian highlands of Guatemala a week later, or in the departure lounge of the Miami airport a week after that, or in the thick of a street demonstration in Santiago de Chile another month down the road.

There were plenty of hotspots in Latin America, but El Salvador was the hottest. The SPCA was more or less an ad hoc organization, run out of the UPI office on the second floor of the Camino Real on the Boulevard los Héroes, across from the Metrocentro, the largest shopping complex in Central America. Its main official function was to issue press cards, and these cards had their uses. They'd help you get through an army roadblock, for example (it didn't hurt if you also had an army *laisser-passer*) or a rebel roadblock (it didn't hurt if you also had some American cigarettes). In addition to press cards, the SPCA also issued distinctive T-shirts for a nominal price. They bore the association's rather sophomoric logo on the front, depicting a cartoonish Izalco volcano spewing lava into the sky. On the back, in bold black letters, the T-shirts were emblazoned with the words, "¡*Periodista!* ¡*No dispare!*"

"Journalist! Don't shoot!"

It was meant to be a joke. But the truth was, journalists *did* get shot. Not every day, or every week, but often enough. Most of the time, that awareness lurked somewhere in the back of your mind. Each morning, you knew that one of you or several of you might not be around by evening. You knew this from direct experience. It had happened before. As a result, you cemented friendships more quickly and with greater urgency than was often true in more peaceful circumstances in more temperate climes. And you learned to share in that general bravado, that cocky *esprit de corps*, that you would find wherever journalists gathered to pick through the bones of someone else's war. Hacks drove into rebel country together in press convoys, got scared halfway to death. They drank together, ate together, got homesick together, hiked up into the hills together, told each other sick jokes about torture victims, went to memorial services together whenever it was time for another memorial service to be held.

You stuck together because you had to. Those were unnerving times. There were guerrilla wars in El Salvador and Guatemala, and the revolutionary Sandinista government in Nicaragua was coming under withering political and military attack from the United States. There were plenty of horrors and terrors to write about. There was no shortage of war or death.

In El Salvador, as in neighbouring Guatemala, the papers

would sometimes report on the individuals who had been seized most recently by *hombres desconocidos vestidos en ropa civil*. Unknown Men Dressed in Civilian Clothing. That was the standard phrase, the accepted euphemism for "death squad". Once you saw that phrase, you knew that some poor soul was gone and would not be coming back.

There was a grim iconography to the business of death. It varied from country to country. In Argentina, for example, during the late 1970s and early '80s, the secret police generally came in 1960s-style Ford Falcons (an Argentine classic; factories there churned them out for years). In Central America, where the roads tend to be more rugged, the vehicles of choice for right-wing death squads were four-wheel-drive Cherokee Chiefs with polarized windows. In Guatemala, right-wing thugs would sometimes send flowers before they struck. I'm not kidding — there might be flowers, a bouquet of yellow roses, delivered right to the door of an intended victim. It was a sporting gesture in a way: it gave the man time to flee, a chance anyway. Thus were the edges of evil traced with a certain bleak poetry, a ghoulish sort of romance.

Plus, there were jokes. People came up with some really tasteless jokes. For example, did you hear about the time the Tutankhamen exhibit toured El Salvador? (It didn't really. This is a joke.) One day, Major Roberto D'Aubuisson showed up to tour the celebrated display, which had just got into town. A cashiered officer in the National Guard, D'Aubuisson happened also to be the reputed mastermind of El Salvador's infamous right-wing death squads. In El Salvador, he was Evil personified. Eventually, he came across one mummy that, alone among the exhibited items, bore no date.

D'Aubuisson didn't like that. So he decided to speak to the visiting curator about it. "How old is this mummy?" he wanted to know.

Turned out, the curator couldn't say. He and his staff had subjected the mummy to the most advanced dating techniques that modern science had so far managed to devise, but they'd had no luck at all. They were stumped on this one. Sorry, Major D'Aubuisson. Sir.

But Major Bob was not a man to be put off so easily. He said that El Salvador, despite being an impoverished developing country under attack by the forces of International Communism, had nonetheless managed to develop some fairly sophisticated dating techniques of its own. How about if he and his men took the mummy away and worked on this problem for a while? Say, a couple of days? Maybe they could sort this thing out.

The curator figured he had nothing to lose. He said okay, good luck. Sir.

A couple of days later, a dishevelled Major Bob returned with the mummy in tow.

"How did it go?" the curator asked.

D'Aubuisson looked terrible, completely worn out. He slapped his palms back and forth against each other in that way that meant he was plumb worn out. Then he tucked in his shirt and heaved an exhausted sigh. "This mummy," he declared, "is 3,654 years old."

The curator couldn't believe what he was hearing. "What?" he exclaimed. "How did you find that out? I've tried everything with this mummy. Nothing has worked. How could you possibly determine that?"

"Well," said Major Bob. His hair was mussed, his tie

askew. "It took a little doing — but we finally got him to talk!"

Ha. Ha. Ha.

You heard that sort of joke a lot in El Salvador. It was a way of dealing with the war, I suppose, a kind of war-time gallows humour, a means of keeping the fear at bay. And, to some degree, it worked. One way or another, you found that you could acclimatize yourself to war. Or at least you were able to persuade yourself that you could, which maybe comes to the same thing.

One Friday afternoon in San Salvador, for example, I was on the phone in my hotel room at the Camino Real. I was dictating a story to the rewrite desk at my newspaper in Toronto. Suddenly, the deep, flat report of an exploding bomb burst through the street outside.

"What was that!" exclaimed the rewrite man in Toronto. "What's going on?"

"I don't know," I said. "Just a sec. I'll see." I put down the phone and went to the window. Off to the right, I saw a trail of dark smoke and some flames. People were hurrying away. It was a car bomb. About half a block from the hotel, on the other side of the street, a car had blown up. I returned to the phone. "Car bomb," I said. I resumed dictating my story.

But the rewrite man couldn't believe it. "Car bomb . . . ?" he kept repeating. "Car bomb . . . ?"

A couple of minutes later, another explosion ripped through the air outside, and the rewrite man got agitated again. I walked over to the window to look. Another car bomb. I returned to the phone, reported what I'd seen, and went back to dictating my story. The rewrite man was beside himself by now, amazed — he'd just heard two car bombs over the phone! This was war!

To be honest, I wasn't nearly as relaxed as I was pretending to be. If I'd been able to, I would have stopped what I was doing and headed straight outside to see about those two bombs. But, right now, I simply couldn't. I was on deadline; I had to file this story. Besides, it really seemed that the car bombs were not all that serious. If there were more to it, I'd find out soon enough. And so I assumed an air of calm that I didn't really feel. Right now, I had to file my story. Apart from those two bombs, I was pretty sure that this was just another quiet afternoon in the capital of El Salvador, a country at war.

But that poor rewrite man. I could imagine the impression he carried away from that day — images of El Salvador as a country in constant, pervasive flames, with fighting everywhere. And that got me thinking. It was quite likely that many people — newspaper readers or TV viewers in Canada or the United States — gained a similar picture of the wars in Central America, a kind of all-consuming subtropical Armageddon. It wasn't difficult to understand how they might come up with such an idea. Unless you've gone through a war yourself, it's easy to get a very wrong-headed impression of the experience. A war is not a simple thing to imagine.

Besides, these were not conventional wars. They were what came to be called "low-intensity wars" — a phrase that has a weird oxymoronic quality in English. In Latin America, they refer to this sort of conflict as *la guerrilla*, or "the little war", the kind of war waged by small irregular armies, a hit-and-run war. (In English, we have somewhat corrupted the word "guerrilla". We use it either as an adjective or else as a noun that refers, not to the war itself, but to someone who wages it. The Spanish term for such a person is really *guerrillero*.)

A guerrilla war tends to be a sporadic affair. Take the war that transfixed El Salvador for a dozen years, from 1979 until 1993. It was certainly an all-consuming conflict, but more in the psychological sense than in the strictly martial. The fact is, you never found the entire country on full combat alert at any one time. One week, for example, there might be fighting in a certain garrison town in the east. And, in that town for that week, war would indeed be hell. It would be loud, intense, and deadly. Bombs would explode. Automatic rifles would stutter. Rebels and government troops would blow each other up. Lots of civilians would be killed while hiding in their homes or while trying to escape. Whole neighbourhoods would be razed. War would be everything it was always cracked up to be. In that week. In that town.

But, if you travelled fifteen kilometres outside that war-battered place, you would find something that looked an awful lot like peace. You'd find peasant farmers diligently tilling their miniscule plots of land. You'd find women sauntering along the sides of roads with pots or baskets atop their heads. You'd find boys mounted on skeletal ponies, cantering through fields of blasted corn husks. You'd find school-children ambling homeward, hoisting their satchels over their shoulders. You'd find ancient Bluebird buses groaning beneath an impossible weight of passengers, goats, chickens, and sacks of grain, spewing clouds of oily black smoke into the shimmering, subtropical air.

A day later, these scenes might be completely reversed. A

day later, or even sooner, there could be fighting in this now peaceful spot. Or maybe not fighting. Maybe something else. Maybe some trouble might erupt while a platoon of soldiers was searching a country bus. A recruit might get skittish or ornery, shoot some poor soul dead. Or the guerrillas might set up a roadblock and start collecting war taxes from motorists, or they might blow up another bridge. Or maybe a gaggle of schoolchildren ambling along this very road might happen upon a ditch suddenly swelling with half a dozen mutilated bodies that weren't there before.

And yet, right now, this minute, in this place, it might seem that there was nothing out of the ordinary at all. Central America at war could look a lot like like Central America at peace.

Peace was not what I had expected when I first travelled to El Salvador in 1981. I expected to find what I had always thought of as war — an undifferentiated canvas of conflict, an entire country in flames. But a guerrilla war, it turns out, is a lot like the weather — one day sunny, next day wham. There were lots of peaceful interludes, and yet you could never really relax.

The strange thing was that you eventually began to *think* that you were relaxing. Things, once alien, came to seem familiar — the flatulent buses that crepitated past along the Boulevard los Héroes, for example; or the security agents, with submachine guns braced at their chests, who stood guard outside the McDonald's restaurant in the capital; or the bomb blasts at night; or the nightly homeward rush as curfew approached; or the maddening loss of electricity whenever the rebels hit another pylon outside the capital; or the army roadblocks; or the guerrilla roadblocks; or the chilling whine of the cicadas as you drove east into rebel country; or the mounting signs that you were already *in* rebel country — the toppled phone lines and blown bridges, the burnt-out carcasses of buses, the peasants' huts sprouting tattered white flags like silent prayers.

Eventually, I would start to think that I was getting used to all this. And maybe, in a way, I was. But then I'd take a taxi out to the Cuscatlán airport on the Pacific coastal flats at the end of another Salvadoran tour. I'd be planning to fly home to my apartment in Mexico City, or maybe I'd be about to head south to Managua or San José. The plane — a small Fokker jet or a Boeing 737, flown by one or another of the Central American airlines, TACA or COPA or AVIATECA or LACSA — would trundle down to the end of the runway, race its engines, and roar past the terminal, to grope for purchase against the sparkling air. Only when the tires had left the tarmac, when the undercarriage had folded into the bays beneath the craft and the plane had tilted out over the Pacific, would I realize once again what it was like for the muscles in my jaw to go slack or for my lungs to breathe easy at last. It wasn't that you ever stopped being tense in El Salvador. It was just that, sometimes, you forgot how tense you were.

One American colleague never quite managed to forget. Whenever he heard a knock at his hotel-room door in San Salvador, he first stepped into the bathroom and then inquired loudly who was there. He liked the initial extra protection of that bathroom wall. Another hack refused to sit down anywhere that required him to put his back to a doorway. Another confessed that he felt safer and, on the whole, more comfortable if he slept in his bathtub. Yet another said that each time he checked into his hotel, he devoted the first few minutes to calculating the trajectory of a line drawn from the street below to various points in his room. That way, when he was alone at night, he'd know how far he had to slouch.

I found myself thinking a lot about bombs. I knew that there were a lot of bombs around. In San Salvador, in Guatemala City, you didn't have to look far for the evidence. The rubble that used to be the head office of some small political party. The boarded-up office towers. The mirrors mounted on long metal handles that were used to inspect the undersides of cars.

One evening, in a hotel lobby in Guatemala City, I was interviewing a certain right-wing politician. Partway through the conversation, he excused himself, got up, and walked away. I soon noticed that he'd left a small parcel on the couch. I looked at it. I looked away. Then I looked back at it — a small, unassuming parcel, nothing to indicate what it was. I looked away again. Eventually I thought, so what if it's a bomb? It *could* have been a bomb. It wasn't impossible. There was no logical impediment in this country that would render impossible the prospect that the parcel on the sofa beside you would turn out to be a bomb. Some sort of plastic explosive, I decided. With a remote detonator.

I said to myself, so why am I still sitting here, assuming this parcel contains a bomb? I mean, if there's even one chance in a thousand that it is a bomb, then why am I still sitting here? Is there something I'm trying to prove? I thought of other places I might reasonably go, all of them located at least a block away. I thought of various people I might warn, before I left the hotel. I wondered, if a bomb went off on the sofa right beside you, would you even hear it? Would you even know? Or would it already be too late? Would there just be a blank, followed an hour or so later by the arrival of the relevant authorities, wading through the debris?

I sat there, on that sofa, and thought of many things. And I was still sitting there when my acquaintance, the right-wing politician, returned and picked up the thread of our conversation. He never did say what was in that package of his, and I didn't like to ask.

I'm still not sure if my decision to remain on that sofa was calculated wisdom or incredible stupidity. Or maybe it was just one of those things. The truth is, you can't run away from every hint of danger. Even in peace time, you have to do lots of dangerous things. Every moment of your life contains the possibility of your death — every shower you step into, every morsel you eat, every car you enter, every street you cross, every day you begin. The hazards are everywhere, and so you have to internalize a certain acceptable level of risk. You have to run those risks. Otherwise, you'd never get anything done. You'd never manage to live, for fear of winding up dead.

In war time, it's not fundamentally different — except that the risks increase pretty dramatically, and so you have to modify your sense of what's acceptable. You have to find a way of taking a greater level of danger in your stride. You have to put yourself on a kind of personal war-footing. And it does happen — not immediately, maybe, but in time. You raise your tolerance for fear.

In most cities in the world, if you heard an explosion in the street, you'd just assume it was a car backfiring and you'd carry right along. In El Salvador, you ducked. And, if you found yourself seated on a sofa beside a suspicious-looking parcel, you either stayed or you left — but you definitely *thought about leaving*. You found yourself taking precautions that simply did not apply in countries that were not at war.

Some precautions were obvious, or should have been. For example, I always thought it was bad policy to patronize or insult an army officer in the field, unless you had some very good reason. In the first place, what would be the point? Besides, they *really, really* didn't like it. And, if there was one thing that was worse than a homicidal army officer, it was a homicidal army officer who'd decided that, on balance, you were *not* his favourite person in the whole wide world.

On an army march into eastern El Salvador, I stood wide-eyed in amazement late one morning while a young woman journalist pointedly refused to shake hands with a Salvadoran colonel and then called him a murderer under her breath. You had to admire her nerve, I guess, and there was certainly no faulting her character judgement, but her timing was way off. Granted, this woman had the good sense to hiss the word "murderer" in English and not in Spanish. But, to me, that merely suggested another safety tip: never simply assume that the other person doesn't speak your language.

On the whole, I found it was a good idea to be sort of chummy with soldiers. It probably reduced the chances that they'd kill you, for one thing — and it increased the likelihood that they might tell you something that you actually wanted to know.

Besides, just for your own peace of mind, you didn't want to be attracting enemies unnecessarily. I always thought it was a good idea to wave at military patrols out on the road in El Salvador or Guatemala. It showed that you didn't mind being noticed, and it made you feel a whole lot better when they waved back. Basically, the rule was simple, and it applied to all civilians in time of war — you did whatever it was you felt you had to do, but you remembered to smile at the guys with the guns. Unless you were armed yourself, you had no choice but to defer.

That isn't to say you had to be a coward. Deference isn't the same as cowardice. In some circumstances, it can be the very stuff of courage. In fact, maybe the most poignant gesture of deference that I recall from the war in El Salvador was also possibly the most courageous, a surprise attack disguised by a deferential smile. Along toward dusk one day, I was marching through rebel country north of San Francisco Gotera, along with a column of government troops, part of a pincer operation. The rebel forces were fleeing ahead of us, which was the usual thing. The guerrillas normally did not try to stand up to a large military mobilization like this.

Many of the civilians in the area had pulled out, too. They'd picked up whatever they could carry and headed for the hills on the Honduran border. They had good reason to flee. People who happened to live in a rebel zone in El Salvador were *ipso facto* rebels themselves, according to the calculations of the Salvadoran army. They were legitimate military targets, or they could be. If you ever wondered why civilian casualties in this war were so appallingly high, then here's your answer, or most of it.

But some people had stayed behind this time, to take their chances. And the soldiers clambered past, heading north on a rough dirt trail, kicking up small clouds of red dust into the darkening air. Apart from the clump of boots and the creak of web harness, it was silent out and still. And then I noticed some movement. I looked up to the right and saw a door opening and a woman emerging from one of the small adobe huts that hugged the hillside above the trail. She was alone, a slender young peasant woman. She stepped out into the twilight, carrying a tray. Upon it she had placed a few hunks of bread, a jug of water, some plastic cups. She carried these down to the dirt trail, to render up these meagre offerings to the soldiers who were marching by. It seemed to me, for all the world, as though she was trying to propitiate the forces of some terrible god.

Of course, I don't know exactly what her motives were or what was going on in this woman's mind, but I can make a good guess. I imagine she had some children — in El Salvador, who didn't? — and they were tucked away behind her in that adobe hut. Apart from that, she was probably all alone. I'm pretty sure her husband was nowhere to be found. You almost never saw young men in this part of the country, unless they were armed.

So there she was, a young and pretty woman, all alone with her children, with the army marching through. I'm pretty sure she had decided that the best way to protect her family, and maybe herself, was by carrying an offering of bread and water down to these soldiers, to launch a sort of pre-emptive strike. Maybe they wouldn't hurt her then. Maybe they'd leave her children alone. As far as I know, it worked. Some of the soldiers ate her bread, drank her water, and then they carried on. She stood and watched them go. She was all right. She'd managed to get through this one. She'd figured out a way.

That was the guiding principle in El Salvador — you had always to be thinking about danger and about how to fend it off. If you found yourself in a large gathering, say, one that might come under attack, you had to have a plan — which way were you going to run? Even if you were out looking for trouble, looking for it on purpose, there were usually some precautions you could devise, some measures that would lessen the risk, something you could try.

If you were travelling in a military convoy through dangerous countryside, for example, you would be pretty much at the mercy of fate, but not completely. You could try to avoid riding in the lead or the trailing vehicle. They were the ones that would get hit first in an ambush — a tactic that trapped everything in between. It was better to ride somewhere in the middle. Or, if you were following a convoy in your own car, you could try to keep as much distance as possible between the vehicle in front of you and the one behind. That gave you at least some protection in case one of them was attacked or happened to run over a mine.

So, you tried to be careful, but everyone got lazy or overconfident once in a while, and sometimes the results were fatal. Sometimes, it didn't seem to matter how careful you were. On a bad day, nothing was going to save you. Of course, some people were just plain dumb. I checked into my room at the Camino Real in San Salvador one time, at the beginning of another trip to the country. I was unpacking my gear — and what did I find lying on the upper shelf in the closet when I started to put my knapsack up there?

A postcard. It had been overlooked by the chambermaid. I flipped the card over and read what someone, some other journalist, had written. "Dear Keith, having a wonderful time here in Salvador. Haven't seen any bang-bang yet, but on Wednesday we're hiking up into a guerrilla camp. Cheers, David."

What an interesting note. I wondered why the guy didn't just take out an ad in the local newspaper while he was at it, let all the death squads know about his plans to socialize with the rebels. Granted, the card was never mailed. But who knew how many other similar messages he did mail? Besides, even to *think* of sending such a card was borderline insane.

But those were crazy years. At times, a kind of summer-camp euphoria would seize the foreign press corps in El Salvador, and a lot of reporters would forget that this was not a movie set after all. Many of us would lapse into a kind of journalistic haze, a realm of banner headlines, front-page bylines, and special TV reports direct from the combat zone. We would forget, temporarily, what country we were in, El Salvador, a place where real people were really dying and where no one was safe.

And then, one fine Salvadoran afternoon, we'd hear that another foreign reporter or photographer or cameraman had just been killed, on some dirt road up in Chalatenango or on the streets of Suchitoto. And suddenly everyone would remember exactly where this was and what we were doing here. Everyone would finally be reminded of what we never should have forgotten in the first place.

Sunrise in
Morazán

I F YOU COULD somehow manage to disregard the war, El Salvador was an idyllic, even tranquil land — a country of varied and almost constant beauty. Along the Pacific coast, you find sagging, sunburnt fishing villages and sprawling beaches, each rimmed by another shiny fretwork of coco palms and sea grapes. Inland, the country is a natural roller-coaster of sudden green mountains and pleated valleys, of tightrope ridges and cone-shaped volcanic spires. Deep blue lakes wash the shores of ancient craters.

San Salvador, the capital, and a city of about half a million, is still divided between the posh, rambling neighbourhoods of the rich — areas like San Benito or Escalón — and the dusty slums that ring the city or tumble through its ravines and disused lots. You also find the bric-a-brac of contemporary commercial culture: a conglomeration of Yankee fast-food joints, tacky amusement arcades, and huge billboards reminding Salvadorans to drink Pepsi, wear Sassoon jeans, and smoke Winstons. San Salvador is cradled between a huge, extinct volcano called el Boquerón (literally, the big mouth) and el Cerro de San Jacinto, a mountain that rises to a height of 3,800 feet above sea level. You can ride to its summit by cable car.

If you prefer, you can drive up into the surrounding heights, to a place called la Puerta del Diablo — the Devil's Gate — that commands a yawning, silent view of the surrounding countryside, including a lovely old Indian village called Panchimilco where the older women weave strips of blue cloth into their long black braids and still go about in traditional dress, one of the last places in El Salvador where this is so.

Most of the time during the country's long civil war, the capital was strangely insulated from the worst effects of the fighting. In the afternoons, I'd often go out for a run, along a route that would take me down a succession of cracked and winding streets, lined by jacaranda trees, past clusters of women grilling *pupusas* on wood-fired braziers, and I would not be thinking that here was a country that lacked for peace. But then an army *tanquete* would thump and rumble down an adjoining street, or a truck loaded with soldiers would groan by; or I'd hear another bomb go off, blowing up another telephone switch box; or I'd notice, not for the first time, that in this city even the traffic police carried automatic rifles.

Or — and this was literally a dead giveaway — I'd see another of those armour-plated Cherokee Chiefs with polarized windows, conveyance of preference for Salvadoran death squads. It would roar past, blare its horn to clear a flock of school children, say, or a gaggle of barefooted women. The vehicle would lurch not quite to a halt and then squeal away, bound for who-knew-where. And then I would remember about the war.

At night, foreign reporters would head out in groups from the lobby bar at the Hotel Camino Real to dine at one or another of the city's finer restaurants — La Ponderosa maybe, or Siete Mares. La Ponderosa was a cavernous place, set on a table-top hill high above the surrounding streets. Here, you'd order beef and it would invariably be excellent. Even during the war, El Salvador raised first-rate beef cattle. Sometimes at La Ponderosa, we'd gather on the darkened terrace in the cool evening air, where we could listen to the occasional muffled blast of bombs going off — the rebels blowing up more telephone switch boxes — or watch whole sections of the city suddenly drop off the map as the lights there went out, thanks to another act of sabotage.

Even at dinner, we could not escape the war, and I don't think anyone really bothered to try. What else was there to talk about over our meals, over plates of beef at La Ponderosa or seafood at Siete Mares? Often we talked about politics, but in Central America in those days politics meant war. There was no other kind. Even if someone changed the subject for a time, the war didn't go away. It was all around us, lurking in the air or somewhere just beneath the surface of the night, context and subtext. From the moment we sat down until we paid the check and trooped back outside, some part of me would be thinking that what was going on here was not simply a meal in a restaurant, but a meal in a restaurant *in a country at war*. And that was a very different thing.

Besides, there was the nightly *toque de queda*, the curfew imposed under the country's perpetual state of siege, renewed every six months. The curfew moved around, depending on how the government security forces were feeling at the time, on how much of the night they wanted as their own. For a time, the curfew fell at seven p.m., and that put a big crimp in everyone's night-life. Mostly, it was pushed back to eleven. In either case, you did not want to be caught out in the dark after the curfew took effect, for then the capital's streets would be turned over to the soldiers, the police, the death squads. From the moment that darkness fell, you could sense the curfew like a dangling weight.

There we would be, gathered in a well-lit restaurant some night in San Salvador, and we would all be talking politics, as usual. On the surface, this would seem thoroughly ordinary, nothing to be remarked upon at all. But, if some stranger were to eavesdrop on the conversation — amid the clatter of dishes, the bursts of laughter, and the snap of cigarette lighters — he'd hear an urgency of tone, an odd manic edge, that had little to do with peace and almost everything to do with war. People spoke a little too quickly, laughed a little too hard, or their hands shook, almost imperceptibly. They were thinking about something terrifying that had happened that day, or that might happen tomorrow.

One evening, a British reporter on her first night in El Salvador would get off the elevator and wander into the lobby bar at the Camino Real, carrying the bullet that had just burst through the window of her room on the fourth floor. Or someone familiar would be killed, someone you knew. Occasionally, this would be another journalist, someone you'd spoken to only that morning, at breakfast.

John Hoagland, for example. He was shot dead in Suchitoto one afternoon, and Bob Nickelsburg came back down with the news. Another time, Dial Torgesson and Richard Cross were blown up by a landmine on the border between Honduras and Nicaragua, along with their Honduran driver. At the time, Richard had an apartment just down the street from me in Mexico City, and we'd gone out for dinner not long before. We'd had a discussion about how to translate "Give me a break" into idiomatic Spanish. *"Déjame en paz"* was the best we could come up with. Not that it made any difference now. Or ever.

One day, a group of journalists set out from San José, Costa Rica, for a press conference in the jungle with Eden Pastora — or Commander Zero, as he was known. There was an imposter in the group, it turned out, an assassin. He had a bomb, and it went off. Linda Fraser was killed. Susie Morgan and Reed Miller ended up down by the river literally holding themselves together with their hands while they waited for help. Another afternoon, in El Salvador, Andries Koster and three other members of a Dutch TV crew got themselves summarily executed along with two young rebels up in Chalatenango. A year or so later, Nick Blake walked off the map in northwestern Guatemala, never to be seen alive again. The list was not exactly a short one.

Maybe this shouldn't have been surprising. Death was a part of the scenery; there was no immunity for journalists, any more than there was for anybody else. And yet, each time someone was killed, someone you knew, the news would come careening down like a thunderbolt, like the last thing you had ever expected, like a bomb exploding out of the blue. You were never prepared for it. Death always seemed like an interloper, an invader — the crank in the crowd who wades out onto the field in the middle of the game and turns out to have a gun. You could never be ready for that. Besides, there are at least two kinds of death. There is anonymous death, and there are the deaths of people you know.

Somehow, you had to deal with them both, and somehow people did. No doubt there are various strategies for coping with a tide of experience so huge it almost overwhelms. I suspect that the most common of these is the simplest — you just avoid dwelling on things. You live in the present. In those years, Central America was spinning like a lethal top. Each new day seemed to obliterate the one that had come before. There would always be another imperative to focus on, another rebel offensive, another threatened coup. For me, it felt as if my psychological metabolism had speeded up to a dizzying degree. I had to work my way through everything so quickly that nothing seemed to stick. Events became memories in a matter of hours, not days, and I rarely allowed myself the time to look back on this accreting fund of experience, to reflect or to brood. In fact, there wasn't time. I had to be looking always ahead, to see what was coming next.

If we refused to dwell on things, maybe we also denied them. In Central America, in those days, a lot of people — a lot of journalists, anyway — spent a good deal of their time in some kind of denial, as if all of this fighting and death were merely a movie or an extended cartoon, something to be played once and then forgotten.

In El Salvador, for example, we would go around once a week to the US Embassy — a true fortress of a building that overlooked the Avenida Gustavo Guerrero — for regular off-the-record press briefings. These were conducted by someone we could refer to in our dispatches only as "the senior US military officer in El Salvador."

For a time, the senior US military officer in El Salvador was an acerbic, cigar-smoking colonel named John Wagelstein, a sharp, intelligent man with pitted cheeks and a rugged sense of humour. The weekly briefings were known as The Wag Show, and the mood was hip and jaded; war was transformed into this really cool activity, a kind of sport, that we pretended to take in our stride, but which we couldn't quite conceal our passion for. In Wag-speak, Salvadoran government troops were "the friendlies"; guerrillas were "the gees"; combat casualty figures were "body counts" or "the score." A soldier didn't draw his pistol; he "cleared leather". Or, if you were flying in a helicopter over rebel country and got hit by rocket fire, it "sure would spoil your day." To say nothing of your mother's.

Almost all of us fell into the same loping linguistic stride of denial. Newspaper reporters — people whom I knew and admired — would actually say things like, "Colonel, what was the score in that firefight up in Morazán last week?" And they'd get another puff of cigar smoke, followed by another dose of John Wagelstein's gruff and morbid insouciance.

Maybe the jargon and the tone weren't quite as inhuman as they sometimes seemed. A lot of people were being killed in El Salvador — journalists, US military advisors, Salvadoran soldiers, guerrillas. And tens of thousands of innocent people were caught in the crossfire or dragged from their beds. You didn't want to join them, although you knew that you very well might. So you did what you needed to do, to stay sane and alive. If words were all you had for a shield, then you shielded yourself with words.

Once, I was on an army march up into rebel country in northeastern El Salvador. There were just two journalists on that march — Jim Bock of the *Baltimore Sun* and I. We'd had a hard go of it. We'd been up all the night before, stumbling through the darkness, afraid of ambush. At dawn, the real fighting began, and we'd spent the day climbing a sudden range of mountains called Ocotepeque under constant rebel

fire. By late afternoon, the government side had dug in on a
mountain ledge, pinned down by guerrilla sharp-shooters
trying to slow the army's advance.

Jim and I were dog-tired by this time and more than a
little rattled from the exertion, the lack of sleep, the fear.
There was nothing to do now but wait the shooting out —
no one was going anywhere. So we got down in the shade
of some trees near an old adobe house, more or less out of
the range of fire. To take our minds off the fighting, we
started to play a spelling game that I knew. You take turns
choosing letters of the alphabet, each one of which should
continue the spelling out of a word you have in your mind.
But you try to avoid *finishing* a word. As soon as one of the
players does finish a word, either by mistake or because
there's no choice, he loses the round. On one round, I
started with "J".

Jim countered with "I".

I said, "T".

Jim said, "T".

I added an "E" and was pretty sure I had this round sewn
up.

Jim said, "R".

"You lose," I said. "You spelled a word. 'Jitter'. That's a
word."

"No, it isn't," he said. "'Jitters' is a word. But 'jitter' isn't
a word."

"It is so a word," I said. "It's the singular of 'jitters'."

"There is no singular of 'jitters'," he said. "There's only
the plural."

I just looked at him. I said, "What the *hell* are you talking
about?"

Crack, crack, crack, went the guns. Boom went the mortars. And on and on we argued about whether or not "jitter" was a word. We got damn angry at each other, I recall. For a while, we flat-out stopped speaking. We just glared off into the distance on this gorgeous afternoon — gorgeous, that is, if you ignored the roar of rifle and machine-gun fire that rattled down the mountainside, the occasional burst of mortars. There was nothing to do but wait, and so we waited. The light that particular afternoon had an almost celestial clarity. I can imagine it now, an uncommonly vivid light that I'll always associate with Central America in the dry season. Everything shone and the sky overhead was the very perfection of blue. For centuries they'd been having afternoons like this in El Salvador. On most of them, people would just now be rousing themselves from another siesta, maybe thinking about dinner. But not this afternoon, not on this mountain. Instead, the government troops up here were making an unholy racket trying to dislodge a nest of rebel snipers, and they weren't having much luck.

It was starting to look as if we'd be stuck up here all night. That wasn't what was bothering me though. What was bothering me right now was my colleague from Baltimore. I couldn't believe this guy. I was completely outraged. Who the hell did he think he was? What kind of an imbecile would argue that "jitter" wasn't a word?

Looking back on that confrontation, that bout of interpersonal friction in time of war, I think I understand what the problem was. Combine the effects of fatigue with a generous allotment of fear, and the j-i-t-t-e-r-s were what you got. Every damn time.

Eventually, we recovered from our little grammatical

contretemps and started to take stock of the situation. It was getting dark by then, time to be thinking about sleep. The troops were still pinned down by those guerrilla snipers, so it was sure that we'd be up on this mountain all night. It was going to be an ordeal, and not just because of the war. The summit of Ocotepeque was a long distance above sea level. When darkness fell, the air turned bloody cold.

Jim and I spent that night on an old concrete pad that in peace time had been used for drying coffee beans. The surface was very flat and extremely hard, which didn't make for much in the way of comfort, but at least it was warm. I could feel the accumulated heat from the daytime sun radiating out through my body and into the darkness. We managed to avoid dying of hypothermia, but we didn't get much sleep. It was a very long night. Finally, daylight broke above the mountains, and a couple of small, Salvadoran air-force planes droned in from the west. They circled overhead and bombed the rebel positions on the ridge above us. This aerial attack was probably unnecessary — the guerrillas had likely pulled out during the night. But, one way or another, it meant we could get going again.

The troops organized themselves, and we climbed down the far slopes of Ocotepeque and continued marching north, farther into the province of Morazán, a part of El Salvador where the rebels were especially strong. The army was aiming for a town called Corinto, which was normally under rebel control. It was tough slogging, through rugged country, and we kept getting ambushed. Every hour or so, we came under fire from another band of rebel sharp-shooters dug into the hills above us.

So far, Jim and I had managed to stay out of real danger,

though. I had a theory about combat coverage: if you were close enough to hear it, you were close enough to write about it. It was a good theory, as far as it went, which wasn't all that far. In practice, you couldn't really control your distance, or anything else, once you got into the thick of combat. But, on this march, we had kept well back from the lead troops, and it had seemed to work.

On this afternoon, we kept trudging north, following a dirt track that wound up through sudden hills, across narrow ridges, and down into torrid valleys. Brush fires raged on the forested slopes that rose on either side. The soldiers had set those fires themselves, in a bid to flush out ambushers, and the air was dense with cinders and smoke.

Even so, the guerrillas always had the advantage. They held the high ground, behind crude fieldstone barricades — small groups of sharp-shooters who were staying back to slow the army advance. Meanwhile, the main rebel forces and their *masas* — their civilian supporters — were fleeing farther north. It was the usual thing, a tactic they probably still teach in Guerrilla Warfare 101. When the army advances, a guerrilla retreats. When the army pulls out, the guerrilla returns.

By this time, Jim and I had got ourselves hooked up with one particular platoon of soldiers. We'd got to know the sergeant, too — a rotund fellow with a grizzled face and a crusty friendliness, sort of a Latin version of a younger Walter Matthau. The day wore on, and we pushed down into a broad valley. This was the height of the dry season, and the heat was withering, the air so dry it could chap your bones. The sun beat down like a hammer. Our throats were constantly raw from thirst, and we had to drink from every stream or pool we stumbled upon, including some pretty murky-looking sources of water.

We knew we'd probably pay for this in twisted guts or in years lopped off our lives, but there was no choice. It was either drink or dessicate. Each time we found another brook or pond, we knelt down by the water's edge, drank what we could hold, said a little prayer, and then soaked our hats and our handkerchiefs and our shirts. Then we clambered back up to our feet and continued slogging north.

Before long, we would walk smack into another barrage of bullets unleashed by another squad of rebel sharp-shooters — or at least the advance troops would. Jim and I were staying back. *Close enough to hear it, close enough to write about it.* We waited out those bursts of fighting along with our platoon, crouching down behind a thicket of trees or beneath some rocky ledge. Shooting over, we would pull ourselves to our feet and resume our trek.

The afternoon wore on like that — the dust, the heat, the sporadic din of war, the constant weight of the sun. We were tired and, I suppose, a little dazed from too little sleep and too much exertion. We just kept marching, not really paying attention to much of anything, and so we somehow failed to notice it when we started *passing* all the other troops. Every-one else seemed to be resting, yet we kept pushing ahead.

Soldiers at our sides flopped down by the road's edge, to dig through their canvas packs for tins of beans or hunks of bread. They tipped back their canteens, fussed with their rifles. But we kept marching north until it seemed that we had become the lead platoon ourselves. We were dumb with fatigue by now, I guess, so we just kept on going. It was our turn to bear the brunt of the advance.

No one spoke much, if at all. We were all too tired to talk. We simply pushed ahead through the crackling heat, the smoke, and the dust. We rounded another bend in the track — and at once the air turned to lead. The outbreak of shooting hit like a thunderclap, just exploded around us, like the beginning of one universe or the end of another.

And, just like that, we were all sprawled in a shallow ditch by the roadside, pressed tight against a low rise that offered some protection from the bullets that sliced through the foliage above our heads. The bullets sang with a whip-saw cry, and shreds of leaves pelted down around us. At my sides, the soldiers wrestled their rifles into position and began to return fire, in single bursts or in cracking *rafagas*. Another column of soldiers must have been advancing through the hills on our right and now started firing long barrages of M-60 machine-gun fire. The shooting thundered through the afternoon heat and the dry, burning hills. Soon, I heard the booming reports of larger weapons — 81-mm and 90-mm mortar shells soaring from behind us towards the guerrilla positions in the hills above.

There was no choice but to stay down, wait, and hope we didn't die. Yet it seemed impossible to be doing so little. It seemed impossible to accept fate so passively. If I'd had a rifle, I probably would have fired it, just for something to do. But I had no rifle. Instead, without really thinking what I was up to, I worked myself over onto my side and pulled my note-book from my hip pocket. I flipped it open, got out my pen, and started to write. At some point, I glanced up and noticed that Jim was doing the same. You're a reporter, you report.

But this wasn't mere dedication to duty. It went deeper than that. It was atavistic in some way. Maybe we were trying, with the movement of our arms, to ward off harm. Or maybe, by maintaining the appearance of normal activity, we thought we could deny the proximity of death. We sure as hell weren't taking notes. I wasn't, anyway. My hand was shaking so hard I couldn't compose a recognizable letter. I would look at that notebook later, and it would be impossible to make out a single line. This was a language without grammar or syntax. It was pure compulsion, something like the written version of glossolalia. Or like an incantation. But, if an incantation was all you had, then that was what you used.

After maybe half an hour of nearly constant fire, the clash trailed off and then ended. In the hills above us, the guerrilla snipers had abandoned their positions and fled father north. The silence roared back around us. Now we pulled ourselves to our feet. At once the laughter hit. I was suddenly laughing uncontrollably. Maybe this was atavistic too. It was just that we were alive, and laugh was what you did. I was laughing, Jim was laughing, and so were we all.

We let another platoon move ahead of us — now they would bear the brunt — and we continued north on foot, with the slanted afternoon sunlight seeming to pop and shimmer all around and with the ground undulating beneath our feet. I wasn't exactly laughing now, but I was still having that high — that slow adrenalin high — the one you always got after being in a firefight and thinking you were probably going to wind up dead. That feeling is one of the reasons that some people fall in love with war.

Later, at dusk, Jim and I followed our platoon — we thought of it now as "our" platoon — up into the hills that overlooked the town of Corinto, with its patchwork of clay-tile roofs, its cypress trees, and its twin-spired church.

We found a hollow beneath a grove of acacia trees and settled in there for the night. The following morning we were up early. We climbed to the summit of a nearby ridge where our platoon acted as forward observers, marking the impact of mortar rounds being lobbed onto suspected rebel positions in the hills north of Corinto.

It was another beautiful day. Pine trees conferred in clusters on the slopes beneath us, shifting in a cool morning breeze that murmured through the needles and flared the golden, feathery grass. In the valley below, the pink blossoms of makilihaut trees dabbed the rusty landscape, like dried rose petals scattered across a crumpled sheet of brown construction paper. Except for the booming reports of outgoing mortar shells, their whistling trajectory overhead, and the bursts of smoke in the distant hills, you wouldn't have known there was a war on.

An hour or so later, we climbed down into Corinto itelf, abandoned by the rebels some time the night before. The town was quiet when we got there, but the people were all out, congregated at the edges of the grassy main plaza, silent and watchful, as the army took control of their town. The troops set up their Yugoslavian-built howitzers at the foot of the bomb-shattered colonial church. Later, two UH-1H helicopters whirled in from the south and set down in the plaza itself, strange as a pair of flying saucers. Army trucks rumbled up from Sociedad.

The man in charge of the operation was already in Corinto when we got there. His name was Lieutenant-Colonel Jorge Adalberto Cruz, and he was a forty-four-year-old officer who commanded the Salvadoran Army garrison in Morazán. A small, rather dour man with a slick

of greasy black hair, Colonel Cruz had set up a temporary
headquarters in a disused office under the clay-tiled porti-
coes that lined the plaza. We went over there to talk to him,
and what caught our attention were the five automatic rifles
that rested in a row against the stucco wall outside Colonel
Cruz's makeshift office. They were a mixed bag — FNs and
G-3s, an M-16. Immediately, we were curious about those
rifles. We wanted to know whose they were.

"Rebels'," said Colonel Cruz. He explained that the
weapons belonged to five guerrillas who had been slain in
combat in the surrounding hills the previous night. The five
men had been killed, he said, in an encounter with troops of
the Conchagua infantry battalion from La Unión province.

We asked, where were the corpses? And Colonel Cruz
explained that the retreating rebels had carried off the bodies
of their fallen comrades.

Now this was incredible on the face of it. It was true that
the Salvadoran rebels did try to clear their dead from the
battlefield. But would they leave the rifles behind? It was
difficult to imagine the People's Revolutionary Army spirit-
ing away the bodies of five dead guerrillas, while leaving five
rifles to be collected at leisure by government troops. One
or two — maybe. It could happen by mistake. But five?

Before long, Jim and I managed to track down several
members of the Conchagua battalion, who were among the
troops occupying Corinto, and they told us quite a different
story about those five rebels. They said that the men were a
guerrilla rearguard that had become trapped during the
army's advance on the town the night before. They hadn't
been killed at all, but had been taken alive after the soldiers
entered Corinto — and they were still alive. They were still

being held prisoner. The soldiers agreed to show us where.

It turned out that they were right — the five rebels were in fact still alive and being held prisoner. We confirmed this to a certainty. And so we returned to Colonel Cruz and asked him again about what had happened. He simply repeated his original story — that the rebels had been killed in battle and that their bodies had been carried off by their comrades. He said he didn't want to discuss the subject any further.

It didn't take a genius to figure out what was happening here. The Salvadoran Army was not in the habit of taking prisoners in its long and bitter war, or anyway not for long. Those it did capture — such as these five poor souls in Corinto — were rarely acknowledged publicly. Obviously, Colonel Cruz could not admit their existence now, for the very simple reason that he planned to kill them. They would be interrogated. Their interrogation would be slow, horrible, and at last fatal. Then they would disappear.

That was now their fate, and there was no escaping it. There was nothing that Jim or I or anyone else could do to prevent it. All we could do was write about those men afterwards, but that wouldn't stop them from dying. In a way, they were dead already, had disappeared already. After all, no one but their interrogators would ever see them again. And yet I knew that they did exist, in that place, on that day — March 13, 1984. They were alive then. A day afterward — I don't know. And now, years later, I imagine their families must still wonder about them, about their fates, must still be haunted by the mystery of five more men who did not come home at the end of the war.

Meanwhile, the war ground on. But, that night, at least

in Corinto, there was a break. A group of soldiers crowded into the town's communal granary, illuminated by a hurricane lantern. They sang melancholy Central American folk songs, taking turns on a guitar. Outside, across the broad plaza, a tall cypress tree stood in a pale lake of moonlight, near the twin spires of the town church. Finally, the songs trailed off, and the hurricane lantern went out. We slept on sacks of grain that night. In the morning, we'd be heading south again, back to the capital. We'd been told a private truck was driving down to Sociedad, and Jim and I planned to be on it. It was time to get back in touch with our newspapers, time to file our reports.

Deep in the darkness before dawn, I heard an engine roar. Immediately, Jim and I got ourselves up and going. We grabbed our things and stumbled across the plaza through air as black as India ink. Right on time, an old truck was waiting to carry peasants south, and we clambered into the wobbling bed. Soon the engine roared again, and the truck wound along the rough gravel road, tottered out of Corinto and then twisted and bounced through the swooping hill country of northern Morazán.

Daylight broke, and the sun gradually swelled above the dry, pine-scented land. The morning mist burned away. And in that slowly rising light, I was astonished to hear some of the women in the truck speaking what turned out to be Lenca, an ancient Indian language. I was sure it had vanished from El Salvador — I'd been told time and again that no one could speak it any more. Yet these women certainly could, and here they were, chatting amiably among themselves in a vanished indigenous tongue, while the morning light expanded over Morazán.

Eventually, we came upon our rented car, still waiting in an open field where we'd left it several days earlier. It made an incongruous sight. But no one seemed to have disturbed the vehicle, and that was reassuring when you thought about it — reassuring to think that, in Central America in time of war, you could still find secure parking. We pounded on the roof of the cab until the driver stopped. Jim and I jumped down from the truck bed, ran around to the driver's window, and asked the man in the cowboy hat behind the wheel how much we owed him. But he just smiled, shook his head, and drove away.

2

FROM THE IVORY COAST TO ZAMBIA

The Sage of Africa

EVEN THE SAGE OF AFRICA, His Excellency Félix
Dia Houphouët-Boigny, finally had to die. While
alive, he did what he could — and it was a lot — to
stave off, or buy off, the gatekeepers of the space-time con-
tinuum. And he managed to live to a venerable age. He was
at least eighty-eight and may well have been older when on
December 7, 1993, he asked his doctors to shut down the
life-support system on which he was being maintained. It
was shortly after dawn on the thirty-third anniversary of his
country's independence.

And it really was *his* country. From 1960 until his death,
Houphouët-Boigny was president of *la République du Côte
d'Ivoire*, or the Ivory Coast. He was in fact the only president
the country had ever known. When he died, only two of his
contemporaries among world leaders had held power longer
— Fidel Castro in Cuba and Kim Il Sung in North Korea,
neither of whom was exactly one of Houphouët-Boigny's
great ideological soul-mates.

Houphouët-Boigny was a capitalist and, under his leadership, the Ivory Coast developed what was probably the

most robust economy in all of black Africa, even if that distinction was eroding by the time of his death. All in all, the Sage of Africa gave private enterprise a pretty good name, on a continent where the image of capitalism had largely turned to post-colonial mud. During his long presidency and his even longer life, Houphouët-Boigny did a great deal that was more than merely good. He transformed the Ivory Coast from a backwater of the French colonial empire into the economic powerhouse of West Africa. Although not what you would call a model democrat, he was certainly a passably benevolent ruler by the standards of the region.

By any standards, his was a remarkable life.

Born into a family of prosperous planters in central Ivory Coast, the young Houphouët-Boigny later studied medicine in Dakar, Senegal and worked as a rural doctor before entering local cantonal politics under French colonial rule. After the Second World War, he was instrumental in the establishment of *le Rassemblement Démocratique Africain*, which sought greater political independence for French West Africa. At the same time, he forged close ties with the French political elite and even served briefly as minister of health in Paris during the government of the Fourth Republic. His heroes were George Washington and Charles de Gaulle.

At independence, Houphouët-Boigny was named president of the Ivory Coast, which in those days was the poor cousin of France's former colonial possessions. "They started from a base of zero," a European diplomat told me. "They had no agriculture, no money. And you see the result."

The result was the Ivorian miracle. While neighbours like Ghana and Guinea sank into decay, the Ivory Coast ploughed ahead, thanks in part to Houphouët-Boigny's willingness to use French technical assistance and mainly to his single-minded conviction that African development had to rest on the shoulders of its small-scale farmers. It wasn't glamourous but it worked. By encouraging those farmers to produce, the Ivory Coast achieved feats of economic growth that were not remotely matched in other emerging African countries, where more elaborate and expensive industrial programmes quickly collapsed, dragging national economies down with them.

By the 1980s, the Ivory Coast had become the world's largest cocoa producer and was second only to Brazil in coffee production. Abidjan, the de facto capital, was transformed into an impressive city of modern skyscrapers towering above a maze of coastal lagoons, its downtown streets sedately plied by Mercedes limousines and luxury Renault-25 sedans. What was even better, Houphouët-Boigny managed these feats of economic growth while avoiding the ferocious political repression or tribal conflict or runaway corruption that hounded so many neighbouring states. To be sure, there was repression, there was conflict, and there was corruption, but they didn't go spinning right off the charts — which, in many other countries, they surely did.

Still, there was undoubtedly a tendency towards material excess. You have only to gaze across the Bay of Cocody from the centre of Abidjan to be pretty clear about that. On a green spit of land across the blue and unruffled bay rises the towering central column and sprawling annexes of the Hôtel Ivoire. The place is a massive complex of boutiques, bars, restaurants, sports facilities, hospitality services, and European-style opulence — not to mention the only artificial ice-skating rink in all of black Africa. Abidjan in the late 1980s was reputed to be the eighth most expensive city in the world. You didn't have to like it, or approve of it, but you certainly had to be impressed. As a symbol of all that Houphouët-Boigny hoped to achieve for his country, and to some extent did achieve, the Hôtel Ivoire is about as eloquent a statement as you are likely to find — at least in Abidjan.

In the country as a whole, however, the Hôtel Ivoire is far from being the last word in Ivorian excess or opulence. In fact, it is little more than a clearing of the presidential throat. You would be astonished by it only if you hadn't made an inland pilgrimage to the city of Yamoussoukro, which is, on paper, the official capital of the Ivory Coast. Now, *here* is a place of truly mind-warping weirdness.

The city is located about two hundred kilometres northwest of Abidjan. Once just a humble farming village, it was abruptly transformed on March 21, 1983, when the Ivorian National Assembly voted unanimously to make it the official capital of *la République du Côte-d'Ivoire*. Like so much else in the Ivory Coast, this thoughtful gesture was intended to honour the president. The president just happened to have been born in Yamoussoukro.

Thus did the Sage of Africa embark upon what may well have been the strangest urban project in the world. Five years later, the new Yamoussoukro rose at the inland edge of the West African coastal forest — an eerie ghost town inhabited by the silent spectres of one man's dreams, where the sumptuous amenities included an eighteen-hole championship golf course and a three-hundred-room five-star hotel, both about equally empty.

In name, Yamoussoukro had become the political and administrative hub of the Ivory Coast. In fact, however, by the late 1980s, no foreign embassies had moved there, almost no government business was conducted there, and even the president tended to avoid the place. Nonetheless, what was once an unassuming collection of mud huts perched amid eucalyptus trees and surrounded by sweltering savannah, had been utterly transformed.

The huts had made way for colossal marble palaces that sprawled over the veld but were mostly empty. An artificial lake had been installed, surrounded by green wrought-iron railings, bordered by replanted palms, and stocked with sacred caimans that slithered up onto the banks each evening to be fed. Outside town, an elaborate air terminal had been constructed — the Yamoussoukro International Airport — capable of handling even the largest Boeing 747 jumbo jets, although no such aircraft flew there.

The undulating terrain of Yamoussoukro was now criss-crossed by yawning six-lane boulevards that had no names, carried almost no traffic, started nowhere, and went nowhere. On the fourteenth floor of the five-star Hôtel Président — which had a grand total of eighteen guests the night I stayed there — Joseph Joubard, chef-de-cuisine at the magnificent revolving Restaurant Panoramique, had composed a regally sophisticated menu. The fare included *salade de langouste au parfum de gingembre, fricassée de rognons et ris de veau à la crème d'ail doux*, and *millefeuille de poire au vin rouge*. Dinner for two, assuming two diners could be found, cost the silently rotating roof.

Almost nobody except Houphouët-Boigny and possibly his closest supporters really seemed to believe that the capital would ever *in fact* be moved to Yamoussoukro, although in theory it already had. Yet the work continued, at mind-boggling expense. Italian and French architects were commissioned. Israeli and French builders were contracted. Huge glass and marble structures were erected. Vast sums were spent on imported marble, European stained glass, Moroccan tapestries, and antique oriental vases.

The six-story presidential palace — which Houphouët-Boigny owned privately — was a commanding structure of glass-paned galleries interspersed by marble beams and pillars. But even that grand mansion seemed to shrink beside the gargantuan marble-and-glass headquarters of the Fondation Félix Houphouët-Boigny. And that structure was about to be dwarfed in turn by the most ambitious and controversial building in Yamoussoukro — the Basilica of Our Lady of Peace.

In 1988, the basilica was still a year or so away from completion, but it was vaulting skyward at an impressive pace and at a staggering cost. The estimates I heard varied from $100 million to $300 million, and they kept rising. More recently, I've heard that the temple wound up costing closer to $800 million. It was eventually offered as a gift to the Vatican. The Holy See dithered for quite some time, but in the end it reluctantly agreed to accept what is now the largest Christian temple of worship in the world — in a country where there are hardly any Catholics, in a city where almost nobody lives.

Whenever the subject of the basilica was raised or indeed whenever the name Yamoussoukro was mentioned, Ivorian officials had a tendency to respond in stiff, brittle voices. "There's no reason Westerners should dictate to Africans how they should develop their countries," one government official reminded me. His office was in Abidjan, naturally.

And that is true — there *is* no reason Westerners should

dictate to Africans. Besides, more than a few Western leaders have erected architectural monuments to themselves that are pretty colossal too. I can think of Jean Drapeau, the long-time mayor of Montreal, whose soaring vision led to the construction of the huge and woefully impractical Olympic Stadium in the city's east end — the Big Owe as they call it. Almost two decades after its construction, residents of Quebec are still paying for the structure through their taxes, and the retractible roof still doesn't work properly.

So it would be a mistake for anyone in North America to feel inherently superior to a Houphouët-Boigny. Besides, although Yamoussoukro was costing hundreds of millions of dollars — billions, probably — at least the money was being spent on bricks and mortar inside the Ivory Coast and not being spirited out of the country for deposit in numbered bank accounts in Switzerland, the fate of more than a little ill-gotten African wealth.

Still, it's hard to believe that Yamoussoukro, or the Ivory Coast — or the entire African continent, for that matter — really requires a basilica quite this regal or nearly this large. When I visited the place, it was still in the throes of construction, but already it was a spectacle to behold — a dazzling array of clustered marble columns and domes connected by soaring archways of stained glass. "It's a very unpopular project," remarked a diplomat I spoke to. "Ivorians at all levels grumble about it."

As well they might. While the basilica was under construction, the Ivory Coast's economic miracle was in a free fall. World prices for many agricultural commodities had plummeted, and the country had been forced to suspend payment on its foreign debts. Besides, only about ten per cent of Ivorians are Roman Catholic (the president, of course, among them). Many of the rest aren't even Christians; most are Muslim. What do they want with the world's largest Christian temple of worship — a Roman Catholic basilica?

And so people were complaining out loud. To be fair, I should note that Houphouët-Boigny was not entirely insensitive to their concerns. He eventually responded by announcing that the basilica wasn't costing the country one red *sou*, because — and this was the best part — because *he* was paying for the place *out of his own pocket*. Unfortunately, the president did not expand on this point. He did not go on to explain just how it was that he had managed to come by such an impressive amount of discretionary cash. Maybe he just saved a lot.

In the erstwhile village of Yamoussoukro, the people seemed to accept all this weird and apparently pointless new construction with the sort of long-suffering equanimity that is far more a part of the African social fabric than are the occasional spasms of anger or violence that receive most of the international attention. Even the basilica failed to arouse real outrage. "For the people, this is nothing new," said Jerome Yonan, a thoughtful and engaging young man who worked at the municipal library in Yamoussoukro. "They're used to big buildings."

Yonan volunteered one morning to show me around the city and to introduce me to some of its grander sights, of which there were quite a few. After several hours spent inspecting a succession of shining but empty mansions and office complexes, and after much earnest discussion of the magnificent stupidity of ambitious men, Yonan and I repaired to a jumble of dirt-floor wooden stalls tucked in the shadow of the Hôtel Président and its Restaurant Panoramique. Here, an earthier side of Africa survived amid the surrounding confusion of glass and steel.

Yonan and I settled ourselves at a rough wooden table by one of several ramshackle stands, and he chatted briefly with the rotund woman who came over to take our order. Here, you could feast upon boiled head of gazelle, sloshed in a dark peppery sauce with lots of warm rice — all for about $2.50. I am not a great partisan of antelope brain, as it happens, but the broth was good.

And so we slurped and ate, as occasional groups of barefoot women padded past outside, along the otherwise vacant boulevard. They all bore some combination of bundles, baskets, and loads of firewood balanced atop their heads and did not bother to look both ways before they crossed the street — they knew they were pretty much the only traffic hereabouts and maybe always would be.

On that slow and easy afternoon, I had the feeling that Félix Dia Houphouët-Boigny, with all his vaulting aspirations, would one day be only a faint memory, and all the temples and palaces of Yamoussoukro would in time be claimed by worms and termites and the ponderous tropical air. Meanwhile, these rickety wooden stalls would still be in place, still doing a fair lunch-time business in peppery gazelle-head soup, as flocks of women ambled past on what remained of an ancient asphalt road.

I imagined that someone very much like Jerome Yonan would still take his midday meal here, still kibbitz with the cook, still nod in amusement as he reflected on the follies of great and powerful men. He'd be speaking in that patient and phlegmatic tone of his, in that unhurried African way.

Africa on
$41.21
a Month

I T'S ONE THING for a country and its people to survive the excesses of a man such as Félix Dia Houphouët-Boigny. After all, he was essentially a benevolent leader; his policies were generally sound, if not downright inspired; and Yamoussoukro, in the end, was just a bunch of construction materials. Other countries in Africa haven't been so lucky. Uganda, for example, had to endure a madman named Idi Amin. That was one reason I wanted to go there. I wanted to see if there was anything left.

But when I travelled to Uganda, I made the mistake of entering the country illegally. This was purely an accident on my part. I flew from Nairobi and landed at Uganda's international airport at Entebbe unaware that, as a foreign newspaper reporter, I needed a special journalist's visa, a document that could be obtained only in advance and only after considerable effort — if it could be obtained at all.

This was not an unusual requirement in Africa. In fact, it was pretty much the norm. But somehow, in this case, I'd overlooked it. It really was an accident. I even wrote "journalist" on my landing card at the airport. But the immigration officer at Entebbe either didn't notice or didn't care. Or maybe he just couldn't make the word out, it was so dark in the immigration hall. The electricity wasn't working.

Still unaware that I was an illegal migrant, I retrieved my bag, passed through customs, and rode a rattling old taxi past the shores of Lake Victoria and up through the shining green hills towards Kampala, a thoroughly decrepit town. All was rust or rubble. Junk-heap cars clanged through the city — miracles of human ingenuity and mechanical resolve; all around, the buildings were literally crumbling. Slabs of concrete lay about the sidewalks where they had toppled from some disintegrating ledge overhead. Garbage was piled everywhere, and great marabou storks — five feet tall if they were an inch — strode through the litter like scraggly and disgruntled waiters at a restaurant where, on careful reflection, you would not care to dine.

I checked into a hotel and immediately went to bed — some Kenyan parasite had got me. The next day, feeling fully recovered, I dropped by a succession of embassies and offices scattered around the city, in order to talk to people there. I was still an illegal migrant, although unaware of the fact. It wasn't until the afternoon that I headed around to the Ugandan government press office. I wanted to enlist their help in arranging interviews with several government officials. At the press office, I was promptly told what I probably should already have known — that I had entered the country without the proper papers.

One of the press officers scowled at me. "Where are your documents?"

"What documents?"

"The documents authorizing your entrance as a foreign

correspondent. Look at your passport. It contains only an ordinary visa." The press officer slapped my passport down on his desk in contempt.

He said he had received no prior and official knowledge of me. I was an illegal journalist, quite likely a spy to boot, and this office could be of no assistance to me whatsoever. By rights, he said, I ought to be expelled, or even jailed, at which point this imperious government employee glanced at his cheap digital wrist watch and saw that it was just about quitting time. Immediately, he relaxed. He adjusted his manner at once, the way you might adjust your clothes. No more talk of expulsion or jail. Instead, he and his mates invited me out for a beer.

And so, at an open-air drinking spot just down a muddy and rutted dirt road, three chatty Ugandans stood me a drink, and then another, and gave an off-the-record assessment of my situation. No, they weren't going to report me to the state-security people (the ones responsible for all these stupid and idiotic rules restricting the entry and movement of foreign journalists). One fellow shrugged. "You're here now," he said. "So why don't you just go ahead and do whatever it was you were going to do?" He and his colleagues couldn't help me, or not officially, but they didn't think there'd be any trouble.

There wasn't. In fact, my time in Uganda — long among the most tormented countries in the world — unfolded like the wings of a dream. I have nothing but fine memories of the country. True, the place was falling apart. Granted, it was crawling out of a past that was as dark, as ghoulish, and as horrible as almost any the modern world has known. And, yes, it was the African country perhaps hardest hit by the scourge of AIDS. The trials and burdens of Uganda were almost too onerous and terrible to list. And yet I wonder if I have ever visited a more joyful land.

It was a land with a past. From 1971 to 1986, Uganda was prey to the dictatorships of Idi Amin and then Milton Obote, a former president returned to power. Hundreds of thousands of Ugandans were murdered in a long frenzy of paranoia, lawlessness, hatred, and revenge. It was difficult to credit some of the things that were done, and yet they happened. People were collared on the streets and battered to death in public, with sledgehammers. Torture chambers burgeoned around the country and the screams of Ugandans welled up by day and exploded through the night.

Uganda literally collapsed, ceased to be a country in any meaningful sense. Soldiers rampaged, murdered, and looted. Tribe fought tribe. And just about everything that could fall apart, did. The exercise of power was capricious and absolute. One morning, for example, Amin awoke from a visionary's dream and saw it as his duty to expel all Asians from the country. Just like that, they were gone — as refugees to India or Britain or Canada. Back in Uganda, their substantial properties were commandeered by Amin and his cronies, who looted what they could before abandoning what was left, leaving it to rot. No one knew how to run the properties, or cared to try. They were condemned to disintegrate.

The years spun by in a whirl of chaos, gunshots, and bloodshed. In response to Ugandan provocation, a ragtag army from Tanzania invaded. There was a comic-opera war. Amin, who had come to power in a coup against Obote, was toppled himself. He was replaced by a succession of dull or dithering or otherwise ineffectual men, until Obote himself returned to power, and the chaos and the killing resumed. In mid-1985, Obote was again overthrown, this time by his army commander, General Tito Okello, a longtime henchman of Idi Amin.

Finally, in January, 1986, following a bitter civil war, a rebel leader named Yoweri Museveni led his National Resistance Army into Kampala, once a splendid city built like Rome upon seven hills. Museveni, it turned out, was a very different manner of leader from the long line of despots and madmen he succeeded. He certainly didn't look the part of a guerrilla warrior. When he put on a business suit, he reminded you rather more of a balding, middle-aged chartered accountant than a rebel commander, much less a national president.

But he was the president now, and things started to change almost at once. Museveni introduced some extraordinary reforms, and Uganda began to turn itself around. The new president actually seemed open to new ideas. He launched a government newspaper, for example, that was *independent* of government control, something almost unheard-of in Africa. It was called *The New Vision* and, to help ensure that the paper did not become a prisoner of tribal politics or a toady to power, Museveni had a professional journalist appointed as its editor, a complete outsider — a white man from England.

The paper took its mission seriously. In part, it operated as a journal of record, but it also did investigative work. Sometimes it uncovered stories about government corruption or incompetence or human-rights abuses, and it published them, often on the front page. As far as Museveni was concerned, this was just fine. He did not shut off the electricity, or jam the presses, or block the supplies of newsprint, or order certain reporters to be assassinated, or throw the editor in jail. The paper was doing precisely what he wanted it to do.

When I travelled to Uganda, Museveni had been in power just three years, but already things were looking up. Here was a battered but oddly hopeful land. The previous month, consumer prices had risen only 1.5 per cent, a dramatic reduction from the one hundred per cent inflation rate of the previous year. International lenders were rescheduling the country's debts. Foreign aid had begun to flow once more. Consumer goods were back in the stores, and some commodities—soap, for example, and beer — were being produced domestically. Human-rights problems persisted, but they were vastly less severe or widespread than they had been in the past. And national elections of a kind, the first since Museveni came to power, had been scheduled.

This wasn't paradise. The country was still a mess by just about every standard other than its own terrible past. It wasn't even peace time. Government forces still had to contend with several rebel groups, mainly in the northern and eastern parts of the country. Until a few months earlier, the Uganda People's Democratic Army, composed mainly of members of the Acholi tribe, had waged a sporadic guerrilla campaign under the leadership of Tito Okello, the man Museveni had replaced in power. When a peace agreement was forged with the UPDA, many of its members decamped and joined an outfit called the Holy Spirit Movement led by one Alice Lakwena. This was the most insanely gallant of the rebel forces Museveni had to cope with.

A former prostitute and an inveterate mystic, Lakwena assured her warriors that protective spirits would render them invulnerable in battle against government forces — the bullets could not possibly harm them. They took her at her word and, in a typical battle, would march straight into the teeth of the munitions fired by the government side, making no effort to protect themselves. Although divinely inspired, this tactic proved to have some serious practical flaws, and the Holy Spirit warriors suffered heavy casualties. With her legions badly depleted, Lakwena eventually fled to Kenya.

Meanwhile, in the east, the government had to contend with a force called the Uganda People's Army that was linked to cronies of the ousted Obote regime. In all, the rebel forces may have consisted of perhaps two thousand men in arms — enough to make trouble, certainly, but not to pose a real political or military threat to the government.

In comparison to the past — and this was the comparison that counted most in Uganda — you could say the country was at peace. You could even say that Ugandans, on the whole, were optimistic about their future. And that was a kind of miracle. In this gorgeous horror story of a country — the land of Idi Amin, of Milton Obote, and of a million horrible screams — I kept stumbling upon all these human outposts of confidence and hope.

When I travelled to Uganda, I had expected to find a physical shambles, but I also thought I would encounter a tide of human wreckage too, a population hounded by misery, horror, despair. Granted, I had lived in Africa long enough to realize that a country or a continent can never be reduced to a single image and especially not to one of those woeful tableaux you so often see on TV or in magazines — a thousand gaunt humans in rags, all gathered helplessly to die on a blasted African plain. You can find such sights, and they're real, but they don't embody Africa or any country in Africa.

Ugandans, on the whole, were neither helpless nor dying. They were very much alive and, despite their troubles, they were getting by. Meanwhile, the fact that I was in the country illegally seemed to make no difference at all. I interviewed plenty of government officials during my stay, all of whom seemed perfectly happy to talk to me and entirely willing to tell me just about anything I wanted to know. They didn't bother to ask whether I had the proper documents or not. They didn't seem to care. What seemed most important to them, as it did to Ugandans in general, was clearing the time to settle down and have good long chat.

For a journalist, there is nothing better. Producing newspaper stories in some countries is a bit like trying to pull teeth from the maw of a large and unhappy hockey player — they're difficult to find and, once you find them, they're the devil to get out. And, if you do get them out, who the hell wants them anyway? Other countries are just the opposite. They're like a stroll through an orchard. You just reach up and pluck the stories down — round and ripe as apples. Uganda was like that.

Kampala, however, was a mess. Once a proud and prosperous east African capital — where even the haughty Kenyans came to shop — the city had been transformed by fifteen years of death and disorder into a topsy-turvy maze of boarded-up, rundown, burnt-out, or crumbling buildings slowly being reclaimed by the irridescent lizards, the cockroaches, the rats, and the seething tropical air, not to mention the huge marabou storks that drifted overhead or floated down to refuel among the garbage.

A similar fate had overtaken the rest of the country. Once, Uganda had vast sugar estates, substantial industries, a bustling network of commerce, and an active tourist trade. Now, everything lay in ruins. Yet there was life in those ruins. One afternoon in Kampala, I ventured into the office of a handsome, deep-voiced man named Eric Edroma, who was chief research officer at the Uganda Institute of Ecology. He had a broad intelligent forehead, wore a white shirt with pale pink stripes, and had that direct easy manner some people seem to possess as a birthright. After five minutes in Edroma's office, you felt you'd been good friends for years.

I wanted to talk to Edroma about elephants — a desperately endangered species in Uganda — and he was happy to oblige. But we also talked a good bit about Edroma himself and his life as a civil servant of no little consequence in a troubled African land. His life, it turned out, was a constant slog.

In almost any other part of the world, a man or woman of Edroma's talents, accomplishments, and credentials would be grazing in the bureaucratic equivalent of clover. After all, he was eminently well-qualified for his position. He held a doctorate in natural science and was recognized internationally for his expertise in the protection of the African environment. But this was Uganda, and so it was a struggle for Edroma just to survive, to turn one day into the next. Somehow, he met the challenge, but it consumed almost all of his energies, leaving little to spare for the actual performance of what was, after all, his job.

He shook his head. "If you were to put down all a civil

servant does in a day," he said, "out of an eight-hour day, a person would put in one hour in effective time. In fact, one hour would be quite a lot. The rest of the time is just spent doing lousy personal things."

Despite his qualifications and his position, Edroma could count on a salary of just 6,800 Ugandan shillings a month. It was all the government could afford; at the official rate of exchange, it worked out to exactly $41.21 US — a *month*. How many days could he, his wife, and their seven children survive on that? "Three days, at the very most," he said. "Nobody in Uganda could survive just on his salary."

And so, nobody even tried. Instead, everybody had to cook up something on the side. Edroma, for example, was regularly invited to regional conferences to speak about ecological issues. He wasn't normally paid for those appearances, but he usually received a per-diem allowance to cover his expenses. The rates were set by the United Nations and amounted to $90 US a day if he happened to be in Nairobi, for example, or slightly less, $80 a day, if he happened to be in Harare, the capital of Zimbabwe.

And what did Edroma do with that money? Well, he didn't spend it on posh hotels or expensive meals. Instead, he squirrelled it away. While abroad, he stayed at the cheapest hotels he could find, ate in the least expensive restaurants, took buses rather than taxis. Then, at the end of his trip, he smuggled the precious US dollars back to Uganda and changed them on the *magendo*, the local black market in foreign currency. At the time, the *magendo* rate for US dollars was roughly triple the official rate. And so, for each day he spent outside Uganda, Edroma stood to make the equivalent of around $200 US or even more. It all added up.

Inside Uganda, he used that money to set himself up in business. Until recently, for instance, he had been the owner of a Land Rover. He'd hired someone else to drive it as a *matutu* — one of the countless unofficial taxis that careened along the blasted streets of Kampala. They were a sight, those taxis — all surplus humanity, with sundry arms and legs sprouting out the windows like so many tassels or streamers. They veered and swerved through the city, defiantly flouting all the rules of the road, not to mention most laws of mechanical engineering.

Eventually — inevitably — the Land Rover fell apart, so that was the end of that. But Edroma had recently managed to buy a small truck, second-hand, which he intended to licence and put back on the street. He planned to engage another driver, maybe two, and hope for the best. "Of course, they'll cheat," he said. "But there's no one you can get to give you one hundred per cent service without any cheating."

I wondered if everyone in Uganda had to cheat in order to survive. Edroma pondered for several moments before answering. He tilted his head to the side. "In a way," he said, "the answer is yes."

It figured. Just in order to make ends meet, secretaries removed reams of paper or cheap plastic pens from their offices. Store clerks filched small amounts of merchandise. At the very least, everybody stole increments of time from their employers. They had no choice. How else could they manage to do the deals, make the informal arrangements, and scout for the bargains that made life possible? It wasn't tidy, and it certainly wasn't efficient, but somehow most people got from one day to the next.

Although they got by, the strain left little time or energy

to spare for other pursuits, such as doing the job for which you were supposedly being paid, albeit not very much. At the time I spoke to him, Edroma was feeling worn out from the exertion of living in Uganda. He said he was considering giving up on the country. He'd received an offer from an international organization that would take him to Harare where a hard-currency salary awaited.

On the other hand, he also had his eye on a possible promotion in his own department. True, the new Ugandan job would pay only 10,000 shillings a month — hardly a huge improvement — but it would mean less travel and therefore leave more time for developing local business prospects. Edroma said he'd worked out a way to buy certain consumer goods directly from government factories at the official rate — commodities such as clothing, cooking oil, and soap. He could then sell them on the *magendo* at a three-fold profit. It wouldn't leave him much time for attending to his "real" job — saving the Ugandan environment and all that — but it would get him through the day. And that, in Uganda, was the main battle and the main victory.

The Last Elephants in Uganda

A T THE TIME I travelled there, Uganda was staging the country's first elections since President Museveni's rise to power. Formerly, all government ministers and all delegates to the country's parliament had been appointed. Now, Museveni ordered the country's leaders — with the exception, it was true, of himself — to return to their villages. They would have to throw themselves upon the mercy of their fellow citizens and let democracy rule.

I spent most of that memorable election day on a rounded savannah by the village of Butolo, roughly an hour's drive outside Kampala, and it was an exhilarating, even rapturous, experience.

Constant sunshine washed over the rolling blue hills on the horizon. A warm breeze kicked up through the neighbouring banana fields, and hawks set their wings against the broad blue sky, to hover and tilt upon the shifting air. Eucalyptus and flamboyant trees stood about in clusters or columns, and a massive mango tree towered by itself almost in the centre of the savannah. This was where the villagers and the farmers from the surrounding countryside customarily met to discuss matters of importance and moment.

It was here that several hundred voters gathered on election day. They arrived on foot or on bicycles or in the backs of trucks. The men had put on their Sunday best for the occasion — cheap ill-fitting jackets, baggy pants, and wide, striped ties. They wore dark fedoras, which they removed in order to mop their foreheads with large handkerchiefs. Their wives were garbed in *gosenis*, the bright billowing gowns with puffed sleeves and broad belts that are the traditional dress of the Baganda women of southern Uganda. They strolled across the savannah, the women straightening and adjusting their dresses. The men used their handkerchiefs to slap away the rich red African dust that had caked upon their clothes.

Eventually, the people assembled near the broad shade of the mango tree, almost five hundred of them in all. Together, they made up a sort of electoral college — each had been elected a week earlier in order to cast a vote today. And what unfolded on this fine afternoon on this green savannah was a piece of pure African magic.

In Butolo, seven candidates were running for national office — a seat on the National Resistance Council, as the country's new parliament was known — and each of them was permitted five minutes to introduce himself and to explain his platform. The men all spoke in Luganda, the local language, and some made extravagant claims about their accomplishments, waving aloft sheafs of documents which they said were their diplomas or degrees. Some of these were from institutions of dubious authenticity — for example, "the University of Minnesota, Wisconsin, USA."

When their speeches were over, the candidates were excused. They headed off in a group to cool their rhetoric beneath a tall, graceful mpafu tree some distance away. The voters, meanwhile, proceeded to discuss the men's suitability for high office. One candidate was roundly criticized for having kept his hands in his pockets while he spoke — a sign of disrespect. Another was darkly accused of having smuggled some of his money out of the country. And there were other complaints. "We want people who are educated and will go to parliament and talk sense," said Saul Katabalwa, a local resident, pretty much summing up the prevailing view.

There were three rounds of voting. During each round, the voters of Butolo expressed their democratic will by marking the green Ugandan ground with their feet: they simply formed a queue behind the candidate of their choice. True, this procedure posed some difficulties in the area of confidentiality, but it certainly streamlined the tabulation process, which was a simple matter of counting heads. It wasn't quite as slapdash an affair as it may sound; for example, candidates were strictly prohibited from turning around to look at who was voting for them, or who wasn't, and so the voters had some protection. There were even some advantages over a secret ballot, where the integrity of the system is largely invisible and has to be taken on faith.

"No one can complain because, if you lose, you can see that you are defeated," said Joseph Lumu, a farmer in a white caftan and a grey jacket, who amassed just eleven supporters in the first round of voting and who did not complain when he lost.

In the end, 258 voters queued up behind a young soap-factory owner named John Mugwanza, putting him just ahead of a dashingly handsome potato farmer named Edward Sengkwangu, who won 214 supporters in the two-man run-off.

After the final round of voting, the people and the candidates repaired to the shade of the mango tree, where the results were announced by the local returning officer — an officious man named Sam Nawitta who carried a pen and a clipboard. Immediately, Sengkwangu — the loser — leapt to his feet and made straight for Mugwanza, his victorious opponent. Backed by their supporters, the two men stood face to face for several instants in what briefly looked, to me, like a Ugandan version of a Mexican stand-off — a confrontation in which both parties wait for the other to strike the first blow — except that both of these men were beaming.

After only a brief hesitation, the two men shook hands and warmly embraced. No one cried fraud. No one pulled out a knife. True, the army was in evidence, in the form of several rifle-toting youths in grubby camouflage fatigues and green rubber boots. They roamed the perimeter of the savannah but did not intervene. And thus were the seeds of democracy planted in Uganda, the land that survived Idi Amin.

Idi Amin was only a man. After surviving decades of despotism, corruption, and bloodshed under his rule — and under the succeeding regime headed by Milton Obote — Ugandans now faced an even deadlier enemy, if that could be imagined. Their country had the terrible misfortune to lie near the buckle of the African AIDS belt, the region of central and east Africa where the human immunodeficiency virus had established its first major bridgehead.

We have learned a good deal about AIDS in Africa, about how the virus travelled along the trucking routes linking Rwanda, Burundi, Uganda, and the Central African Republic, carried by truck drivers who frequented the many brothels located along those roads. The virus took hold in these congenial circumstances and advanced from there, east to Tanzania and Kenya, south to Zambia, Malawi, Zimbabwe, and beyond. No one can say for certain where AIDS began its spread around the world. But it certainly made big and early inroads in Africa, and Uganda was among the earliest and the worst.

Considering all the horrors the country had already endured, AIDS in Uganda seemed like a dirty prank played by a thoroughly demonic god. And yet, unlike some other countries, where AIDS posed a threat that was just as great, Uganda didn't shrink from this affliction. Other African governments sought to deny the existence of the disease, not so surprising a reaction, really, when you counted all the other burdens they faced. But not Uganda.

The Ugandan health ministry carefully charted the disease's spread and published quarterly reports showing its relentless advance. The news was invariably grim, but it was significant that the information was available at all. It was of huge benefit in understanding how and where the virus was spreading and — with luck — in devising strategies for curbing its progress. At least in the early days, few other African governments were remotely so open. Health officials in those countries could only dream about being able to compile the kinds of records that were being kept in Uganda.

But those records were awfully depressing. In Uganda,

by 1989, the virus was rampant in children under the age of five. *In utero* transfer had become the leading route of transmission, after heterosexual intercourse. And women were more at risk than men. In the twenty- to twenty-four-year-old age group, women were two times more likely to be infected than were men. Among those aged fifteen to nineteen, it was worse — three times more girls carried the virus than did boys.

At the time, only a single age group was largely unscathed — children aged five to fifteen years. They'd had the good luck to be born before *in utero* transmission became a common vector for the virus, and they were not yet sexually active. Health officials took a hard look at those numbers and concluded that the best strategy in the fight against AIDS in Uganda, maybe the only strategy, was to isolate that narrow demographic stratum, those aged five to fifteen in the late 1980s, and try to nurse them safely through life. Too bad for everyone else.

Cold-blooded stuff, maybe. But in a poor African country there really wasn't much choice. Consider the numbers. In the United States, for example, a *single* course of treatment with AZT — a drug that slows or delays the onset of AIDS — carries a cost of about $80,000. Meanwhile, the national health-care budget in Tanzania, for example, works out to about $1 a year per person. Now what can be done with that? There is simply no way of comparing the health-care dollars available in North America to those in Africa. In Africa, the battle against AIDS is a desperate rearguard campaign waged with the paltriest resources.

It wasn't long before people in Uganda stopped talking about fighting AIDS in the sense of saving lives from the disease. Instead, they talked about helping ravaged communities to find ways of holding themselves together in spite of the losses that AIDS had already caused and would continue to inflict. This wasn't mere desperation. It was a strategy for survival, an example of people finding a way to get through their lives, despite the diseases, the obstacles, and the odds. I felt that if Uganda — of all countries — could weather its storms and not quite implode, then surely there was hope, not only for this country, but for the rest of Africa, too.

The fact is, conditions in Africa are rarely quite as dreadful as they are sometimes painted. Africa is not the mess it is often depicted to be. The continent has its troubles, obviously, and AIDS is certainly one of them. But what North Americans or Europeans often see as evidence of African collapse — the crumbling apartment towers, the rusting electrical pylons, the washed-out macadam roads, the gutted remains of buses — are really not signs of African collapse at all. They are signs of *European* collapse *in* Africa. Most Africans never had apartment towers, or electricity, or running water, or inter-urban buses, and so their loss or decline for an average rural African is not quite the blow it would be for a resident of Boston, say, or Birmingham or Bonn.

Power blackouts in Africa aren't a good thing, of course, but neither are they the end of civilization as most Africans know it. When you look at the sagging hulk of an African city—Luanda or Dar es Salaam or Lagos — you might well conclude that nothing good is happening there, but it isn't so. After two decades of terror and destruction, something good remains in Uganda. There is wreckage, but there is life. Even AIDS won't destroy the country. Most Ugandans will survive, to live out their lives however they can. Their

survival probably won't provide much in the way of consolation to those whom AIDS will claim, but something good
will remain in Uganda and, given a chance, it will grow.

If this sounds callous, I don't mean it to. Obviously, it
would be wonderful if medical science were to find a cure
for AIDS tomorrow or a vaccine against the disease. But,
right now, medical science seems to be a considerable distance from doing either. AIDS is one of many problems in
the world that we don't seem able to solve just now, and so
countries like Uganda have to cope the best way they can.
Uganda has to deal with AIDS, just as it has had to grapple
with countless other troubles — tyranny, inter-tribal hostilities, poverty — that the world has engendered. The wonder
of Uganda is not that all or even any of these problems have
magically been overcome. The wonder is at once more
modest and more stirring. It's that Ugandans face up to these
problems and make do.

For all its many woes, Uganda is nowadays in pretty good
shape compared to some of its neighbours, especially its
neighbour to the north, Sudan. At the same time I was in
Uganda, international relief organizations were using
Kampala and the airport at Entebbe as a secure base from
which to fly emergency food supplies up into the beseiged
city of Juba in southern Sudan. At breakfast each morning,
the dining room at the Kampala Sheraton boomed with the
deep drawling accents of paunchy American men — flyers
or support crew for the international relief effort to feed
Sudan. By comparison, Uganda was a haven of peace and
stability.

I flew into Juba myself once, not long after I left Uganda,

although I made the trip from the other direction, south from Khartoum. After a nearly interminable amount of lobbying, I had managed to get on board a relief plane, a clanking old Boeing 707 flown by a Cairo company with an Egyptian crew, and we headed south to Juba. The crew had been reluctant to make the trip — relief planes were being shot at — and there'd been a long, testy meeting in Khartoum before we took off. Now, the pilot had to corkscrew down directly over the city, to avoid flying low over rebel-held territory. He made a couple of passes over the airport before landing, just to see how things looked. Then he began his final approach and brought the aircraft down.

What a place. The largest city in southern Sudan, Juba seemed to be in a state of total collapse. Nonetheless, a Sudanese army officer declared the opposite shortly after I arrived. "Everything is peaceful," he assured me. "Everything is normal." He should have tried telling that to the dozens of people gathered directly behind him, with their suitcases, their hampers, and their cardboard boxes bound with cord. They were so eager to push their way onto the tarmac at the Juba airport that soldiers in olive-green fatigues had to wade among them, imposing order with whips. "Oh, that's natural," the officer explained. "Some people come. Some people go."

In those days, in Juba, a lot of people were bent on going. Those with connections to the outside — and with enough money to cover the fare, not to mention a welter of informal add-on costs — were cramming themselves aboard the relief aircraft to flee their swollen and hungry city, which was stranded along the shores of the White Nile, deep in rebel-controlled territory. There was no electricity here any more, no running water, no telephone service, almost no medicine, and not nearly enough food. The only commodities in plentiful supply were the gathering storm clouds of war, as the Sudanese People's Liberation Army amassed on the city's outskirts.

The rebels had blocked almost all movement into Juba by road and had begun shelling the city. At least ten people had been killed and another fifty wounded in an artillery bombardment the previous Saturday. "This used to be a nice place," a local merchant lamented. He was preparing to abandon Juba, along with his family. "We had electricity, water. We got tinned goods from Kenya."

Now, as peasants streamed into the city by the thousands to escape hunger and war in the countryside, Juba had quickly bloated to about three times its normal population of 100,000, and the only food available was what could be flown in by emergency aircraft. The scene each day at the airport was one of barely restrained bedlam, reminiscent of the set of a movie depicting the final panic-stricken days of a toppling regime. Boeing 707 jets disgorged military equipment and more soldiers — reinforcements sent in to bolster the government side — while Hercules C-130s flew in from Nairobi or Entebbe with loads of food.

Sandwiched between a pair of armoured cars, four dark green army trucks rolled onto the tarmac one afternoon, carrying dozens of soldiers returning from patrol. In a show of bravado, the soldiers kicked up their boots, let out a chorus of war whoops, and waved their weapons above their heads, an assortment of automatic rifles and grenade- and rocket-launchers.

But the local civilians didn't seem inspired. A Boeing 707

operated by a Khartoum company — Nile Safaris — stood on the tarmac. As soon its cargo bay had been emptied of soldiers, a mob of civilians scrambled onto the apron and made straight for the aircraft. They clambered onto a cargo elevator and were raised aboard for the flight to Khartoum and what they hoped was safety from war and from the threat of famine, both of which were becoming almost chronic fixtures of life — and death — in southern Sudan. A year earlier, according to the best estimates of international relief organizations, some 200,000 Sudanese had starved to death. Now it looked as if the same thing could happen again.

It's surprising how little it takes to get a serious famine going, or for that famine to repeat itself year after year. Never mind the weather, all you need is a decent military conflict. War on its own can cause massive hunger, through the destruction of facilities for the production and storage of food, for example, or the disruption of supply routes. And armies regularly use food as a military weapon. In Mozambique — as part of a campaign to sabotage the economy — anti-government rebels sowed landmines along the footpaths that connected villagers to their farmland. Before long, no one was willing to venture out to the fields. Here in Sudan, both sides in the civil war consistently interfered with international efforts to bring food to the needy. Their reasoning was ruthlessly logical. They wanted their enemies to go hungry. They wanted their own supporters fed.

Already, a combination of war and other factors — including deforestation and over-farming — had turned much of Sudan into desert. Just twenty years earlier, for example, the country was considered a land of enormous agricultural potential. It could have been a bread basket for Africa. Now, it was pretty much a basket case. Ten years earlier, Sudan had been the world's leading exporter of gum arabic, a product of acacia trees. Today, there are no acacia trees left — they've all been cut down. I once spoke to a Sudanese political scientist who had studied these phenomena in depth, a man named Abdelgalil Elmekki. He estimated that in northern Sudan some five million hectares of land have been completely deforested in recent years. About half of that has now been swallowed by the Sahara Desert. "You just see huge sand dunes, and that's all," he told me. "Ten or fifteen years ago, it was green. Now, there is nothing, absolutely nothing."

With drought comes famine, at least in degraded regions where the people are poor to begin with. Because of the drought, they will obviously have no food. But, even worse, they will have few alternative resources and no employment — nothing that would permit them to earn some money to buy food from elsewhere. In desperation, they will take the only measures they can to stay alive — and thereby merely ensure for themselves a worsening of their poverty and an extension of their hunger.

If they have stocks of seeds for planting, they will eat them. If they have livestock, they will either sell it for cash or slaughter it for food. Now, they will be left with nothing for the following year, no seeds to plant, no fallback resources, not even an ox to shoulder the plough. This is how famine transforms itself into chronic famine — a miserable cycle that soon becomes self-perpetuating. Drought leads to famine; famine increases the stress on the land and leads to more drought. Add war to the mix — as has long been done in Sudan — and famine quickly turns to catastrophe.

Sometimes it really does seem that parts of Africa are a lost cause, on a continent without hope. But that isn't really Africa's fault. There's nothing fundamentally wrong with Africa. In fact, most of Africa's problems nowadays are not even inherently *Africa's* problems. They're mainly the result of a nearly apocalyptic turn of events that, for most of the continent, is only about a century old — the collision of Europe with Africa. Unfortunately, that collision did take place. There's no going back now.

It would be absurd to suggest that Africa was untouched by antagonism or hardship prior to the colonial age. Of course there were wars in Africa before the Europeans arrived. But the Europeans dramatically exacerbated those conflicts. They did so in two main ways. First, they divided in order to conquer. All the European colonial powers in Africa did the same. They ruled their domains by broadly similiar means. They favoured one tribe with all sorts of perks and privileges — including guns and military power — and they relied on that tribe to keep the others in line. When the Europeans pulled out, they left behind totalitarian tribal rulers, who squatted atop a maze of jealous, embittered, and resentful peoples in territories that in some cases had become little more than seething and almost ungovernable powder-kegs.

That wasn't all. The colonial powers had also imposed a map upon Africa that horribly distorted African reality. They carved up the continent to reflect European political imperatives — this territory for Belgium, that one for France; this one for Britain, that one for Portugal. There is little about Africa's present-day borders that even remotely approximates the verities of African political or cultural life. Instead, tribes have been cut in half by the stroke of a European cartographer's pen, for the convenience of Europe. Or, separate and mutually antagonistic tribes have been forced to share the same national identities — except that there *are* no national identities, not in Africa. There never have been, not really. Even now, there are only the vaguest stirrings of the modern nation-state, the complex and unwieldy political contraption developed in Europe and imposed on Africa without regard to African history, geography, or demographics.

When independence came to the continent in the 1950s and 1960s, Africa's new black leaders faced an impossible choice: either scrap all these phony borders and start over, or accept them and try to make the best of a very bad business. They chose to adopt the borders they'd inherited from the colonial powers. They really had no workable choice. The alternative would surely have led to an explosion of territorial wars even more devastating than the post-colonial conflicts that have nonetheless broken out. And these have been terrible enough, rendered all the more horrific by the willingness of the industrialized powers — especially the United States and the Soviet Union — to get involved, to choose sides and to supply them with modern weapons.

One of the more astonishing revelations of recent African history is the speed with which many of the continent's bloodiest and most intractable wars have lurched to a peaceful conclusion following the collapse of the Soviet Union. This is what happened in Mozambique, in Ethiopia, and to some degree in Angola. Once the outside world stopped interfering, Africans were able to start the job of sorting out their differences for themselves.

It hasn't worked in every case. Africa's conflicts did not begin with the arrival of the Europeans, and they won't necessarily end thanks only to Europe's withdrawal. Still, to understand war in Africa, you have to look back to the colonial experience. Sudan, for example, has been at war with itself more often than not ever since independence four decades ago, and the underlying reason is absurdly simple — the country makes no sense. In a rational world, it would never have become a country. But, in the late 1800s, Britain was keenly interested in securing control of the Nile and in containing the expansion of French colonial power drifting eastward from West Africa. A succession of British adventurers and mercenaries sought to conquer Sudan, often with miserable results. General Charles Gordon once peered out across the dusty cityscape of Khartoum, set upon a Nile flood plain, punctuated by Islamic minarets and date palms. He shook his head and uttered some bleakly prescient words. "All those who have lived in Sudan cannot fail to reflect on the pointlessness of possessing this country," he lamented. Gordon, of course, was himself killed in the attempt, along with all of his men.

Eventually, however, the British did possess Sudan. By the turn of the century, the territory had become a British colony. And so, following independence in 1956, it was fated to become a single nation-state, at least in name. In practice, the idea has never remotely taken hold. The north of Sudan is Muslim in religion and Arabic in culture, the south is either Christian or animist, and the two sides are locked in a war that looks to be endless. Sometimes it seems that the only possible solution to Sudan's many sorrows would be the partition of the country into two, but that doesn't seem likely. And so the war grinds on, and famine remains a perennial spectre for hundreds of thousands of Sudanese.

It needn't be that way. Famine can be overcome. The really surprising thing, as the millennium approaches, is not how pervasive the grip of famine remains on many parts of the globe. It's just the opposite — how much of the world is now free from the threat of famine. India is a good example. Between 1770 and 1880, the country was struck by at least four massive drought-induced famines, each of which claimed a million lives or more. Much more recently, in 1943, some three million died of hunger in Bengal alone. Since then, although chronic malnutrition persists in many regions, famine has been unknown in India.

Part of the explanation for this turnaround lies in improved land management and in better crops. Hardy new varieties of rice and other grains have proved more resistant to drought. Meanwhile, the Indian government has devised emergency plans that provide alternative employment for people whose crops fail. Instead of starving to death, they work on government infrastructural projects, and buy the food they cannot grow.

There is nothing to prevent similar schemes from being introduced in drought-ridden parts of Africa — nothing, that is, apart from war, instability, a lack of management skills, and an absence of political will. But, given peace and time, parts of Africa that now seem blighted and hopeless — like much of Sudan — could yet be reclaimed. "I would think a lot could be recovered," said William Tossell, a Canadian agronomist I once spoke to. "It's amazing what can be recovered. I would be suprised if they couldn't recover a lot of these areas that on television look completely bare. It's surprising what can be done. People are very resilient."

People are indeed resilient. Still, it would certainly help if some of them would stop fighting. When the fighting does end, however, it's often astonishing what you will find. Near the end of my time in Uganda — where, unlike Sudan, the fighting had mostly wound down — I decided to travel west by road toward the border with Zaïre. I wanted to look for elephants, a species that had pretty much been wiped out in the country during the long years of war. Only a handful remained, and they were said to be damned hard to find. But I wanted to look for them anyway. I wanted to locate the survivors.

My driver for the overland journey turned out to be that rare thing in Uganda — a dour individual. He glared at the rutted and ravaged road ahead and said almost nothing the entire way, an extraordinary thing in this voluble land. But the main problem on that long drive was not the lack of conversation. The main problem was the car.

The car was equipped with a device that was meant to discourage speeding but whose main effect was to drive me nuts. Each time the driver exceeded eighty kilometres an hour — not an easy thing to do on these roads, but he managed it — an alarm would go off in the form of musical bells playing a mindlessly repetitive jingle. After about ten seconds, the noise would just about split my head open, it was so irritating. It didn't seem to bother the driver, though. I had to beg and plead with him to slow down. It wasn't the potholes. It wasn't that I feared for the car's suspension or my back. It was that damn music.

And so, alternately speeding up and slowing down, to the fragmented accompaniment of simulated bells, not to mention my anguished groans, we rattled south across the equator and then west toward the border with Zaïre, where the sprawling savannahs and wetlands of Uganda's Ruwenzori National Park unfold in the shadow of the Mountains of the Moon. I was looking for the last elephants in Uganda, and this was where I'd been told I might find them.

The last elephants in Uganda: the phrase itself has an ominous, almost apocalyptic ring. But, after two decades of war, Uganda had just about run out of the creatures. The fighting had claimed human lives by the tens of thousands. Meanwhile, it had pretty well gutted the country's wildlife. Soldiers on all sides had run amok, moonlighting as big-game poachers, marauding through Uganda's parks, butchering the elephants for their ivory tusks and the rhinoceroses for their horns. The rhino horns went mostly to the Yemeni republics, where they were fashioned into dagger handles — a popular symbol of virility there. And the ivory was spirited abroad, to be carved into jewellery or knick-knacks. Now, the rhinos were completely wiped out, and the elephants had just about vanished, too. Result: the poachers had also gone, at least from the Ruwenzori Park. There was, quite simply, nothing left to kill.

"The elephants here are so far reduced that, as far as we can tell, nobody can be bothered to hunt them," Robert Olivier told me. He was a Kenyan conservation expert working in southwestern Uganda. I met him shortly after arriving at the Mweya Safari Lodge, a rambling old hostelry (great view, appalling food) set upon a high peninsula that overlooks a misty Lake Rutanzige and the border with Zaïre. "The elephants are showing every sign of making a recovery," Olivier said, "but it will take fifty years to get back to where they were."

He meant fifty years if there was peace. There was no hope at all if there was war. In parts of the country, in the north and in the east, the fighting continued and so did the poaching. At the time, Uganda was trying to bolster its anti-poaching campaign, by hiring and training park rangers and equipping them with radios, vehicles, and camping gear — but not new weapons. Park rangers were still armed mostly with antique .303 bolt-action carbines, and they were vastly outgunned. The poachers — who now were mainly army deserters — carried AK-47 assault rifles. One solution would have been to issue the wardens with heavier arms, but President Museveni was understandably leery of putting yet more powerful weapons into yet more unpredictable hands.

Here in the western part of the country there was relative calm. But the region's wildlife had already taken a terrible beating. Two decades earlier, roughly five thousand elephants roamed the territory covered by what was then called the Queen Elizabeth Park — two thousand square kilometres of savannah and marshland sprawling along Uganda's border with Zaïre. Now, there were maybe four hundred.

They were called Uganda's last elephants, but they could well have been Uganda's newest elephants. Maybe they had wandered across the border from Zaïre to sample the new atmosphere of peace now flourishing in this part of the continent. It was, after all, a tricky business to determine the precise nationality of an elephant. Either way, their presence in this benighted, almost shattered land was little short of miraculous — a species returning to its own graveyard. But Olivier was almost buoyant about their prospects. "Given a plan, given a well-deployed team of rangers with mobility," he told me, "and they're back in business."

Back in businesss maybe, but not so easy to find. I spent several days roaming the Ruwenzori Park without any luck at all. And then, one hazy, humid morning, someone said a herd had been sighted and told us where. I hopped into a Land Rover with a pair of rangers and, less than an hour later, we stood upon the brow of a crater-like basin and watched what struck me then as a kind of African renaissance.

To the accompaniment of countless birds, about thirty of Uganda's surviving giants paraded down toward a shallow salt lake to drink at its fresh-water springs. Surrounding the lake and its rounded basin, the land seemed to come alive, or maybe it had been alive all along, only I hadn't noticed. A red-breasted cuckoo glided towards its nest in a vine-entangled cactus. A flock of pink flamingos probed for insects near the lake's glassy shore. A scattering of lemon doves called to each other across the surrounding grasslands. Off to the west, the faint grey foothills of the Mountains of the Moon reared up through the haze.

And the elephants floated down. They moved with surprising grace, as if in slow motion, like four-legged schooners breasting through a sea of their own imagining. Their great grey ears flapped like canvas sails; their trunks furled and unfurled in the still morning air. And, at least for these few moments, on this one morning, in this small and distant corner of a troubled land, Africa seemed for all the world like a kind of paradise, regained.

A Good Man in Nigeria

THE NIGERIAN CITY of Maiduguri is probably not what you would call a paradise, unless you happen to like your paradise dry. In that case, Maiduguri is pretty much made to order. After all, it's slowly disappearing beneath an ocean of sand. If you're partial to deserts, Maiduguri's your place. But be forewarned — getting there can be a problem.

Maiduguri is in Nigeria, and in Nigeria almost *everything* is a problem. I once met a Swiss businessman in Lagos — now *that* was a combination conceived in hell — who told me that his personal credo based on several years in the country ran as follows: Never Trust A Nigerian. It was a dictum that thoroughly offended me when I heard it, but I've got to admit that I started to change my mind, maybe just a little, while I was trying to get to Maiduguri.

I wanted to go to Maiduguri in order to do research for an article about desertification — in this case, the gradual but apparently relentless southward advance of the Sahara. I had thought I would just get on a plane in Lagos and fly up there. But this was Nigeria. In Nigeria, you don't just get on a plane and fly somewhere. That would make too much sense and no one would make any money.

The thing is, Nigerians *like* to make money and they aren't too fussy about how they go about it. What sand is to Maiduguri, corruption is to Nigeria — a thing that threatens to bury you. When I travelled to the country, the oil boom of the early 1980s had collapsed — taking the Nigerian economy down with it — and so the horrendous graft of those years had diminished somewhat, if only because there was a lot less money around to steal. But the garden-variety extortion known in Nigeria as "dash" had not declined at all.

In Nigeria, the term is used either as a noun or as a transitive verb, as in, "You can dash me." That pungent phrase is mouthed shamelessly by Nigerian officials of almost every description at almost every opportunity. Dash is ubiquitous in Nigeria, encoded in the social landscape. It's so pervasive that it seems at times to have an odd kind of innocence. Once, while strolling along a city street in broad daylight, I was stopped by a policeman who wanted to know what I was doing and where I was from. I explained that I was a journalist from Canada.

"Ah," he said. "And how can I get a journalist from Canada to dash me?"

I just looked at him. "Well, don't ask *me*," was what I wanted to say. "*You're* the policeman."

In Nigeria, dash is taken for granted. But it can have a debilitating, almost cancerous effect. It is surely insidious. In those days, for example, employees of the National Electrical Power Authority regularly insisted on being dashed by their customers in exchange for not presenting them with their bills. In theory, it looked like a great system, albeit illegal.

NEPA employees made some extra cash, and their customers saved money by not having to pay their electricity bills — and everyone was happy. Right?

Not really. The other main result was that NEPA didn't collect much in the way of revenue from its clients and so was regularly unable to pay for the oil it needed to fuel its generators. The result? Regular brownouts or blackouts. By paying dash instead of their electrical bills, NEPA customers were not beating the system. They were losing. They were paying out good money in graft and getting electricity shortages in return. But what could they do? The NEPA bill collectors refused to present customers with their bills — they wanted dash instead. If a customer finally balked at paying dash and insisted on footing his legitimate bill, the NEPA employees would simply threaten to cut off his electricity outright. After all, had not the customer failed to pay his bills?

This, it seemed, was Nigeria in microcosm — an open palm in want of greasing.

But back to Maiduguri.

Home to about 300,000 people and capital of the northern Nigerian state of Bornu, Maiduguri is perched at the edge of the Sahel, that broad band of semi-desert land that runs along the southern border of the Sahara and seems to be turning into desert itself. I planned to travel north from Maiduguri, overland, up to Lake Chad — the vast "desert of water" sought by nineteenth-century European explorers with a zeal exceeded only by their passion to locate Timbuktu.

The day before my intended departure, I bought an airplane ticket to Maiduguri at the Nigerian Airways office in

downtown Lagos. I made a reservation on the flight departing the following morning, the only flight to Maiduguri that
day. The people at Nigerian Airways thoughtfully warned
me to make sure I got to the airport in plenty of time. There
was bound to be a crowd. Well, this was no surprise. In
Nigeria, there is always a crowd.

The next morning, I was up early to brave the traffic out
to the airport. As instructed, I reported to the domestic terminal, a hangar-like building crammed with Nigerians and
their stacks of luggage. I had lots of time to spare, or so I
thought. But the line was *extremely* long, and, what was
worse, it didn't seem to be moving. I don't mean that it
didn't seem to be moving very quickly. I mean it wasn't
moving at all.

Time passed, and the line (a) got longer and (b) continued not to move. From my vantage point quite far back I
could see that there was some commotion at the front —
people horning their way in and then hurrying away. Were
they line-crashers? Hard to say. Nobody else seemed to be
making a fuss, so I didn't either. After all, I was the only
white person around.

Eventually, a voice over the public-address system announced the imminent departure of the Nigerian Airways flight
to Maiduguri. Now we'll start moving, I thought. Yet still
the line failed to advance by as much as an inch. Before long,
more announcements were made.

The flight was departing soon.

All passengers should now have cleared security.

All passengers should now be on board.

The flight was about to depart.

The flight was departing.

But the line-up still didn't budge. Everybody just stood in place, patiently waiting — for what? This was probably the first orderly line-up I'd ever encountered in Nigeria, but it wasn't going anywhere. And, now, another announcement came over the PA system.

The Nigerian Airways flight to Maiduguri had departed.

It had gone.

Here on the ground, we all looked around at each other in dull amazement. The flight was *gone*? How could the flight be gone? We all had our tickets, our reservations. And yet it seemed to be true — the flight was a *fait accompli*. Up ahead, the counter was closing. The Nigerian Airways personnel were traipsing away. At this point, most of the frustrated would-be passengers picked up their luggage and shuffled out of sight as well. They seemed to accept this set-back without complaint — admittedly, an odd way for Nigerians to behave, but there you go.

A few of us refused to. We remained where we were, standing in a daze, where the line-up used to be. We were bewildered. This made no sense at all. We checked each other's tickets. Everything was in order, the dates, the flight numbers — everything. For my part, I was furious. I was operating on a tight schedule. I had deadlines to meet. I couldn't afford to waste a day. If I didn't get to Maiduguri today, the desertification piece was off. There wouldn't be time to do it. I'd have to phone my editors, report a failure, and they wouldn't understand. What did they know of Nigeria? They would blame this on me.

Just then, a young man in plain clothes sidled up behind me. He said, "Do you want to go to Maiduguri?"

I turned and looked at him. I wondered for a moment if

he was crazy. Or who knows? Maybe he thought we could *drive.* "Do I want to go to Maiduguri?" I repeated. "Yes, I do — but . . . " I shrugged. "But the plane has gone."

He shook his head. "No, it hasn't."

"Yes, it has. They just announced it. It's gone."

Again, he shook his head. "No, it hasn't gone."

"But the *announcement* — they said it's gone."

"Oh, they always do that. But it hasn't gone." Again, he asked, "Do you want to go to Maiduguri?"

"Yes."

"Your ticket? May I see your ticket?"

And in his voice I thought I heard it, that tell-tale under-current — the *soto voce* resonance of . . . *graft.* I handed my ticket over to him. What did I have to lose?

It was the right thing to do because the young man was telling the truth. In fact, the aircraft *was* still on the ground. Its departure had been announced only to ensure that all the passengers who hadn't got on board would go away without causing a riot. It turned out that the only people who suc-cessfully boarded the plane were those willing and able to pay the hefty bribes. This explained the commotion I had earlier seen at the head of the queue. People who under-stood the system had been cutting into line in order to bribe their way onto the plane — the *only* way to get aboard. Those, like me, who stood patiently in line either didn't understand the system or couldn't afford it.

And so I managed to get on the flight to Maiduguri that morning, after all. Granted, I had to pay two considerable bribes to do it, both of which were negotiated for me by this resourceful young man, who pocketed the larger of the pay-ments himself, naturally. In total, the bribes came to about one-and-a-half times the face value of my ticket, but by this time I didn't care. I had to get on the plane and I managed to. And I even got a seat, a good one, by a window.

Some other passengers were not so fortunate — it seemed the bribery system was prone to error. In this case, the flight to Maiduguri was over-bribed by about twenty passengers. They gathered in the aisle of the plane — a modern French Airbus — and refused to leave. They were deeply upset, which was understandable. After all, had they not obeyed all the rules, paid out good money to all the right people?

In the end, the army had to intervene. Several soldiers armed with automatic rifles climbed aboard the plane and were eventually able to strong-arm the shrieking supernumeraries off the craft without — it should be recorded — quite having to shoot them in the process. At last, the doors were closed, and the airplane pulled away from the terminal. It lumbered across the tarmac, hit the runway, raced its engines, and took off for the flight north to Maiduguri.

I sat hunched in my seat, shaking my head. I was thinking: this *country*, these *people*. If passengers had to bribe their way onto a plane operated by the state airline, then what did you have to do to ensure that the maintenance crew did its job, or the flight crew, or the people responsible for refuelling the damn thing? Had *they* been properly bribed? I stared out the window at the long and suddenly very fragile-looking wing, now undulating through the blue skies over Africa. Was this airplane a metaphor for all Nigeria? And, if so, what on earth was holding the whole enterprise up? *Bribes*?

As it happened, the airplane flew like a charm, and we

landed at Maiduguri without mishap. I could tell at once that we were on the edge of the Sahara. The harmattan drifted overhead, bearing a fine haze of sand down from the desert. The sun beat earthward, a pale silver disc in an opaque sky. It was broiling hot, about forty-two degrees Celsius in the early afternoon. You dehydrated at break-neck speed up here. There wasn't even time to perspire properly — the sweat evaporated instantly on your skin.

As I strolled across the tarmac toward the airport terminal, it was the heat and the dryness that I noticed first, but it was the sand that caught my attention next. The sand was everywhere, covering everything, an element almost as pervasive as the baking, semi-desert air. No matter where I went in Maiduguri, I could not stop marvelling at the apparent inexhaustibility of the sand. Outside the city, nomadic goatherds swathed themselves in black robes and trudged behind their flocks across an endless carpet of sand, desperately seeking fodder. Kanuri villages rose above the sand — clusters of thatched, dome-shaped huts peaked by twisted cupolas. Camels shambled across a treeless expanse of sand through the blast-furnace heat. And Maiduguri itself — an African otherworld of mosques and minarets — was encrusted with sand. Men knelt on their rugs in sand-covered alley-ways to pray to Mecca. Their lips as they murmured were flecked with bits of sand.

There were several ways to escape the heat. You could repair to the bar of the Lake Chad Hotel, a gloomy and windowless place, a depressing little pit — but an air-conditioned pit! It was furnished with saggy brown sofas and filled for much of the day with Nigerian businessmen — commercial travellers, mostly — in their billowing caftans and intricately striped caps. They quaffed ice-cold beer by the quart and stared, blank-faced, at endlessly repeated reruns of "Charlie's Angels" on TV. They were escaping the heat.

But it was just about impossible to escape the sand. Especially now, during the harmattan, when the sand was air-lifted here from the Sahara, there wasn't much that a human being could do. The sand burrowed into your clothes, your pockets, your hair. It formed a fine gritty glaze on every exposed area of your skin. But what was most impressive about the sand was what it did to the surface of Maiduguri itself.

It covered the city. Every two weeks, workers went out with shovels and brooms to dig and sweep the sand away. A week later, it was back — about two inches deep and spread like a crystalline shroud over the sidewalks and the streets. Unlike snow, which you can watch as it falls, the sand didn't seem to come from anywhere. It just appeared out of thin air and then drifted in dun-coloured waves through the pale-green, saw-tooth foliage of the Indian neem trees. It was an ominous effect, this eerily materializing sand, and its consequences were more than merely psychological. Unless something changed and soon, Maiduguri and all of northern Bornu state would be swallowed whole by the stuff.

That was why I was here. I hired a car and a driver and headed north, bound for Lake Chad. The scenery along the way was pretty much what I'd come to expect — sand. When I got to Lake Chad, however, the lake wasn't there. Or, to be more precise, it had moved. Lake Chad was now a shrunken, evaporating shadow of its former self. Maps only eight years old showed the Kanuri town of Baga as being set on a promontory jutting far out into the lake. But when I got to Baga, there was no lake in sight. There was just a shallow pool of water maybe five hundred metres long, where local fishermen waded, clutching their nets, in search of towada or carapasa fish. The main body of the lake, they told me, was a good fifty kilometres away, across the border in Chad.

The shrinking of the lake may have been an act of Allah, or it may have been the work of man, but it was certainly dramatic — a powerful illustration of the increasing aridity plaguing this part of the world. If even Lake Chad was drying up, what hope did Maiduguri have?

That was the question on a lot of people's minds. And Nigeria, unlike Sudan, did not have war as an excuse. The problem here was almost prosaically simple — not enough rain. On the other hand, it isn't always an easy matter to say why the rain refuses to fall. For millennia, people have resorted to a kind of answer — the belief that droughts are sent by the gods to punish humankind for its sins. Nowadays, of course, this seems like mere superstition. It seems absurd. But, in fact, it's basically what happens.

Across the Sahel, men had cut down the trees, scattered the soil, and angered the gods. Put another way, they had disrupted the transpiration cycle. Denuded land emits little moisture and so gets little or no rain. Meteorologists explain that in many subtropical areas, water tends to be recycled locally. What falls as rain in any single region is the exact same moisture that returns to the air — as transpired water from trees or the ground — in order to fall again. But if the trees have all been cut down, and if the topsoil has all blown or washed away because there were no trees or root systems left to hold it, then the water that falls from the sky just runs off the land. There's nothing to retain it — and it doesn't come back. With no moisture returning to the air, clouds stop forming. The rains cease and drought becomes a permanent affair. The land turns to desert.

Land may become denuded for many different reasons, but most of them bear human fingerprints. Perversely, many of these fingerprints are applied in a good cause. International aid organizations, for example, have long encouraged the sinking of bore-holes in marginal areas, in order to bring water and fertility to the surface. But this, it turns out, only hastens the destruction of the land. Livestock congregate in their thousands near such bore-holes. The land is soon overgrazed, and the soil is further eroded by the effects of massive trampling.

Modern agriculture has had even more onerous consequences. The introduction of large-scale commercial farming has been disastrous in some parts of Africa. To clear the land for ploughing, the farmers cut down the trees, just as peasants have long done, but with a crucial difference. The modern farmers don't merely axe the trunks. They also haul out the stumps and the root systems to facilitate deep ploughing. And they remove all of the trees, every last one, to make ploughing more efficient. Nothing is left to hold the topsoil in place.

Meanwhile, commercial farmers, eager to expand their properties, displace the small producers and drive them onto ever more marginal lands, which are quickly exhausted. In order to supplement their dwindling incomes, the poor are then forced to cut down more and more trees to obtain wood to sell, either as charcoal or as firewood.

Around Baga, there was now little vegetation left, apart

from the occasional eerie shape of a rickety baobab tree. Midday temperatures in April would soar to nearly forty-five degrees Celsius, and it hardly rained at all. The terrain had turned to a flat plate of sand. You might think that an obvious solution to the problem was to plant trees, and you would be right. Trees were being planted. Foreign forestry experts had come to northern Nigeria to administer refor-estation programmes. But even they admitted that planting trees alone would not provide the answer.

The problem is that trees — even fast-growing species such as eucalyptus or Indian neems — still take a good while to grow. And, when they do reach a decent height, they aren't of much direct economic benefit. They don't even make very good firewood, because they burn too fast. But the people cut them down again, anyway. Casey said it would be far better to plant trees with a clear commercial value — citrus or mango trees, for example, or indigenous species such as gum arabic, whose sap is used in the produc-tion of cosmetics and candies. Deserts, he insisted, can be stopped.

For the time being, however, this desert wasn't stopping for any one. It continued to accumulate over northern Nigeria and to spread south. On my return from Lake Chad, or from where Lake Chad used to be, I was greeted by a Maiduguri that was still visible, albeit barely, beneath its cus-tomary mantle of sand. The businessmen were still drinking beer and scrutinizing "Charlie's Angels" on TV in the sub-terranean bar at the Lake Chad Hotel, escaping the heat. I couldn't join them, for this was my last day in the north before I was to head back to Lagos. There were some people I wanted to see.

I hired a driver for the day, an amiable, articulate young man named Alhaji Ali Mai Mamman. We got along extremely well, the two of us. He was an avid reader, it turned out, and we talked a good deal about books. He'd been to Mecca, too, and we talked about that. When the day was over and it was time for us to settle up, I had to overpay him by ten naira, for he had no change with him. Never mind, he said. He promised he would make up the difference the following day. We arranged that he would pick me up at my hotel at six a.m. in order to drive me to the airport.

And so, sharp at six o'clock, I was standing outside my hotel with my knapsack at my feet and a new coat of sand already accumulating upon my skin. But there was no sign of Mamman or of my ten naira. I waited a while but he didn't show. Well, I thought, this was Nigeria, so what did I expect? I set about finding another taxi and eventually headed out to the airport. I checked in for my flight, picked up my boarding pass, and found a seat in the sparsely furnished but densely populated departure lounge.

So far this morning, I'd had to pay no bribes. But this was Nigeria. Before long, an airport security guard happened by and told me to come with him. He took me outside and then into a small and vacant hangar. In a low tentative voice he tried to shake me down, but I just pretended that I didn't understand what he was getting at and he let me go. It seemed that a lot of Nigerian corruption was like this. There wasn't any malice involved; it was just the custom around here to troll for bribes. If it didn't work, no hard feelings. I returned to the departure lounge.

I couldn't say I was too surprised that Mamman hadn't

made an appearance that morning, but I *was* a little disappointed. It wasn't the ten naira that I missed. After all, the money was worth only about three dollars to me, although it meant a good deal more than that to him. No, I was upset that this man hadn't kept his word. The thing was, I'd had a good feeling about him, and it irritated me to be proven wrong. Of course, this was Nigeria, and it was the custom here to take what you could get, and Mamman was a Nigerian. I remembered what that Swiss businessman had said — *Never Trust A Nigerian* — and I shook my head.

It was then that Mamamn himself came bursting into the terminal. He looked around, caught sight of me, and hurried over. He was brimming with apologies. "Sorry, so sorry," he blurted out. "Please to forgive me." It turned out that his car had failed to start that morning. He hadn't been able to phone because he didn't *have* a phone. When he'd finally got his car going, he drove straight to my hotel — only to find me gone. So he jumped back into his car and raced flat out to the airport.

Now, he produced a ten-naira note. He had come all the way out to the airport in order to pay me back. I didn't want to take the money, but of course I had to. To have done otherwise would have made a mockery of his gesture. So I pocketed the cash and thanked him as warmly as I could.

Over the public-address system, they were announcing the departure of the flight to Lagos. This time, the announcement would turn out to be accurate. So I said goodbye to Mamman — a good man in Nigeria and one more African friend whom I'd probably never see again. I headed outside to board my plane.

Requiem for a Lioness

ANNIE CHAILUNGA was one of many Africans whom, having met once or twice, I would never see again.

Just twenty-six years old, Annie had once been among the bright young hopes of Africa. If I hadn't known better, I'd have thought she still was.

When I met her, on a shimmering winter's afternoon in Zambia, Annie was lounging in the living-room of her aunt's house. It was a rambling, airy bungalow surrounded by cypress shrubs and flowering trees in Rhodes Park, a prosperous suburb of Lusaka, the Zambian capital.

A pair of ivory bracelets jangled at her wrists, and she had on a black-and-white sweater above a brightly coloured wraparound skirt called a *chitenje*. She had an aquiline nose and a fine sheen to her dark-brown skin. She wore her hair straightened and combed back from her broad brow. She had painted her fingernails with burgundy polish. To keep her feet warm from a wintry nip in the morning air, she'd put on a pair of thick silvery socks. She looked cosy and comfortable, subdued but friendly. That was the good news.

The bad news was that Annie Chailunga would be dead before very long—and, with her death, another rare flicker of hope for Africa would be extinguished.

Annie had once seemed the embodiment of someone's best wishes for a troubled continent. She had a good job, working as a secretary at a Lusaka travel agency. She was newly married, and her husband was highly trained in a sophisticated technical skill, the kind of skill that modern Africa so desperately needs. His name was Agnusdei Chailunga, and he was an electrical engineer. True to his given name — which is Latin for Lamb of God — he was also a church-going man, "a staunch Catholic," according to Annie.

In May, 1991, the couple had a child, a daughter. They named her Nkalamo, a word that means "lioness" in the Nyanja dialect spoken by most people in this part of Zambia. By rights, their three lives should have been as promising as any in Africa. The Chailungas were what much of this continent is striving to become. But the little lioness was never well. She died in August, 1991, aged three months. Officially, the cause of Nkalamo's death was registered as pneumonia, but Annie had her suspicions. She thought that something else was involved in the fate of her daughter, something even more sinister.

Shortly after the death of their child, Agnusdei Chailunga fell ill himself, and he was soon diagnosed as having AIDS. Unlike some in Africa, when they learn that their spouses are suffering from this spectral disease, Annie did not desert her husband. He carried on for five debilitating months, fading slowly all the time, until he died in June, 1992. Annie was with him to the end. "I stayed with him," she said. "And my husband died in my arms."

After his death, Annie discovered that she was HIV-positive. It probably should not have come as a great surprise — but, of course, it did — and she reacted just as anybody would. "Oh — shattered," she told me. "But I've really come to accept it now."

She had little choice. Now, she was in the early stages of AIDS, a disease without a cure. There was really nothing to do but soldier on. Annie was lucky, too — or luckier than some. She wasn't abandoned. Her own family and the family of her dead husband stood by. "I've lost most of my friends," she told me. "I lost my best, best friends. They just stopped visiting. If it hadn't been for my family, I would have died."

The cold hard truth, of course, was that Annie *would* die, and before too long. In Zambia, as in so much of Africa, AIDS is ravaging the population with an aim that is both harsh and merciless, targeting women even more than men, leaving orphans by the thousand and crippling whole communities. In its first wave, the disease hit hardest at upwardly mobile, urbanized Africans, at people very like the Chailungas — that stratum of African society that has made the great leap to modernity. Those people are now dying, and they are taking with them their precious technical skills and three decades of spotty, hard-won economic gains.

Result? The fragile advances that Africa has made during thirty years of post-colonial development are now being lost, borne away in a long procession of coffins, because of a scourge that no one could have predicted, a disaster that is no one's fault.

Even without the burden of AIDS, Africa would be weighed down by an excess of troubles — wars, ethnic conflict, environmental degradation, collapsing institutions, financial corruption. Add AIDS to the total, and you almost have to wonder if realistic answers are possible or if there is any hope left at all. A lot of people are apparently concluding that there isn't and that a continent that is home to seven hundred million people is pretty much a lost cause. But they're wrong. There is cause for hope in Africa. Consider Florence Lungu.

If you believed even half the bad things you hear about Africa, you'd probably think that someone of Lungu's background would be living in a luxury villa overlooking the Mediterranean, on the interest from her husband's numbered Swiss bank accounts. Her husband, after all, had been a minister in the government of Kenneth Kaunda that ruled Zambia from independence in 1964 until it was turned out of office in democratic elections in 1991. At the time of the elections, he had been serving as Zambia's ambassador to the United Nations in New York.

If stereotypes held true, Florence Lungu would be a rich woman — the wife, after all, of a top official in a long-ruling African political party. But it isn't so. Florence Lungu is not wallowing in the avails of ministerial graft. Since losing his government job, her husband — the former minister — has gone back to earning an honest living another way, as a farmer outside Lusaka. Partly to make ends meet and partly for reasons of her own, Lungu returned to work, too.

A registered nurse by profession, she got a job with a non-governmental organization called the Family Health Trust that operates a home-based care project for AIDS patients. She spends her days visiting people like Annie Chailunga, people with AIDS. She monitors their health and advises them about straightforward ways to keep their bodies' defences up — drink lots of milk, stick to purified water, watch diets carefully. Many of her patients are destitute, so Lungu also distributes food — two twenty-five-kilogram bags of corn meal to each patient per month, some cooking oil, some dietary supplements. Just as important, she provides a sympathetic ear and lots of moral support.

On the day I met her, Florence Lungu marched into the house in Rhodes Park where Annie Chailunga was staying and she immediately took control. "You're feeding well?" she asked. Annie nodded and crossed her arms, jangling her ivory bracelets. The older woman produced a thermometer from her blue medical bag and proceeded to take Annie's temperature. It was normal. Later, she checked Annie's blood pressure and talked about diet. She measured out some Aspirin and warned Annie that she might hear a ringing in her ears, maybe suffer some nausea. She should drink lots of milk. Annie nodded again. As she went about her duties, the older woman comforted Annie in a dozen ways, chatted with her about this and that, tried constantly to buoy up her spirits. And it seemed to work.

"I have to fight this disease," Annie declared. "This can't be the end."

And it won't be. The harsh truth is that Annie Chailunga herself would die, long before her time. And so will many millions of others — men, women and, increasingly, children. Yet, one way or another, Africa is going to survive. The continent will continue to have its widely heralded disasters but also its triumphs. What is Florence Lungu, after all, if not a triumph?

A handsome woman with a serious air, Lungu was wearing a long brown khaki dress and navy-blue running shoes on the day I met her. Her hair was done up in long plaits, and she had on a pair of glasses with large frames. Her schedule that day took us to both sides of Lusaka, from the colonial-style comfort of Rhodes Park to the parts of town where the other ninety per cent lived — for example, a matchbox cinder-block house in a slum called Matero.

Here, in a dark little room, Lungu hauled out a portable scale from her bag and checked the weight of a haggard, sickly-looking man named Robert Tembo. He was bald and wore a woollen vest, beige corduroy pants, and a pair of plastic flip-flops. He had a sombre, defeated air. He'd had more than his share of bad news lately, but today there was some good — he was still forty-nine kilograms.

"There isn't any loss," Lungu remarked as she jotted the information down in her folder. "He was forty-nine the last visit, which was two weeks ago."

As she worked through the items on her list, Lungu kept up a running commentary, mainly for Tembo's benefit. It seemed he could use both the patter and the encouragement. Out of work and abandoned by his wife, the man was clearly down in the dumps. He did not look well and his spirits were sagging. His blood-pressure, however, was a heartening one hundred over eighty.

"That's very good," said Lungu. "It's full and bounding."

Later, back out in the crystalline Lusaka sunshine, as she set off for the next of her morning appointments, Lungu reflected on Tembo's predicament. "If he had a good diet and good living conditions, he could live another one to two years," she said. She didn't need to add the obvious — that Tembo had never had a proper diet or good living conditions and never would. He was, after all, a poor man in

Africa, and all he had to get him through what remained of his life was the support of his closest relatives and these twice-monthly visits from Lungu.

That may not seem like much, but to Tembo, a little probably looked like a lot. No one pretends that AIDS is not a horror, or that Africa's problems can simply be wished away. There is no magic cure — not for AIDS and not for the other ills plaguing the continent. Nonetheless, a lot of good people are doing what they can. They have some sort of faith in some kind of future, never mind how grim that future might look to others.

Remember Kampala. In Kampala, one bright green morning, I had walked into a room bathed in sunshine where I met a woman I'll call Maggie Owara. At twenty-five, she was a smashing beauty. She had close-cropped hair clustered around a large oval face, with flashing eyes, a button nose, and perfect white teeth. She kicked off a pair of flat-soled pumps and settled herself upon a deep window sill. She wore a pale raspberry skirt, a trim cream-coloured jacket, and a high-necked blouse with narrow pink stripes. She laughed easily, talked enthusiastically, listened attentively. At one point, with a beaming smile, she made me promise never to forget her. And I said I never would.

Of course, Owara was only flirting with me, nothing more. It turned out that she was having a far more serious affair with a vastly more formidable presence. She was another young African woman with AIDS. She told me she thought she'd been infected by a former boyfriend. When I met her, she had known of her condition for about a year, but she was far from giving in. "We have to fight the virus so we can live more years," she said.

Owara and many other Ugandans were doing exactly that — fighting the virus and living more years — thanks to an agency called The AIDS Support Organization (TASO), which operated out of a nondescript tin-covered building tucked in the shadow of Kampala's large Mulago hospital. TASO was founded in 1987 by a Ugandan physiotherapist named Noerine Kaleeba after her husband died of AIDS.

When I met Kaleeba in late 1989, she was carrying a photo album that contained a picture of her and the six other Ugandans who had set up TASO. Now, two years on, all but Kaleeba were dead, victims of AIDS. "Subsequently, they have all died," she said with a sad shrug. "I'm the last of the first."

A large and garrulous woman, Kaleeba had few remaining inhibitions about sex, human foibles, or death. "One of the hurdles is to talk about death, but in my counselling sessions, I always talk about death. The person might not want to talk about death, but he has to."

At TASO, Kaleeba had twenty full-time co-workers, thirteen of whom themselves carried the AIDS virus and seven of whom had not been tested and so weren't sure. Kaleeba herself had been tested on several occasions — negative each time.

"Once you come to TASO, you have to accept that other people will know you have AIDS," said Dr. Elly Katabira, a Ugandan physician who ran a weekly clinic for TASO's 140 clients. "That's the way we want it. We want people to accept that this is a disease that is a part of us."

Even so, TASO's approach was discreet. Nothing about the building — actually, a former polio clinic — identified it as having anything to do with AIDS. That was an important consideration for Isabel Nakendo, twenty-four, whose husband had ordered her never to tell him if she learned that she had the disease. As it turned out, she did have it — and her husband didn't know, even though it was almost certainly he who had given it to her. Neither did he know that their two children, both under four, were also infected with HIV, which meant that they too would suffer and die before long.

Like Maggie Owara, Isabel Nakendo seemed healthy, brimming with life. But that was an illusion. Both women were not merely HIV-positive — they had the disease. For now, however, the symptoms came and went, and they soldiered on. A devout Roman Catholic, Maggie Owara was keeping her spirits up by a combination of grit and faith. "From what I have seen, faith is very important," she told me, and then softly ran her lips over the words a second time, and then a third, as though they were the beads on a rosary that was steadily slipping through her hands. "Faith is very important. Faith is very important . . . "

But faith alone will not be enough, for Africa is to AIDS like butter to a hot knife. Why is the disease spreading so much faster and so much more widely in Africa than in western Europe or North America? A lot of people look at the figures and conclude that Africans must be more promiscuous sexually than other people. Or something. But it isn't so. There is really no great mystery about the spread of AIDS in Africa. In most cases, it is transmitted by straightforward sexual intercourse between men and women, the sort of thing that goes on all over the world, every day, every night. Still, there are some sexual patterns in Africa that make the continent a paradise for HIV, and a purgatory for the men and women it infects.

Allan Ronald, head of internal medicine at the University of Manitoba, has spent considerable time studying the transmission of HIV in Nairobi, the Kenyan capital. He told me there were three principal factors that accelerated the spread of AIDS in many parts of sub-Saharan Africa, particularly the cities. Typically, there are large numbers of women engaged in prostitution. There is also widespread genital ulceration, caused by untreated venereal disease. And, finally, there is a high proportion of uncircumcised men.

These three factors don't prevail in all African cities. But where they do, according to Ronald, the AIDS virus is able to spread at a rapid rate. In Nairobi, for example, there was no HIV infection prior to 1980. A decade later, it was deeply rooted. "In two or three years," Ronald said, "over half the deaths in Nairobi will be HIV-related."

One of the main problems in Africa is the prevalence of prostitution. At least in the cities, and along trucking routes, it's a very common practice. In Kenya, this is largely attributable to the country's colonial past, when men were drawn from the countryside to perform wage labour in the cities. They had to leave their wives behind to mind their rural lands.

Nowadays, despite Africa's political independence, such migratory labour practices remain firmly embedded in the economy. In Nairobi, three decades after Kenya gained its independence, the ratio of men to women is almost two to one. Women in the cities are poor, they often have to support children on their own, and there is a high demand for sex. Prostitution is an obvious result. Venereal disease is another. Ronald said that HIV-positive women with genital ulceration carry one hundred times as much virus in their genital tracts as do similarly infected women without ulceration.

Ronald's final conclusion — about the increased likeli-hood that uncircumcised men will contract HIV — is some-what more controversial but has come to attract wide acceptance among epidemiologists. "The only places where you get rapid transmission of HIV is where you get a signifi-cant proportion of men with foreskins," he told me. "That's definitely true in Africa." The foreskin, it seems, acts as a kind of incubator for the virus and so increases the likeli-hood of infection.

International efforts to slow the epidemic in sub-Saharan Africa have mainly focused on intensive, community-based education programmes — and there is evidence that they help. But there is also considerable pessimism, given the extent to which the virus has spread already. Worse, the social factors that sped the transmission of HIV in central and east Africa are, if anything, even more prevalent in southern Africa, where the disease is fast gaining hold. Ronald spoke of "a sense of helplessness" among epidemiologists and med-ical experts who look at Africa.

Still, the people themselves haven't given up. One thing you can do is promote a little caution, and a lot of Africans — a lot of African women, anyway — have been trying to do just that.

One Friday afternoon in eastern Zimbabwe, I went out to a place called Sakubva, a low-income black settlement near the city of Mutare. About thirty women had gathered by a street market and were now preparing to carry the mes-sage about safe sex into the very lion's den. "Be wise and talk about AIDS," urged the slogans emblazoned across the fronts of their white T-shirts.

Nearby, from rickety wooden stands, vendors were selling tomatoes, bunches of bananas, hot peppers, shafts of sugar cane, heads of lettuce, lemons, and limes, while Zimbabwean pop music — known as jit — echoed from a radio somewhere. The market throbbed with life, but life can be a fleeting thing, and that was why these women were here. They were all members of the Mutare AIDS Prevention Project.

Soon they formed themselves into a line, put their shoulders back, and marched through the tall steel gates of the Rufaro Beer Hall, a large, walled enclosure where local men gather of an evening to drink, chat, and maybe pick up women who, in this setting, are almost certain to be professionals. As it happened, the women of the Mutare AIDS Prevention Project were also professionals. All were current or former "commercial sex workers", as the now standard euphemism puts it.

Inside its tall surrounding walls, the Rufaro Beer Hall was a sprawling open-air operation, punctuated by small brick-walled drinking stalls and ornamented with tulip trees and flamboyants. In a vacant area in the centre of the hall, the women of the AIDS Prevention Project assembled in their white T-shirts and matching rose-coloured skirts and running shoes. They soon started to perform a series of songs, dances, and skits aimed at encouraging men to take precautions about sex. At one point in the routine, the women each produced a condom in a silver foil wrapper and waved them in the air, like soft-shoe dancers with miniature straw boaters. "Use condoms to prevent AIDS, and your life shall be a sweet one," they sang. "Have one partner to prevent AIDS, and your life shall be a sweet one."

Meanwhile, the beer hall's patrons — masculine, all —

peered on from the drinking stalls. Many others gathered in
a semi-circle around the women. They sipped from large
plastic jugs of *chibuku* beer — a yeasty, naturally fermenting
corn brew — and for the most part they paid close attention,
both to the women and to the message.

Still, it is one thing to send out a warning about AIDS and
quite another to make the warning sink in. It is certainly a
good thing for a man to put a condom in his pocket on a
Friday afternoon. But that is no guarantee he'll remember it,
or be inclined to take it back out, later that evening when he
will probably be drunk and may well have thoughts other
than disease-prevention on his mind. It would be easier to
feel encouraged by condom distribution of whatever magni-
tude if only there were more signs that men, as well as
women, were really committed to the struggle against AIDS
in Africa. Unfortunately, most signs point the opposite way.

One afternoon, I drove out to Chirovakamwe, a small
rural settlement outside Mutare, and came upon a dozen
local residents gathered on a pair of wooden benches by a tall
mushumha tree. In the distance, a range of craggy mountains
pressed their cathedral arches to the sky above the dry, rock-
strewn earth, where scattered stands of corn stalks clattered
in the midday breeze. Barefoot women strolled by, with bags
of mealie meal on their heads. Children in green uniforms
ambled home from school, past the Chitsora Brothers Bottle
Store and General Dealer.

The people under the *mushumha* tree were dutifully
attending their weekly AIDS education class, but there was a
conspicuous absence of men. All the people in the class were
women. The class leader, Georgina Manyanga, was also a
woman. The only man in the picture was Stanford Kambeu,

supervisor of the local anti-AIDS campaign, who hovered in the background. Otherwise, the campaign against AIDS in Chirovakamwe was all too typical of the campaign in other parts of Zimbabwe — women talking to women, about a subject that most assuredly involves men.

"Are you talking to your men about it?" asked Manyanga. The women shifted uncomfortably in their seats, but they did not reply.

Later, Lydia Chiname, aged thirty-seven, spoke to me about her concerns. An earnest women with a noble round face, she wore a blue wool vest over a blue-and-white smock and had a red kerchief knotted around her head. She conceded that she had never spoken to her husband about AIDS. He was away most of the time — working in a municipal office in Harare, a long day's bus ride to the west. When he came home for occasional visits, they did not use condoms.

I asked, was her husband faithful to her?

She hesitated, then nodded. "I think he is honest." She admitted that she'd never actually asked him.

Would she now talk to him about AIDS?

Another nod. "Yes. I think I will tell him."

Would he like that?

A shrug. "I don't know."

In fact, she probably did know. The truth is, in Zimbabwe, men don't like to talk about AIDS, at least not in the way women want to. In Zimbabwe, as in other African countries, men have a name for AIDS. They call it "woman disease". In other words, it is a plague visited upon men by women. Never mind that all the hard evidence points, if anything, in the opposite direction — that isn't what most

African men want to hear. They tend to blame women. And they are largely absent from efforts to curb transmission of the virus. It would certainly be comforting to think that these entrenched perceptions are at last changing, that younger men are taking a more enlightened view. But I never found much evidence of that.

In Mutare, for example, as in other parts of Zimbabwe and southern Africa, many public schools have started anti-AIDS clubs — voluntary organizations for youngsters keen on learning about the disease and how to protect themselves and others from its impact. I headed out one weekday morning to the Dangamvura High School just outside Mutare. The afternoon anti-AIDS club there had twenty-five members, and all but two of them were girls. In their school uniforms — burgundy sweaters, turquoise skirts or beige shorts — they gathered on the grass beside an empty soccer pitch. A small willow tree provided some shade from the winter sun. A grove of tulip trees stood nearby, in brilliant orange blossom, framed by the dry eastern hills in the distance.

Lovemore Magwere, a grinning man in a grey suit, quizzed the children on their knowledge about AIDS and its prevention. He was assisted by Gladys Mapanzure, a teacher at the school. At one point, there was some debate about whether kissing was a safe activity. It was eventually agreed that ordinary kissing was all right, while heavy kissing was maybe a problem.

"What's heavy kissing?" asked Mr. Magwere.

One of the two boys in the group piped up: "Heavy kissing is *vigorous* kissing."

It was a good line, and everyone laughed. But mostly

these kids were serious. After all, they were the storm troopers in the fight against AIDS. The main goal of such anti-AIDS clubs is to produce a critical mass of youngsters who are well-informed and highly motivated about preventing the disease. They are then encouraged to pass that knowledge and energy on to their peers. Unfortunately, the gender split at the afternoon anti-AIDS club at the Dangamvura High School (twenty-three girls to two boys) was about typical. "Normally, it's more girls than boys," conceded Mr. Magwere.

Meanwhile, in Africa, it is the male of the species who tends to make the final decisions about condom use or multiple sexual partners. So all the sex education in the world isn't likely to have much impact as long as it is confined to women and eschewed by men.

Following the group's meeting that Friday afternoon, several of the students stayed behind to chat with me about the club and its impact on their lives. "Yes, it is really helpful," said Rose Munyebru, fifteen. "We are now able to know what spreads AIDS." But she and several of her friends admitted that most students at the school didn't seem to share their concern. In fact, those who joined the anti-AIDS clubs were apt to be accused of being already infected. Why else would they have joined?

"Others say we are the carriers," said Rose.

"They treat sex as a game, entertainment," complained one of her friends.

Still, the children insisted that they would make every effort to keep themselves safe. "We'll try by all means," declared Lynette Vdzembwe, fourteen. She nodded her young head.

"We *promise*," said Sarah Ben, fifteen, her brow furrowed, an earnest gaze on her shining oval face.

Later, Sarah and several other members of the anti-AIDS club at the Dangamvura High School strolled with me out to the parking lot. They pleaded with me for the names and addresses of people in Canada whom they could write to, people their own age — they were starving for pen pals. I jotted down the name and address of my niece, a seventeen-year-old student in Toronto. And, sure enough, several weeks later, a letter arrived in Canada, plastered with Zimbabwean stamps. It was from Sarah Ben.

"I would be very happy if you would send me your photograph and if we can share the message of AIDS and how to prevent this deadly virus," she wrote in part. "P.S. What grade/form are you?"

I thought, now here was a good thing — a friendly letter to a distant person in a rough world. But no amount of friendly letters — no amount of any commodity known — is going to save all these bright young hopes of Africa. Many thousands of lives have already been lost to AIDS, and God knows how many more will soon be gone. Yet Africa itself will survive, despite its wounds, its sorrows, its endless parade of coffins. In fact, despite the ravages of AIDS, there will be more, not fewer, Africans a generation from now than there are today — living, breathing people attending to their affairs. Demographers are certain of this. Countless Africans will live long and memorable lives. Many of them will flourish. True, Annie Chailunga will not be among them, or Maggie Owara, or Robert Tembo, and those are immense losses, immeasurable losses — human lives foregone. But maybe in the Africa of the future, the Africa of the living, there will be a place for Lynette Vdzembwe or Florence Lungu, for Noerine Kaleeba or Sarah Ben.

"Personally I believe in the fortitude of man," said an official I once spoke to, a senior epidemiologist at the World Health Organization in Geneva. "I do not believe societies will disintegrate. But they may go very close to that."

You have only to look at Kampala, the Ugandan capital. Every epidemic has a "saturation point" — a stable level of infection — and AIDS may already have reached that level in Kampala. Here, the human immuno-deficiency virus has already spread about as widely through a society as it is ever likely to go. Kampala is already living Africa's future, and it is not what many of us would consider a happy place. In Kampala, the buildings are crumbling, people are dying, and life is hard. And yet shops are open, cars clatter along the pot-holed streets, men and women go about their business. You can hear the squabbling of children. If you stop on a Kampala street corner some warm and luminous evening, you will detect the scent of roasted corn drifting from a charcoal fire; you will catch the brief tremolo of a woman's laughter; you will hear a church choir sing.

3

FROM
GUATEMALA
TO
BOLIVIA

The Pale
Morning
Mist

IGH IN THE CUCHUMATANES MOUNTAINS in
the province of El Quiché in northwestern Guatemala, a natural belvedere of land juts out from
the surrounding terrain to overlook the remote Indian town
of Nebaj, where Ixil women trek along the dirt lanes in the
first faint light of dawn. They walk barefoot, wearing scarlet
faldas and bulky white *huipiles*, they have bolts of red fabric
piled atop their heads, and in the milky light of morning they
seem to resemble the high priestesses of some ancient faith.

But they are merely local women, accompanied by their
daughters, and they are heading off for the day, to gather
firewood or to work in the cornfields outside their town.
Pillars of wood smoke drift above them and above the community, with its pastel stucco walls, its mottled clay-tile roofs.
The smoke twists into the grey morning air, vanishes into the
early light, and the Indian women dwindle beyond the trees
and the undulations of land as they fan out into the countryside. This could be today. It could be four hundred years ago.

On such a morning, when a pale rose mist slinks among
the hilltops, you can climb up onto this ridge above Nebaj

and peer out across the rounded green walls of the mountains that recede north toward the border with Mexico, maybe seventy-five kilometres away as the *quetzal* flies. Off to the west, at a similar distance, lies the provincial garrison town of Huehuetenango, invisible from here, hidden by the curvature of the earth, the green mountain spires, and a sprawling archipelago of clouds.

You would not think it would be an immense challenge to cross that distance on foot. But this is rugged country at any time. In the mid-1980s, it was dangerous and lawless land, roamed by Guatemalan rebels, government troops, and rural civil defense patrols. It would have taken several days for a pair of men to trek the modest distance from Huehuetenango to Nebaj. And maybe they wouldn't manage it. Maybe they would venture on foot out into these treacherous highlands and never be heard from again. Maybe they would die. Or maybe they would do something worse, something vastly more difficult to absorb. Maybe they would simply disappear.

In Latin America during the 1980s, this was not an uncommon fate. Many people did not merely die — they vanished. One moment, you saw them. The next moment, they were gone. Disappeared. In Latin America, they have a name for these people — or these non-people. They call them *los desaparecidos*. The disappeared ones.

And this, it seemed, was the fate that befell two Americans named Nick Blake and Griffith Davis, a pair of unlikely travelling companions who ventured into Guatemala's northwestern highlands one day in late March, 1985, and did not return. On April 18, a couple of weeks after the men were reported missing, two US vice-consuls made a tour of the region by helicopter, collecting what information they could from the residents of several isolated Indian hamlets. It didn't amount to much. A week later, a single-engine plane flew over the area and dropped 4,500 leaflets containing photographs of the two men and a message asking anyone with any information to contact the US Embassy in Guatemala City. That came to nothing at all. About the same time, at US behest, the Guatemalan Army sent a total of eight thirty-six-man patrols into the region, to search for the two Americans. But they evidently came up empty as well.

Blake's family in Philadelphia — a family of considerable financial means — launched investigations of its own. For years, those efforts turned up little or nothing, and it was impossible to say with any confidence what happened to Nick Blake and Griffith Davis. Up to a point, their story could be told, but it ended with an ellipsis rather than a period. It just trailed off into the thin mountain air. It was as if the earth simply opened up late one March afternoon in northwestern Guatemala and swallowed them whole. One moment, they were two men, hiking through the green Indian highlands. The next moment . . . gone.

Apart from the shared mystery of their fate, the two men did not have much in common. They were both American. Both lived in Guatemala. Both apparently were hiking enthusiasts. But there the similarities pretty much came to an end.

Blake was the adventurer of the two. A twenty-seven-year-old freelance newspaper reporter, originally from Philadephia, he'd been living in Guatemala on and off for about a year, renting a room at the Posada Refugio in the old colonial capital of Antigua, not far from Guatemala City.

He was frequently away on forays to other parts of Central America, and he'd had his share of dangerous times. He once spent forty-two days with the rebels in El Salvador and, on another occasion, he'd written a much admired how-to article about hitchhiking through Central America's war zones. It was reprinted in *Harper's* magazine.

One colleague in the itinerant Central American press corps remembered Blake as a "Hemingwayesque" figure. And Carlos Aviles, owner of the Posada Refugio, recalled how the American would sometimes be away for weeks at a time until, without warning, he'd suddenly materialize in the lobby of the hotel. "Hi, man!" he'd exclaim, and he'd be bursting to recount his latest adventures of war. Later, he would relax by himself on the balcony outside his room on the second floor. He'd tip back a Guatemalan beer straight from the bottle. He'd gaze down at the hotel's small interior courtyard and just smile to himself.

Blake was the kind of man you might very well expect to set off on a dangerous trek up into Guatemalan rebel territory. And so he did. On the morning of March 25, 1985, he rode a country bus up to the northwestern mining town of Huehuetenango. There, as planned, he hooked up with Griffith Davis. The two proposed to head east into El Quiché toward Nebaj, a nine-day journey through glorious hiking terrain. God's country.

It really is splendid land — green, mountainous, and wild — a region of cathedral hills and cavernous valleys, of rambling coniferous forests and gushing rivers. It is inhabited by Mayan Indians, envoys from a distant past who still wear their traditional costumes, dazzling affairs that differ in style from village to village and tribe to tribe, all but unchanged from colonial times. As they've done for centuries, the Indians still plant corn on the precipitous mountain slopes of El Quiché, still dwell in rambling villages of smoke-charred adobe houses with mossy clay-tile roofs. In each village, you will find a white-stucco church, glinting in the sun like a huge piece of quartz — but in 1985, you would not have found a priest. The army had expelled all of the priests from El Quiché.

And that should have been a warning, one of the many signs that this was, in fact, a tormented corner of a deeply troubled land. There was nothing benign about the recent history of the northern Quiché. For a short time, in the rebellious early 1980s, the province had been roamed by a force of anti-government rebels known as the EGP, Spanish abbreviation for the Guerrilla Army of the Poor. But the rebels had lately been forced into retreat.

Now the government troops were able to ravage their way through these hills pretty much at will. And they did. The soldiers had already razed whole villages, staged mock trials and mass executions, massacred countless civilians, and driven far more into flight, northward, up across the border into Chiapas state in southern Mexico. What little remained of the EGP was now confined to a slender swath of territory that hugged the Mexican frontier — a guerrilla army in retreat. These were bitter times, and emotions were raw.

But that, it seemed, was exactly what appealed to Nick Blake about the proposed trek — this romantic and defiant rump of Guatemalan rebels. He hoped to link up with the EGP somehow. It would be dangerous and exciting. And it would make a great newspaper story.

It was much less clear why Griffith Davis had let himself

in for so risky an enterprise. Davis wasn't a journalist, and he wasn't an adventurer. In fact, it was a bit difficult to make out exactly what he was. He was in his late thirties and had lived in Guatemala for the previous ten years, in a place called Panajachel on the shores of Lake Atitlán. Among other things, Panajachel was home to an eccentric community of European or North American drop-outs, and Griffith Davis was one.

Even in peaceful times, Panajachel was a jarring hybrid, where white-skinned refugees from the industrialized world wandered around in tie-dyed robes, with flowers in their hair. They crossed paths, but not much else, with sombre-faced Indian women, mostly of the Cakchiquel or Tzutuhil nations. The women trudged home in the fading afternoon light, bound for the villages that punctuated the steep green shores of the lake, most bearing the names of Christian apostles. But these were twitchy times. Even here, near Panajachel, left-wing guerrillas were on the loose. Government troops were on the prowl.

Yet, in Panajachel, the often blurry-eyed expats carried on. Or at least a few of them did, the few who remained. During the height of Guatemala's armed strife in the early 1980s, Panajachel's foreign population plummeted. But a few hardy gringos stayed on throughout, despite blown bridges, car bombs, downed power lines, and proliferating firearms. When the sun went down, they would gather in local dives with names like Restaurant Sicodélico where they would listen to Cat Stevens songs, order vegetarian dinners, and prepare to party.

During the mid-1980s, when the government's counter-insurgency drives finally forced the rebels into retreat, the ranks of the expats quickly swelled back almost to pre-war levels. It wasn't difficult to see why. Surrounded by towering volcanoes, overlooking a deep and sparkling lake, Panajachel commands a view of almost staggering splendour. Alduous Huxley once called Atitlán the most beautiful lake on earth, and he may well have been right.

It was here that Davis had lived with his common-law wife, a German woman named Mikki Lindken. Whatever his other interests may have been, it seems that Davis was also something of a hiking enthusiast. He had met Nick Blake some weeks earlier, and the two men had hatched this plan of theirs to venture up through the isolated, almost pre-Columbian world of El Quiché, a part of Guatemala — a part of the earth — that was galaxies removed from the druggy, flower-child atmosphere of Panajachel.

And so, late on March 25, Blake and Davis linked up in the western provincial capital of Huehuetenango. They checked in under their own names at a gloomy establishment on Fifth Street not far from the main plaza. This was the Hotel Central, a dreary box-shaped building with brown and yellow walls.

The following morning, the two men set off by country bus for the Indian town of San Juan Ixcoy. There, they began their journey on foot, what was to be a nine-day adventure. Their trek took them east and then southeast through the Cuchumatanes Mountains. By the afternoon of the second day, they had reached Mixlaj, a village on the border between the provinces of Huehuetenango and El Quiché. Here, they spent the night sleeping in the local school. They departed Mixlaj on the morning of March 29 and, that evening, reached a hamlet called El Llano, where they spent the night. The next day, they apparently headed for a village called Salquil. But they didn't make it. Somewhere between El Llano and Salquil, Nick Blake and Griffith Davis dropped off the map. They were supposed to show up in Nebaj on April 3, where some friends had agreed to meet them. But the two men did not show up in Nebaj at the appointed time. In fact, they didn't show up anywhere at all. Instead, they vanished. They simply disappeared.

Were the two men killed? If so, who killed them? It could have been almost anyone. It could have been government troops, thinking the Americans were rebel sympathizers. It could have been the rebels themselves, thinking the two hikers were CIA operatives or something of the sort. Or it could have been one of the government's ragtag civil defense patrols, local men who marched along the steep mountain trails, toting battered old Mauser carbines. What motive could they have had? Fear, perhaps. Or avarice. Maybe the two Americans were killed without regard to politics. It could be that they were done in for their watches and cameras. Possibly, they just got lost and strolled off a cliff.

In the wake of those two disappearances, I heard all sorts of theories and no end of conjecture, but nothing that approached solid evidence of some clear truth. Soon enough, the theories and the speculation simply burned away, like the pale rose mist that teased the shoulders of the Cuchumatanes at dawn. All that anyone could say for certain was that Nick Blake and Griffith Davis were gone.

Roughly two months after their disappearance, I made an attempt of my own to find them, or at least to gather information about their fate. I poked around in Guatemala

City, where the authorities were, and in Antigua, where Blake had been living, and in Huehuetenango, where they had begun their journey. I also drove up to Nebaj in the heart of the Ixil Indian region of the northern Quiché, where the two men had been expected to show up at the end of their trek.

Until three years earlier, Nebaj itself and the nearby Ixil towns of San Juan Cotzal and Chajul had been under guerrilla control. Many of the people here had been guerrilla supporters and so had fled to Mexico when the rebels retreated or else now dwelled nervously under the watchful eyes of the Guatemalan army. This was a place of mistrust, resentment, and fear. "I'm only telling you this because you are a journalist," said a seventeen-year-old Indian girl who hitched a ride with me for the lonely two-hour drive along gravel switchbacks from Sacapulas up over the Cuchumatanes Mountains to Nebaj. "Be very careful," she whispered. "The army captures people and kills them to blame it on the guerrillas. Often."

Later that night, I spoke to Major Jesús Carbojal Marín, commander of the Guatemalan Army garrison in Nebaj. He said it had been an act of insanity for Blake and Davis to wander into an area of such acute political and military tension, especially as they had apparently made no prior contact with the rebels. "This was stupidity on their part," Major Marín told me. "Here, the guerrillas are very different from the guerrillas in El Salvador. Here, the *indígena* distrusts all that is white or gringo. They believe they're all from the CIA."

In the end, I wasn't able to determine what had happened to Nick Blake and Griffith Davis. The best I could do was sketch the outlines of a mystery, and it looked then as if that was all anybody would ever be able to do. Already, when I retraced a portion of their steps, the rainy season had settled in. The terrain was soaked and hostile. In those conditions, a lot could disappear without a trace. It wouldn't take much to transform a man into ether.

It had certainly happened before. Tens of thousands of Guatemalans vanished during the 1980s, and they have never been found again. Sometimes foreigners were caught in that invisible web. Just four years before Blake and Davis disappeared, another American named Jack Ross Shelton, from small-town Tennessee, crossed into Huehuetenango province by bus from Mexico. He spent his first night in Guatemala at the Hotel Central, just off the main plaza, in the town of Huehuetenango, the same town and the same hotel in which Blake and Davis slept on the eve of their last trek. The next day, Shelton went missing. He has never been seen again.

In 1985, and for seven long years after, it seemed the same fate had befallen Nick Blake and Griffith Davis. Still, Blake's family persevered in its efforts to solve the mystery. Finally, a Guatemalan schoolteacher in the village of El Llano spoke up: the two men had been shot and killed by a band of government-organized civil defense patrollers. In June, 1992, their remains were unearthed — some bones, some teeth, a fragment of Nick Blake's eyeglasses. In both cases, positive identifications were made. And so a mystery was solved. A pair of disappearances became a verifiable event: the deaths of two men. In Guatemala, that was a rare transformation, even a kind of miracle.

It was a miracle that still lay some years in the future

when I decided to return to Guatemala City from the Indian town of Nebaj early one morning back in 1985. On the way, I took a detour to the town of Panajachel on the northeastern shore of Lake Atitlán, where Griffith Davis had lived off and on for a decade or so. At an outdoor café called El Patio, across the street from the Restaurant Sicodélico, I was directed to a man who identified himself only as Larry. He told me he'd known Davis well.

Larry wore a T-shirt and shorts. He had wavy black hair, turning grey, and his appearance made me think of a matinée idol gone to seed. His eyes were red, he stuttered as he spoke, and one of his legs pumped compulsively. "Yeah, what's the latest on Griff?" he wanted to know.

I told him what I knew, and Larry said that Davis had done "nothing" for a living, owned "a nice piece of property down by the lake", and made great manicotti. He asked me about Nick Blake, who had written occasionally for the same newspaper that employed me, although I had never met the man. Nonetheless, I found myself describing Blake as a good journalist, friendly, a hard worker, a bit of a risk-taker, maybe a little naive. This was the sense I'd got from talking to others.

Larry shrugged. He didn't really seem very interested in talking about *desaparecidos*. "Hey, you should plan on sticking around," he told me. I was getting up to leave — it was time to drive back to Guatemala City. Larry settled back into his chair and grinned. He said, "Things get pretty *alegre* around here, later on."

I nodded. I figured they probably did.

The
Suddenness
of Mountains

ONE MORNING, a decade or so into the dictatorship of General Augusto Pinochet, I happened to be at the Canadian Embassy in Santiago de Chile when a group of six Chileans stepped off an elevator and tried to "take over" the embassy's chancery.

The chancery was on the tenth floor of an office building in a downtown pedestrian mall, Avenida Ahumada. The people said they were from a place called Pudahuel, out near the airport, an impoverished Santiago barrio that was the target of some of the country's most brutal police repression. They had come to the embassy in order to read a statement denouncing the Chilean government.

I knew about this sort of thing. It was a bit of a ploy, really. The group's members would later be able to claim that they had temporarily "occupied" the Canadian Embassy. It would become a "diplomatic incident". They would issue some sort of press release to that effect and hope that this extra twist would entice some of the international wire services — the Associated Press, Reuters, and so on — to pick up the story and distribute it abroad. But the "occupation" would be strictly pro forma. These people were not threatening or aggressive — just the opposite, in fact. They were calm and deferential, perfectly well-behaved.

But the Canadian diplomats on the scene were understandably cool toward the idea of having their embassy occupied, peacefully or otherwise. Donald McGillivray, who was the Canadian consul, came out to speak to the group. He said they would have to leave without reading their statement. And they just nodded politely. Okay. All right. They were ready to accept that. McGillivray made them a counter-offer. The Canadian ambassador, he said, would be willing to meet one member of the group later that afternoon. They could discuss the group's concerns at length and in private at that time. The people from Pudahuel nodded their assent. They seemed quite happy with this. They made a date for four o'clock.

Meanwhile, four Chilean police arrived at the chancery. I'm not sure how they knew that something was going on, but they did. They were told by the embassy staff that the situation was under control, and they soon left. Not long after, McGillivray accompanied the Pudahuel group on foot to the Roman Catholic human-rights office, which was located about five blocks away, beside the Metropolitan Cathedral, overlooking the Plaza de Armas. The six Chileans said they felt they'd be safe there.

But I had a feeling that something was going to go wrong. And so, a little before four that afternoon, I decided to return to the embassy. I strolled east along Ahumada through the dense afternoon throng of pedestrians. The Andes drifted above the city to the east, like spinnakers of ice and granite billowing against a powder-blue sky. In their loud croaking voices, news vendors called out the names of the afternoon papers, and the good people of Santiago picked their way past the buskers, the street hawkers, the beggars, and the police.

A lot of police. The area was suddenly thick with *carabineros*, in their olive-green uniforms, with their holstered guns, their wooden batons and walkie-talkies. They lurked along side-streets or roamed back and forth in front of the tall office building that housed the Canadian chancery. They were keeping an eye out — that much was clear. They had the erect expectant look that policemen get when they know that something is about to happen. But Chileans were used to seeing a lot of *carabineros* in a small space, and so they mostly just continued on their way, bustling along the mall or lolly-gagging past the shop windows or nipping into one of the stand-up coffee bars on Ahumada, where the waitresses worked in scanty Lycra dresses on raised platforms. The bars had the kind of West Indian names that Chileans consider exotic — Haití or Caribe.

At first I thought I would just hang out on the mall, waiting for something to happen. I was pretty sure that all this police activity was related to the delegation from Pudahuel I'd seen that morning. Then I started to worry that the Canadians would try to sneak the Pudahuel representative out the back way, which was what they probably should have done. Just in case, I hurried into the building and rode the elevator up to the tenth floor. I was right on time. A few minutes after I reached the foyer of the chancery, one of the interior security doors swung open. Don McGillivray emerged, along with a woman named Rita Beauchamp, who was the Canadian vice-consul. Between them walked an elderly grey-haired man in dark clothing. He was one of the six people from Pudahuel whom I'd seen that morning. He had concluded his meeting with the Canadian ambassador, and now the two diplomats at his side were going to accompany him back to the Catholic human-rights office. I tagged along.

During the elevator ride down to street level, the Chilean man barely answered any of my questions. He declined to give his name and only nodded in a vague approving way when I asked about his meeting with the ambassador. He did let it be known that he was sixty-five years old. That was about it. He didn't seem to be in a very talkative mood. He kept his gaze fixed straight ahead, as if he knew full well what was about to happen. When we reached the ground floor, the elevator doors slid open, and we stepped into the lobby of the building. We turned and headed out onto Ahumada. Here, we swung right for the five-block walk to the Plaza de Armas and the Catholic human-rights office. It was pretty clear from the start that we weren't going to get that far.

A group of *carabineros* promptly marched across the street and fell in behind us. "You should have brought your running shoes," Beauchamp whispered to her boss. The police soon drew alongside and kept pace as we strode along the mall. It was a cool afternoon, late in the southern winter, and the pedestrians who flocked through the street sported tweed jackets or heavy sweaters and woollen scarves against the faint chill. The *carabineros* wore their customary uniforms, olive-green jackets with epaulets and stiff Sam Browne belts, their pistols at their sides in brown leather holsters. The news vendors bellowed through the evening calm, and Santiago's portly Mercedes buses groaned and gasped along the side-streets ahead. We pushed straight on.

At the corner of Ahumada and Moneda, less than a block along our way, a second group of police suddenly appeared. They simply burst through the crowd and thrust themselves in front of us. So now we were blocked, fore, side, and aft. The police didn't say a word, just stepped up and grabbed the man from Pudahuel. There was a brief and completely useless struggle. McGillivray waved his diplomatic identification and shouted and jumped about, but he was quickly shouldered aside. I had no diplomatic privileges, so I just stood where I was, clutching my notebook and my pen. The *carabineros* hustled their prisoner aboard a waiting police van and sped away. And so, just like that, a man was gone.

The two Canadian diplomats turned and raced back to the embassy, where McGillivray reported to the ambassador about what had occurred. The ambassador, a man named Clayton Bullis, said he would complain immediately to the Chilean authorities. An hour or so later, McGillivray phoned me at my hotel to say the embassy had been informed by the Chileans that the seizure had been a mistake, greatly regretted, all highly irregular, et cetera, et cetera. They'd assured him that the man had been released immediately upon the discovery of the error. But of course there was no guarantee of any of this, beyond the Chileans' say-so. Neither I nor anyone at the Canadian embassy even knew the man's name. For all any of us knew, the man from Pudahuel was gone — gone for good. It could happen, just like that. It already had happened to tens of thousands of people, in Chile, Argentina, Guatemala, El Salvador.

You might think, at such a time, that it would be a reassuring thing to have a pair of Canadian diplomats at your

side, with all their documents and formal privileges and their
supposed immunity. But it evidently didn't make much difference to this particular man on this particular day. Chile
was a police state, after all. And, in a police state, if the police
have your number, there's really only one thing that anyone
can say. *Adiós, mi amigo.*

That was Chile during the long days and even longer nights
of the dictator. Of all the countries I have travelled through
or lived in, none has burned itself more indelibly into my
mind. The first time I travelled to Santiago, it was late winter in South America, and at first the city seemed grey and
dull and cold. I arrived early in the morning, on a Saturday.
The sky was deeply overcast, and you couldn't see much.
But the weather cleared before long, and so I headed out
from my downtown hotel for a stroll. After several minutes,
I turned a corner — and at once, through a blind of palms, I
caught my first glimpse of the snow-covered Andes where
they soar above Santiago. They literally make you dizzy,
those mountains. My knees wobbled. I almost fell down.
Nothing quite prepares you for the suddenness of mountains, or of these mountains, their alarming bulk and proximity, how they seem to curve overhead, cantilevered roofs
in a stadium of the gods. They're unearthly. In the austral
winter, they float above Santiago like a range of jagged and
frozen moons.

The Andes over Santiago have a vertiginous, almost surreal power, and they made a perfect backdrop for Chile during the 1980s — a vertiginous and surreal time. There was
something about Santiago in those years that was wildly out
of kilter, its air of reserve and civility so at odds with the

underlying reality of the country in the time of Pinochet — the brute fact that Chile was a state run on the basis of police terror. Meanwhile, the city's parks were a carefully tended delight, from the Japanese groves on the Santa Lucía hill to the sunken gardens along the Mapocho River. Such decorum. Such propriety. In winter, the weather was distinctly cool but not thoroughly cold. The women went about in heavy winter coats, their hair in brittle perms, while the men dressed in business suits or tweed jackets, always with woollen sweaters and plaid scarves, always with their jet-black hair slicked straight back.

Even in the depths of the dictatorship, what was astounding about Santiago was the warmth of those who lived there. I have sometimes found myself slipping into the careless habit of commenting on "the friendliness of the people" in certain countries I have visited, without really thinking about it, just in order to have something nice to say. Concerning Santiago, no pretense was required. In those days, I would almost hesitate to ask anyone for directions on the street, for fear that he or she would renounce family, church, and career in order to guide me in person to my destination, no matter where it lay. I once made a journey into the far south of Chile, a trip that took a few days longer than I'd arranged with my Santiago hotel. On my return, I was greeted with an almost maternal relief by doormen, bellhops, chambermaids, and telephone operators. "Where have you *been*?" they wanted to know. "We have been so *worried* about you." This was not just some hotel manager's idea of good customer service. It was Chile.

But other aspects of Santiago were less prepossessing. In a city whose downtown area had the appearance of being

well-maintained, sophisticated, and prosperous, it was both
disconcerting and discouraging to stroll along the intersect-
ing pedestrian malls, Huerfanos and Ahumada, past the posh
shops and the smart urbanites, and suddenly to encounter a
human tide of beggars, cripples, and the blind, all pretty
much abandoned to their fate. Santiago lulled you into
thinking that Chile was not that kind of country. But of
course it was. Amidst the news kiosks and the fashionable
stores, and considerably outnumbering them, Santiago's
derelicts sought their daily bread in the constant rattle of so
many dented tin cups. And then there were the police.
Everywhere you went, you'd see them, the green-clad paramilitary *carabineros* who seemed to haunt the place. They
seemed always to be getting ready for something, preparing
for some trouble, and a lot of the time they were.

In Chile, some of the most shop-worn clichés of life
under a dictator turned out to be exactly true. The passenger
trains that journeyed into southern Chile from the Estación
Central on the Alameda O'Higgins really did run on time —
mostly. One Friday afternoon in late winter, I boarded a
train for the five-hour journey south to Chillán in order to
make a brief escape from the constant political storms in
Santiago. I had planned a weekend of skiing. The train left
precisely on schedule — one-thirty sharp — and rolled
through the vineyards of the Chilean heartland, past *álamo*
windbreaks and the lime-green fountains of willow trees,
with the snow-covered Andes glimmering off to the east. At
least to my eyes, there was a quaint almost Old World aura to
the passing scenery — antique stone cottages with curlicues
of smoke drifting from their chimneys, tucked amid golden
hedgerows of gorse and groves of gnarled fruit trees — peach

and apricot — that exploded with bright yellow blossoms. At road-crossings, there'd be *gauchos* mounted on shaggy bay horses. They'd be bundled in layers of wool and leather, with their dark, round-brimmed hats pulled low over their eyes. They'd be smoking hand-rolled cigarettes, staring into the distance. Like much else in Chile in those days, they exuded an air of portent and mystery.

I got in my weekend of skiing, at a place called las Termas de Chillán, which boasted the longest chair-lift in South America and had natural mineral baths at the base, a choice of sulphur or iron. Indoors at the hotel, the waiters wore dinner jackets, and South America's most somnolent orchestra played a succession of barely audible show tunes. Most of the guests were Chilean, but there was a smattering of Argentines and Brazilians, plus a smashing Italian woman and a pair of young American men, both of whom played in the brass section of the Santiago Symphony.

I also met a medical doctor from Concepción, Chile's third-largest city, who had come to Chillán for the weekend, along with his wife and four grown daughters, the eldest of whom played on the field hockey team at the University of Concepción and had a remarkably lovely Christian name. Her full name was María Victoria, but, in Latin America, a vast number of women are named María. It's by far the most common feminine name, no surprise in a region where Roman Catholicism has long dominated and where there's a special, almost cultish fascination with the Virgin Mary. And so, in order to help distinguish a given María from the others, the name is often combined in some way with whatever follows. Thus, someone named María Luisa might be called Malú. Someone with the name of

María Teresa might be known as Mayté. For some reason, María Victoria becomes Malala, with the emphasis on the middle syllable. This particular Malala, as I recall, had flashing eyes, twin sprays of freckles on her cheeks, and thick brown hair. Off the slopes, she went about in cowboy boots, a woollen sweater, and a long peasant skirt.

But I digress. At the end of a full day of skiing at las Termas de Chillán, the wood-panelled lounge quickly filled with après-skiers, who crowded around the massive stone fireplace or gathered in quiet corners. Soon, a bevy of waiters in white jackets swarmed inside, bearing trays of glasses and huge bowls of steaming *gluwein*, which they ladled out and distributed about the room. Before long, the decibel level began to rise amid the cackle of laughter and bellowed jokes until, from the dining room, the muted strains of South America's most somnolent dinner orchestra beckoned us in to dine.

On Monday morning, the weekend over, I rode a bus down through three-metre banks of snow to the city of Chillán, along with several other departing skiers. The bus deposited us at the railway station, where we promptly discovered that, even under a General Pinochet, the trains do not *always* run on time. In fact, they were no longer running at all and wouldn't be for the foreseeable future. The previous night, three railway bridges between here and Santiago had been blown up by leftist saboteurs. And so, brusquely summoned back to the sterner realities of Chilean political life, I caught a slow bus north to Santiago.

In those days, there was a crackling electric undercurrent to life in the Chilean capital. The place bristled with intrigue — politicians, labour leaders, and academics plotting another attempt to discredit the dictatorship. Cigarette smoke hovered over every whispered and clandestine conversation, and I was forever having secret meetings in subterranean cafés with opposition politicians who cautioned me to take a roundabout route back to my hotel. Once a month — at least in winter, when the universities were in session — Santiago erupted in city-wide protest against the dictatorship. Other Chilean cities did the same.

On the eve of protest days, as the Andean peaks burned brick-red in the last desperate light and as dusk tumbled down from the foothills, the central part of Santiago would suddenly start to echo with the rattle and slam of metal shutters — merchants racing to secure their premises so they could scurry home to safety before the curfew fell. Sirens wailed in the distance. Now a wind would kick up, sheets of newspapers would suddenly scatter and flap through the streets, like flocks of low-flying birds, and soon a pale moon rose above the clusters of office buildings by the Plaza de Armas. When it came to assuming an air of danger and foreboding, Santiago had a kind of genius.

On protest nights, we'd sometimes do a tour of the city by car, never mind the curfew. There'd be three or four of us, all reporters. We'd head for one of the squatters' settlements that surrounded Santiago, and the journey would be a slow one, despite the complete absence of traffic. Instead of other cars, we'd have to negotiate our way through one police roadblock after another, each manned by another squad of *carabineros* clad in anti-riot gear with thick balaclavas pulled down over their faces. They'd be clutching Uzi submachine guns, and they'd loom up out of the darkness, sinister as ghosts, their breath forming clouds of condensation in the glare of the headlights. If they let us pass, we'd push on until we got to another roadblock. Then we'd try to talk our way through that.

When we hit the poor areas on the outskirts of town, the power would almost invariably be out — more sabotage — and there would be fires burning at intersections, heaps of old tires set alight. We'd pick our way through scattered debris and rubble, turn up a narrow unlit street, and suddenly there would be rocks, raining down on us from the darkness. Whoever was driving would hit the brakes, slam the shift into reverse, and squeal backwards until we were clear. All right, we'd say. No big deal. No harm done. Wrong street. We'll just try another. And, slowly, gingerly, we would drive on.

It astonishes me sometimes, looking back on Chile in those years, to think of the near infinity of moments that we experience in our lives and how very few of them we remember for longer than it takes them to pass us by. Most of my life is a blank. I couldn't say what I was doing, or thinking, or feeling at almost any given time. I might be able to guess at a memory or deduce one ("If it was a weekday afternoon in September, 1973, then I must have been . . . "), but I wouldn't truly remember. Try as I might, I wouldn't really recall. And yet there are certain moments that you cannot escape — images that force themselves upon you, that scald their way into your mind. You couldn't forget them, ever, even if you tried.

Late one night in the Santiago winter, a protest night, I was driving through an outlying area of the city along with Simon Alterman, the Reuters bureau chief, and his wife, Malgoshe. As usual, the electricity had gone out in this part of town, and the darkness was nearly palpable, broken only by the scattered orange flames of bonfires, twisting in the night. We were embarked upon another of those journalistic forays that didn't really have a name or a specific purpose. This was a sort of reconnaissance, I guess. We weren't likely to come up with any hard news, but simply by being out here, at this time, we'd get a feel for what was going on. People would surely be killed this night, and we would have to write about their deaths the following day. We'd need some context and some colour — some direct experience of our own — and that was what we were gathering now.

We'd already been hit by hails of rocks a couple of times. Now we turned a corner and were promptly pulled up short by several *carabineros* in parkas and balaclavas. One of them kept the muzzle of his submachine gun poking through the window on the driver's side as he demanded to know our business. He was nervous and barking. We were all nervous. I looked past him. By the shifting light of a bonfire, I could make out a vacant lot and, on the ground, in the unkempt grass, at least a dozen men were lying prone, each man with his hands cupped on the back of his head. Half a dozen *carabineros* stood above the prisoners, with their weapons trained at their captives' skulls. Behind them, by the light of the bonfire, the shadows of the *carabineros* writhed and danced on a bare brick wall. Eventually, we were dismissed, ordered to drive on. And we did. We crept past whatever grim drama was being played out in that lot, and we headed back downtown.

Simon and Malgoshe came in for a drink at my hotel that night, and we talked a good long while. It was too late by then for us to file anything anyway. I don't know what had been happening, or been about to happen, in that vacant lot. But some moments of the past, some images, are easy to recall — and this was one. In those days, Chile really did possess a dark, even demonic side. During seventeen years of military dictatorship, the country became almost an international icon of authoritarian rule, governed by a mustachioed tyrant who ranted in a gravelly voice reminiscent of Marlon Brando in *The Godfather* and who strutted about in a white dress uniform decorated with an absurd surfeit of medals and military braid. In the 1980s, when people in North America thought of this crazily elongated land, squeezed between the southern *cordillera* of the Andes and the Pacific Ocean, they probably thought of goose-stepping, Prussian-style soldiers on parade, or of soccer stadiums crammed with detained opponents of the junta, or of subterranean torture chambers, or of lightning police raids at dawn.

None of those images was inaccurate, exactly, but they didn't tell the whole story. Chile was populated by 11.3 million people, and they didn't all fit their appointed stereotypes. Still, enough of them *did* that the image of Chile as a sort of stark Latin America morality play gained wide and at least partly deserved currency. You had only to witness an anti-government demonstration near the Plaza de Armas in the centre of Santiago to conclude that the Chile of the popular imagination was not exactly a work of fantasy. The whole brutish nightmare was played out in public view over and over again in those days — the truncheon-wielding paramilitary police, the attack dogs, the clouds of tear gas, the pluming water cannons, the prone and bloodied bodies of students who had all been engaged in a *peaceful* demonstration.

When I think of a protest day in Chile, I think of a day in

the southern winter. The sky is chiaroscuro of dense grey clouds and streaks of stunning blue. A brisk wind blows through the aspen trees, the oaks, the *araucarías*, and the chubby palms. On weekdays, Santiago normally thronged with pedestrians and automobiles, with black Peugot taxis and crepitating Mercedes buses, but on such a day as this it becomes a deserted warren, its boxy turn-of-the-century office buildings and narrow one-way streets almost empty. The only people about now are demonstrators, journalists, and police. All is deathly quiet until, suddenly, it begins. You hear the first tear-gas cannisters explode, followed by the first shrieks of panic — women's voices, mostly. The *carabineros* almost always went at the women first. I never really determined why. I imagine they just liked hitting women.

At times like those, Chile really did fulfil its image as the definitive Latin American military dictatorship. The *carabineros* seemed to be everywhere. They had their attack dogs and truncheons, their water cannons and tear gas, and they didn't give an inch. Oh, to be a policeman in a police state.

One weekday afternoon in late winter in Santiago, I got on a city bus and headed out to a squatters' settlement on the outskirts of the city, a place called Lo Hermida. It was pretty certain there would be trouble out there.

I had two companions on that journey, both Chileans. One of them was the grandson of Salvador Allende, the Marxist president who died in the 1973 coup that brought General Pinochet to power. His name was Gonzalo Neto, and he'd recently returned from eleven years of exile in Mexico, in order to join the struggle against the dictatorship.

Neto and his girlfriend, a community activist in Santiago, had contacts in Lo Hermida.

At the time, the campaign of protest against military rule was at its height, and our trip turned out to be even more unnerving than we had reckoned. We ran into one disturbance after another until finally we reached the eastern outskirts of the city, where the huge wall of the Andes shouldered the lowering South American sky. Here, we came upon an almost apocalyptic scene, and the bus driver refused to go any farther. He started to jimmy his vehicle around, to head back into town. We told him we'd just get off here, thanks. We were the only passengers left. The driver shook his head, shrugged, and opened the door.

We climbed down onto the street, the driver raced the vehicle's engine, and the bus tottered away. Just ahead of us, a dark-green police van sagged in the middle of the street, its tires deflated, its sides crumpled in. A squad of *carabineros* guarded the vehicle. They all wore bullet-proof vests and riot helmets over their olive-green uniforms. They clutched submachine guns at the ready, and stood amid a rubble of stones, bricks, blocks of wood, and shards of glass from shattered bottle bombs.

Farther up the way, pillars of smoke twisted into the cold grey air from bonfires and burning tires. I couldn't see them now, but there was no doubt that gangs of young men with bandannas wrapped over their faces were huddling off to the side somewhere, in the welter of rabbit-warren alleys that criss-crossed the surrounding slums. They would be regrouping for another attack.

It seemed that this was maybe a good time to think about turning back. But none of us wanted to be the first to suggest it, so no one did. We'd come this far, so we just kept going. We took a few deep breaths and then picked our way up the street, past the disabled police van. We stepped gingerly through the debris, directly under the glare and shifting gun barrels of the *carabineros*, expecting at any moment that something would explode. Having firearms pointed in your direction — it isn't a thing you ever learn to enjoy.

But we got past the *carabineros* safely and, after that, it didn't take long for us to reach our destination — the Chapel of the Holy Spirit. This was a small blue wooden building that slumped some distance from the avenue beside a narrow rutted alley scattered with deep puddles. A makeshift emergency clinic had been set up here, staffed by a Chilean medical student, several political organizers, and three young nuns from a Chilean order called La Hospitalaria de San José. The medical student and the others planned to spend the night in the unheated wooden chapel, just as they had done during previous times of protest. We proposed to do the same.

These were hard times in Chile. There was a global economic recession, and the country's narrow economic base, highly dependent on copper exports, had been thoroughly battered. The economic trials made for turbulent politics — days and nights of protest, often violent. Once a month the cities erupted, as opponents of military rule — poor people, the unemployed, students, academics, labour leaders, and others — rose up against the dictatorship. It was easy to find trouble, especially out in the slums that ringed Santiago like a fraying human noose, places just like Lo Hermida. There was little gainful employment out here in the best of times, and these were not the best of times.

It wasn't long before my two companions decided it was just too risky for them to remain in Lo Hermida that night. Things felt wrong, worse than they'd expected. If discovered by police, Gonzalo Neto would certainly be expelled from the country all over again — if he was lucky. As matters stood, the sun was still up, though buried beyond dense clouds, and they could probably get back into the city before dark.

I decided to stay on without them. I wanted to see what a night of protest out in the slums was like for the people who lived here. Besides, I thought the experience might make a story for my newspaper. My friends set off on foot, out into the spreading dusk. I watched them leave and then I turned to head back into the chapel, where a pair of students named Cristian and Juan José — both political organizers from the University of Chile — promptly befriended me. After darkness fell, the three of us ventured out into the surrounding slums to see what was going on.

We headed north along a darkened alley toward the Chapel of Christ the King. Along the way, we crossed paths with a small red Citroën flying a white flag. Inside, bundled into the back seat, a young man in his mid-twenties lay wrapped in blankets, with a smashed head — the result of blows inflicted during a confrontation with the *carabineros*. This was a serious injury, one that required more than first aid. The driver of the car proposed to try sneaking through the surrounding obstacle course of fires and roadblocks in hopes of getting his passenger to a hospital downtown. A little farther along, we stopped to talk to a group of young people gathered at a street fire. Somebody up the alley cried out, "¡*Pacos!*" and everyone scrambled for cover. A police vehicle roared past some distance away. After a nervous silence, the protesters re-emerged and gathered around the fire again.

We ventured out to Avenida Lo Hermida, the broad roadway that ran past the settlement. It was deserted now, except for fires and scattered stone barricades. Gangs of youths lurked in the shadows, ready to heave rocks at any vehicle that tried to enter. Occasionally, the night was split by an eerie flash of light as demonstrators snapped overhead electrical cables by tossing steel chains at them. Not far off to the west, through the cold darkness, we could hear an unholy racket — people beating their saucepans in protest against the dictatorship, interspersed with occasional gun-shots. The night air bore the sting and reek of tear gas, and our eyes began to water. Shortly before the midnight cur-few, we made our way back to the Chapel of the Holy Spirit where more casualties of the protests had arrived for treat-ment. They included a thirteen-year-old girl, a young woman, a man. All said they'd been beaten by police.

By two a.m. a few of the people in the chapel decided they'd had enough. They pulled some of the wooden pews together, climbed into their sleeping bags, rolled onto their sides, and rooted about for sleep. I was too restless to do the same. Instead I shuffled over to a vacant corner and hun-kered down on the floor. I turned up the collar of my unlined overcoat, which was all I'd brought with me, and prepared to spend the rest of that cold night staring at my breath and listening to the reports of gunfire.

One of the sisters of La Hospitalaria de San José had other ideas. She was a young woman, in her mid-twenties, not beautiful exactly, but pretty in a bright, animated way, a way that exuded energy and purpose. Now she squared her shoulders and marched over to me. She took my arms, yanked me to my feet, and herded me back to the others. She helped me get a wooden pew arranged by the wall. Under her instructions, I stretched out on that. It was better to sleep, she said. There was nothing else to be done now.

I did sleep, more or less. But it was not a quiet night. Some 340 people would be detained before dawn. At least forty would be wounded. Several would be killed. They would include a forty-three-year-old French priest named Father André Jarlan, shot dead by police as he huddled in the study of his presbytery, reading a Bible. That killing — two bullets to the forehead — took place in La Victoria, another squatters' settlement on the Santiago perimeter. During the ensuing thirty-six hours, a total of nine people would die in political disturbances. Hundreds more would be injured, at least sixty of them from bullet wounds.

Several times that night, I half awoke and saw through a blur that the same young nun who'd bossed me around earlier was now perched on the pew at my side, silhouetted above me, shoulders back, spine erect, wearing her habit of beige and Marian blue. In the early morning, I awoke to find that she was still floating above me. She had barely shifted her weight all night and evidently hadn't slept at all. She had removed her woollen poncho, though, to drape it over my chest. A blanket was wrapped around my legs. And dawn spilled its pale light down the sudden wall of the Andes.

A Fist
of Irony

"EVERYONE HERE is right-wing. We *are* the right
wing." That said, the speaker settled back into his
chair. He took another sip of coffee from a fine
china demi-tasse and waited for a reaction.

We had just got up from dinner and were gathered now
in the living room of a house in Vitacura, a prosperous residential district of Santiago. A pair of french doors overlooked a darkened terrace and garden. It was winter outside
and distinctly cold. But here inside it was warm. The living
room was brightly lit and skilfully furnished with a profusion
of antique wooden chests, potted plants, and chesterfields
uphostered in a dark corduroy fabric or elegant chintz. The
room managed to be cosy without seeming cluttered. A
wood fire blazed in the grate, a balm against the outdoor
chill.

On the mantle, among other pictures, mementos, and
keepsakes, stood a framed black-and-white photograph
showing Bernardo, our host. He was mounted on a polo
pony, nonchalantly gripping his mallet while flanked by his
team mates at el Club de Polo e Equitación San Cristóbal.
Here was firm evidence that I was among the Santiago hor-
sy set, or a part of it. Not surprisingly, none of the other

Chileans in attendance that night volunteered to contradict their friend's blanket assessment of the prevailing political ideology in the room. The truth was, they *were* the right wing.

They were all in their early thirties, all wealthy, all politically conservative, socially elitist — and determined to remain so — in a country riven by economic divisions and ruled by an authoritarian military dictatorship. On the other hand, they were individual human beings, too. They had their differences.

Karín, for example. This was her house, and it was she who had invited me to join her husband and their friends for dinner. The mother of four young children, she was in the process of completing a graduate university degree in political science. She also did weekly political commentaries for the evening news programme on the Universidad Católica TV station. I met her at the station one day, and we hit it off immediately. Among other things, she was a woman of quite extraordinary beauty. She had a rippling laugh, buoyant charm, and a huge fund of girlish enthusiasms. To say that I met her is probably an understatement. Karín was not the sort of woman you met. She was more the sort of woman you bumped into and promptly fell in love with, although you'd have to keep the truth to yourself. Married as she was. The mother of four.

Karín was also the sort of woman who on a sudden whim would look up at you, pat the empty seat beside her, and say, "*Cuéntame cosas.*" Tell me things. And dutifully you would sit down beside her and proceed to tell her whatever was on your mind. I didn't share her politics, but that didn't seem to matter. She wasn't what you'd call strident or doctrinaire.

She liked to get ideas out in the open, where she could walk around them and see how they looked from different angles. But let's face it — she was also very rich. She was a rich South American and a creature of her class. She had aristocratic ways and interests. She stabled her horse at the San Cristóbal riding club, where husband Bernardo was on the polo team, and she spoke with genuine expertise about the South American show-jumping circuit. As it happened, this gave her and me something of a non-political nature to discuss. In my pampered youth, I'd had occasion to acquire more than a rudimentary familiarity with the Canadian show-jumping scene. It was not an interest I had maintained, to put it mildly, but I could still talk about horses with a certain muted confidence. During lulls in the conversation, Karín had a sweet way of drifting off on her own. She'd sing American pop tunes to herself in lightly accented English.

Or she'd suddenly snap her fingers, remembering something, and she would drag me upstairs to the master bedroom, where she'd pop a tape into the VCR — a recording of one of her political commentaries. She wanted my considered opinion of what she'd said or of the way she'd said it. Honestly, now — what did I think? We'd sit there on the bed, like kids, and I'd tell her things, and she'd tell me things. She was a difficult person *not* to fall in love with. For me, anyway.

But, like other Chileans of her class, Karín was pretty darn conservative. She had vigorously supported the 1973 coup that toppled the socialist government of Salvador Allende, and now she backed military rule. She agreed that there was something of an inconsistency here. After all,

General Pinochet initially justified his coup by arguing that the action had been necessary in order to *restore* Chilean democracy. And here was Chile, eleven years on, still squirming under the fist of the same bloody tyrant.

Back in the living room, the political discussion continued. Another guest that evening — an urbane young man who was one of Chile's leading television journalists — said he considered himself to be right-wing politically, and yet he no longer supported the dictatorship. He said that, by holding his nose, he could accept the coup that brought Pinochet to power, but he was firmly opposed to the continuation of military rule. He said it should have ended long before.

Another guest — a childhood friend and former schoolmate of Karín's — jumped in at this point. She announced that she too was vehemently opposed to Pinochet. She very nearly spluttered with contempt when she spoke of him — but not because he was too harsh or autocratic. Just the opposite. She considered him *weak*. He'd gone too soft for her. He was straying, she believed, from the strict free-market economic policies advocated for Chile by Milton Friedman at the University of Chicago. Of the six Chileans in the room, this woman alone raised her hand and declared *Sí* when I asked if anyone there considered himself or herself to be, not merely right-wing, but *ultra* right-wing.

This woman agreed that the poor should not actually starve, but she appeared to suspect, as did one or two others at dinner that night, that the *real* problem with the poor was that they didn't wish to work. She was also critical of the rich. "We like to think of ourselves as Europeans," she told me, "but we're really just *tropicales*." She meant, tropical people — a bit of an exaggeration. Santiago isn't in the tropics or even the subtropics.

There may have been a faint trace of antagonism in the air, and so Karín moved promptly and expertly to dispell it. Seated upon a plush dark-brown chesterfield, she looked up and asked if anyone wanted more coffee. She proceeded to fill the cups assembled beside her on a silver tray. She turned to me. In a stage whisper, she apologised most abjectly on account of the coffee being instant. "We're just uncultured people, really," she said. She gave me a shrug and a theatrical sigh. "But you may as well know our faults."

At the time, I laughed. I considered this to be another winning remark. It made me like her more. Now, some years later, it occurs to me that if a similar sentiment had been expressed by an equally wealthy man — and not by a woman I found attractive — I might well have considered the comment to be pretty suspect. Let's say the same thought had been voiced by Pepe Dutríz, the Salvadoran oligarch who once took me to lunch at the Sports Club in San Salvador. I might well have considered it further evidence of a crude and unfeeling nature. I tend to exercise something of a double standard in these matters.

On the other hand, I can think of at least one other factor that distinguished Karín and her remark from Pepe Dutríz and something he might say. The fact is, Karín spoke with a consciously ironic edge. She understood the implications of what she was saying — she, a wealthy and fortunate woman in a land where many were poor, hungry, and angry. But I don't think that Pepe Dutríz had any sense of irony at all. I doubt if he had ever in his life even broached the notion that there might be a disparity between the apparent and the real or between two different sets of appearances. I don't think he had an especially subtle mind. I'm not saying that this somehow justifies Karín's position and not his. It probably doesn't. Still, in the Republic of Chile during the years of the General, a sense of the ironic was a valuable thing. Its uses were certainly manifold, if not always manifest.

Several months after dinner that night at Karín's, I found myself in Chile once again. I was aboard a ferry ploughing across an ocean strait, bound for an island called Chiloé in the wild and rocky archipelago that is southern Chile. I was leaning against the railing on the upper deck beside a young Chilean woman who was blonde, like Karín, and also, like Karín, attached to another man. Her name was Julieta.

"You're here to see the *relegados*, right?" she said at one point.

We were peering out at an astonishing view — long gashes of blue and purple ocean torn by rows of sawtooth whitecaps and bursting with sudden jets of foam. The sky roared overhead, electric blue, and gulls wheeled past like kamikaze kites. On the northern horizon the Chilean mainland squinted above the surging sea, a tangle of variegated green.

I had met Julieta shortly after boarding the ferry. She was in her early thirties, and her wavy blonde hair — a rarity in Chile — was not so uncommon down here in the far south where there was a substantial Germanic population. She told me she ran a small office-supply distributorship in the settled, rather teutonic city of Puerto Montt, back on the mainland. It seemed that her boyfriend — name of Jorge — had wandered off for a chat with the ferry captain, and so she and I had struck up a conversation. Jorge was from

Santiago and was based in the area only temporarily. He was a commander in the Chilean Air Force.

By *relegados*, Julieta meant Chile's internal exiles. At the time, they were legion. General Pinochet had declared a state of siege only a month earlier, and more than two hundred dissidents had been sent to remote corners of the country, not to mention more than four hundred others who had been confined to a special military detention compound in the far northern desert. Directly ahead, on the island of Chiloé — a traditional destination for Chile's *relegados* — there were currently twenty-four dissidents being held under house arrest. I pondered whether to answer Julieta's question truthfully or to dissimulate. In fact, I was on my way to the island to visit some *relegados*. I was to contact three of them, all members of the left-wing Bloque Socialista.

"Right," I said at last. I spared her the details.

It turned out that the three of us — Jorge, Julieta, and I — were all planning to spend that night in Ancud, Chiloé's second-largest town. My two new acquaintances offered to give me a lift in their car, and I was glad to accept, both because I needed the ride — I was hitchhiking at the time — and because it wasn't every day that you got a Chilean Air Force commander on such casual terms. And so, after the ferry landed at Chacao, we climbed into Jorge's car and set out for Ancud. Along the way I tried as discreetly as I could to ease the conversation around to politics. This seemed to amuse Julieta no end. It was just what she'd expected — and so, every few moments, she twisted around in her seat and shot me another knowing smile.

What I wanted to find out was this — to what extent did the air force dissent from General Pinochet's army-backed political programme? It was an important issue at the time. The dictatorship was into its second decade, and most sensible people had now accepted that there was no realistic way of toppling it from the outside. If change came, it would have to come from within — a rift in the armed forces themselves. The air force was thought to be the most dovish branch of the military and so would be the most likely source of a division within the junta. Or so the thinking went.

Unfortunately, I never really got an answer, mainly because Jorge didn't seem to know, but also because we kept being interrupted by the stunning island vistas — pale green meadows glazed with evening sunshine and interspersed with darker wooded thickets that shot from the earth like great tufts of pillow feathers pushing through rents in the emerald fabric of the hills.

In Ancud, population about thirteen thousand, we pulled up in front of a very comfortable-looking hotel — the Hostería Ancud — with a magical misty view out across a sprawling Pacific bay. The hotel was set on a hillside overlooking the town's jumble of shingled, hardwood houses. Columns of smoke drifted from the scattered assembly of tin-pipe chimneys, all staircased against the surrounding hills in the cool, slowly setting sun.

We trooped inside, registered, and split up to go to our rooms. I had my own plans worked out. I meant to head south the following morning to a place called Chonchi, where those three members of the Bloque Socialista were being held. I'd been given their names and was carrying some messages for them from people I knew in Santiago, which gave my trip what I liked to think of as a cloak-and-dagger air. I'd also been given the name of a man who worked for a radio station here in Ancud. And so, shortly after dropping off my bag at the hotel, I headed out on my own to look him up. This turned out to be a straightforward task. I soon found him at the radio station, in his office, and one of the things he did before we parted was to set me up with a certain driver who was, he said, *confiable* — a fellow you could trust. This reliable man would drive me down to Chonchi and back.

Later that evening, at my hotel, I bumped into Jorge and Julieta again, and they asked me to join them for a drink. We met in the bar — a warm, well-lit, wood-panelled spot — and we each ordered a *pisco* sour (a tart, lemony libation that Chile claims as its national cocktail, as do both Peru and Bolivia). My two new friends already knew my general plans — to continue south in the morning to Chonchi to meet some exiled political dissidents there. I really hadn't seen any point in pretending otherwise. There were some places in the world — El Salvador, Guatemala — where you wouldn't dream of broadcasting that kind of news. But, in Chile, I didn't really worry. Everybody knew there were dissidents, and any thinking person would understand that a foreign journalist would likely want to talk to them on occasion. I didn't fuss about it much beyond that. Nobody would arrest me, or break into my room at night to do his worst. Still, I wasn't prepared for what happened next. It seemed that I had badly misjudged the situation.

A trifle awkwardly — as though he were working around to something that had already been discussed in private — Jorge announced that he and Julieta had no fixed agenda for the weekend. So . . . well, the thing was . . . ah . . . why didn't they drive me to Chonchi themselves? Jorge looked up and shrugged. They could drop me off to conduct my interviews, he said, then pick me up and bring me back. How about it? It would be no problem for them, and they'd enjoy the company. Jorge explained that it wasn't often that they ran into foreigners way down here. If it would make me feel more comfortable, I could pay for my share of the gas. It was up to me. With that, Jorge sat back and took another sip of his drink.

Now this was a switch — a reasonably senior Chilean military officer proposing to provide convenient transportation to a foreign reporter who was seeking to interview left-wing political dissidents living under house arrest in a remote part of his country. Only catch — to be honourable, I'd have to pick up my share of the gas.

I have to admit, I considered the idea. It wouldn't have yielded much in the way of classified military information — we'd already established that. But it probably would have been more interesting than travelling on my own, and I'd have got to know two more Chileans, something I never minded doing. And so I wavered. But in the end I decided that there were some things better done *without* a military escort, and so I said no thanks. I thought I'd better travel south to Chonchi alone.

Jorge and Julieta both seemed a bit disappointed, but they didn't press the point. We wound up having dinner together that night, and we spoke of other things. Still, it occurred to me then that there can't be many military dictatorships in the world where a foreign journalist travelling to meet a group of exiled political dissidents would have a commander in the national air force offer to do the driving. Great country, I thought at the time. Such remarkable people.

Mind you, *I* wasn't on the receiving end of political repression, Chilean-style. *I* wasn't a Chilean journalist who'd run afoul of the government and been tossed in jail. *I* wasn't an opposition politician barred from engaging in active politics. *I* wasn't a student demonstrator nursing a cracked skull. And *I* didn't happen to be under house arrest in a distant part of southern Chile — at least, not then.

But once I had been. I had travelled into the farthest southern reaches of the country, to Punta Arenas on the Strait of Magellan just across the cold thrashing waters from Tierra del Fuego. It was wintertime — it *always* seemed to be wintertime when I travelled to Chile — and the ground was dusted with a light covering of snow. A harsh wind blew across the strait and howled through the city, which was a surprisingly elaborate and settled community considering how remote it was.

In Punta Arenas, I boarded a small twin-prop aircraft piloted by a man named Gustavo Leigh.

"Any relation to the other Gustavo Leigh?" I asked. I meant *the* Gustavo Leigh. General Gustavo Leigh.

"Yes," the pilot replied. "I'm his son."

That got my attention. General Gustavo Leigh had been commander of the Chilean Air Force at the time of the Pinochet coup and, in fact, had personally ordered the aerial bombardment of the national palace that infamous day, September 11, 1973. Later, in the rubble of the palace, they would find the body of Salvador Allende, the president who'd been toppled in the coup. It has never been absolutely established how Allende met his end — was it murder or suicide? — but it seems that suicide is the greater likelihood.

Five years after the coup, General Leigh broke with Pinochet. He retired from the air force and settled down to what you'd think would be a more peaceful life as a Santiago real-estate broker. I interviewed him once at his office in Providencia, an affluent section of Santiago, and he railed *against* the dictatorship. He thought the whole thing should be over and done. He thought Pinochet was destroying Chile. It was a strange thing — this former air force commander, a leader of the coup, having become an outspoken *opponent* of military rule.

Now, with the younger Gustavo Leigh at the controls, I flew to a miniscule settlement called Puerto Williams in the far south of Chile. The flight took us over the Strait of Magellan and then above the Chilean half of Tierra del Fuego and the snow-covered Martial Mountains. Eventually, the plane coasted down past the mountains' southern slopes, banked to port, and traced the Beagle Channel east to Isla Navarino, the southernmost place on earth with a permanent human population.

If it is isolation you are after, here is the ideal spot. Puerto Williams clings to the northern shore of the island, part naval base and part village. The town has a church, a small museum, some low wooden houses, a school, and that's about it. When I arrived, in late winter, the place was blanketed with snow. Not a lot of foreigners ventured to Puerto Williams in those days — in fact, none did — and so I was immediately conspicuous. What on earth was a North American doing here? After all, these were tense times. Across the grey waters from Isla Navarino loomed the hatchet-blade peaks of the Martial Mountains on the Argentine side of Tierra del Fuego — and Argentina was the enemy now.

The Beagle Channel — the same waterway explored by Charles Darwin aboard the HMS *Beagle* in the late 1800s — was in those days the site of one of the world's more obscure and eccentric border disputes. True, at the time, both Chile and Argentina were governed by right-wing military dictatorships, and you might have thought this would engender something of a political bond. And maybe it did, but the bond disintegrated pretty quickly when the two countries fell out over a bunch of rocks called Nueva, Picton, and Lennox.

Okay — not rocks. Islands. But very small islands, and very nearly uninhabited. Those three specks of land are part of a remote archipelago that forms the final parcels of real estate that South America has on offer as the Andes finally give up the ghost and tumble beneath the cold southern seas at Cape Horn. The disputed territory happened to be in Chilean hands, but it was claimed by Argentina.

More than once, the two countries had tottered to the brink of war over those three outcrops of the earth. On the face of it, this was pretty absurd. After all, the land in question hardly amounted to much — a trio of almost barren boulders good only for grazing a few no doubt anemic sheep. But it wasn't the islands themselves that really mattered. What really mattered was the southern projection of the Chilean and Argentine land masses. Under international treaty, that factor was critical in determining how much either country would control of Antarctica and of the potentially resource-rich waters in between. So Argentina wanted those three islands. But Chile had them.

In 1978, the two countries had come within hours of an armed clash over the territory. Only last-minute intervention by the Vatican prevented a shooting war. Years later, the dispute remained unresolved, and there were still occasional brushes between the two sides, as they tested each other's state of preparedness. When I arrived in Puerto Williams one bright Saturday morning in the late austral winter, I was walking straight into a tense international stand-off that few people outside the region even knew existed. But it did, and so it was quite possibly inevitable that the Chileans would so quickly become convinced that I was not really a journalist at all. They concluded that I had to be a spy.

I have to confess that I didn't anticipate the problem. I was just a Canadian journalist doing his job. I intended to research some articles about the Southernmost Place on Earth With a Permanent Human Population, with probably a sidebar or two about this strange territorial dispute between Chile and Argentina. And so that was what I proceeded to do, oblivious to the suspicion I was arousing.

Of course, in Puerto Williams, it wouldn't take much to arouse suspicion. Puerto Williams in those days was not what you'd have called an intensely cosmopolitan place. Home to about 1,500 people — at least some of them on a permanent basis — the town was a modest collection of small wooden or prefab buildings clustered below the hardwood forests that scaled the precipitous central hills of Isla Navarino. Most of its residents were connected in some way to the thirty-year-old Chilean naval base there. The rest were fishermen, farmers, or small-scale merchants serving the local market.

There was one hotel — a suprisingly commodious, sixteen-room affair called the Hostería Wala — located about half an hour's walk outside Puerto Williams. There was also an acute shortage of guests — apart, that was, from me. Once upon a time, an occasional inveterate traveller had wandered this way and would wind up at the Wala, there being no place else. But that didn't happen any more for the simple reason that any outsider who came here was now promptly identified as an agent of Argentine espionage. "They're always put under surveillance," explained a portly hard-working fellow named Juan Ruís, who was the cook, housekeeper, bartender, and sole employee at the Wala.

At the time, I pulled out my notebook and wrote his comment down — it was an interesting quotation. But it somehow didn't cross my mind that the remark might very well apply to me. I was more concerned with what a shame it was that more people couldn't take advantage of the attractions that Isla Navarino had to offer. Puerto Williams itself was a fairly humdrum spot, but the surrounding countryside and mountains brimmed with interest and life — ideal for adventurous backpackers. The forests teemed with fox, deer, otter, beaver, wildcat, and juanaco, a smaller cousin of the llama. On the southern coast, flocks of emperor penguins tottered about, and the waters swirled with seals. Eagles, condors, petrels, and cormorants sailed overhead.

I myself saw little of the vaunted austral wildlife of Isla Navarino. The Chilean Navy made certain of that. As soon as I arrived from Punta Arenas, I'd been taken in hand by the military, to be documented, questioned, and then briefed on which areas of the town were off limits. I suppose that this should have tipped me off to the fact that already I was under suspicion, but I simply didn't think about it.

I was turned over to a polite but unusually dour Chilean named First Sergeant Guillermo Ortega, who identified himself as a navy public-relations representative but who was in fact my guard. I went nowhere without him. Each morning, Sergeant Ortega was waiting for me at the entrance of the Hostería Wala. He walked with me into town, through dense deciduous forests, past shaggy grey and chestnut ponies that poked for sustenance through the foot-deep snow. He remained with me all day. Then, each evening, he walked me back.

Once, for no particular reason, I invited Sergeant Ortega in for a drink, but he frowned at me as if I'd just made some dangerously subversive remark or as if he suspected me of trying to buy him off. He behaved as though I were not a person to be trusted, and I guess it was then that I started to wonder in what light I was regarded by the local military authorities.

On the whole, I was glad that Sergeant Ortega *hadn't* stepped in for a drink. Normally, I enjoyed the company of Chileans, but I found that his almost constant presence was starting to get on my nerves. He was a shady, taciturn fellow to boot, and he gave me the creeps. Still, Sergeant Ortega did not become deeply and irrevocably irritating until the military put me under house arrest.

I had found out that a small supply boat regularly chugged out of the harbour at Puerto Williams to plough along the Beagle Channel and then out onto the stormy open waters of the converging Atlantic and Pacific oceans. It was bound for Picton Island, one of the three bits of terra firma possessed by Chile but claimed by Argentina. A couple of Chilean families lived on the place, tending flocks of bony sheep on the thin, unforgiving soil.

As soon as I heard about the boat, I decided that I wanted

to make the trip. It would be so utterly cool. After all, Picton Island was contested territory, an absurdly innocuous part of the earth that two Latin American military dictatorships nonetheless seemed not unwilling to go to war over. Besides, I thought it would be interesting to discover — and write about — whoever it was who had deliberately chosen to live on a miniscule rock of an island just a stone's throw from Cape Horn. It was hard to imagine what their lives were like. And the trip itself would be a bit of an adventure.

So I sought permission from the boat's owner to make the journey, and he said fine, no problem. The only catch was, I needed clearance from the military authorities. But that didn't seem to be a major obstacle, either. Captain Jorge Chacon, commander of the Chilean naval base at Puerto Williams, readily gave his approval. It was all set. I could go. But then, just hours before the supply boat was to depart on its thirty-six-hour voyage, the owner called me into his office, put up his arms, and informed me that it would no longer be possible to have me on board as a passenger. The military instructions had changed, he said. That was all. Beyond that, he couldn't explain.

I went straight around to Captain Chacon's office at the base. He told me that a sudden order had been received from higher authorities to restrict access to the area "for the moment." If it was any consolation, he added, I could always return to Puerto Williams — granted, one of the most remote spots on earth — in order to make the trip to Picton at . . . oh, at some other time. On some more propitious occasion. He smiled at me, with that sly infectious charm that is so much a part of the professional military personality.

Sure, I thought. Just give me a call. I'll be ready at a

moment's notice to climb on an airplane in order to fly back down to the Southernmost Place on Earth With a Permanent Human Population so that I can take a supply boat to Picton Island. Thanks a lot.

I did my best to change Captain Chacon's mind, but he was just following orders, it seemed. Probably, I reacted with just a shade too much vehemence. Eventually, Captain Chacon seemed to read something other than simple professional zeal in my manner. He didn't put his thoughts into words, but an additional coolness in his voice seemed to betray his suspicions. What was he confronted with here — a spy in the pay of Argentine espionage?

The following morning, I found Sergeant Ortega waiting at the entrance to the Hostería Wala as usual. But this time *his* orders had changed as well. He informed me that I was not going anywhere that day. I was staying right where I was. My appointments for the day had been cancelled.

I wanted to know if this meant that I was under arrest.

Sergeant Ortega seemed downright offended, as if he'd never heard that particular term before, or as if the very words were deeply mortifying to him personally and to his tender sensibilities as a Professional Public Relations Representative. He assured me that my situation was nothing of the sort, had nothing at all in common with — what was that phrase I had used? — with being *under arrest*. I simply wasn't permitted to leave the hotel. Not the same kind of thing at all. He said arrangements were being made to put me on the next military flight back to Punta Arenas, over on the other side of Tierra del Fuego.

And so I spent the rest of that day at the Hostería Wala, under something that apparently wasn't, but certainly bore a striking resemblance to, house arrest. I grant you, as periods of incarceration go, this was not among the most disagreeable that I could imagine. I had endured one or two more onerous ordeals in my life. But it was the principle of the thing.

While I raged at my captivity, Juan Ruís served me lunch and then a light tea and then a substantial dinner in the otherwise vacant dining room, with its soaring picture windows overlooking a snow-covered meadow that sloped down toward the steel-grey waters of the Beagle Channel. Beyond, the rough-hewn mountains of southern Argentina massed against the tattered skies over Tierra del Fuego.

Later, after dinner, I sipped a *pisco* sour or two and read by a roaring fire in the lounge. A Julio Iglesias recording — not my choice, but I was only an inmate here — was playing in the background. In this way, I whiled away my sojourn under military detention on Navarino Island in the southern archipelago near Cape Horn.

It was pretty ironic. This was the same country, after all, in which I'd once watched a gang of *carabineros* mass around the helpless body of a young man — Miguel Angel Raúl Leyva was his name. They kicked and clubbed his prone body for ten or fifteen seconds, which is a very long time to be kicked or clubbed. Later, unconscious, Leyva was borne away, and all that remained where he had lain was a large pool of blood, a blood-soaked rag, and a blood-soiled pamphlet calling on Chileans to protest in peace against military rule.

And now here was I at the Hostería Wala, with Julio Iglesias crooning out a succession of catchy Latin pop ballads as I read by a crackling fire. The following morning, I was put on a military transport plane and flown back to Punta Arenas. My brief career as a suspected Argentine spy was over. During the flight, I struck up a conversation with a fellow passenger, a young Chilean Navy officer. When we got to Punta Arenas I helped him and his wife with their bags, and I'll be damned if they didn't ask me over to their house for dinner that night. I didn't tell them that I had just been released from military detention or that I was suspected of espionage on behalf of an enemy power. After all, they didn't ask.

Lunch
With the
General

MEET General Arturo Durazo Moreno.
He was surely a monster, albeit a little monster,
a tyrant in a minor key. He was no Idi Amin but
for a time he was quite likely the most reviled man in his
country, which happened to be Mexico. General Durazo
was the chief of the Mexico City police force, and he once
took me to lunch.

At the time of our meal together, I did not know that
General Durazo was fast becoming the most reviled man in
Mexico. I was researching a newspaper article, the first piece
I would write after arriving in Mexico City as a newspaper correspondent. I planned to compose a straightforward story about Mexico City's environmental and demographic problems.

I called up the office of the Mexico City police chief one
afternoon in order to request some statistics on crime and
traffic conditions. I wound up getting lunch instead —
lunch with Arturo Durazo Moreno. The day would come
when the mightiest powers in Mexico, from the president
on down, would try to turn Durazo into a sort of national

fall guy. They would try to make him carry the can for a long and unsavoury tradition of government, one that had spawned six decades of graft, abuse, and brute force.

Durazo was chief of the Federal District police department — which, in Mexico, makes you a general. One day, I telephoned his office, and his secretary answered the call. For some reason, she immediately grew agitated and put me on hold. When she came back on the line, it was not to provide me with a few crime stats. It was to inform me that she had scheduled a personal interview with the chief himself for late the following morning. Wonderful, I said. *Muchas gracias.* I supposed that here was an example of Mexican hospitality.

It turned out that Mexican hospitality was not exactly what was going on. General Durazo rarely if ever made himself available to the foreign press. In my case, however, he made an exception, and this seemed to be a matter of nationality — not his, but mine. I had introduced myself on the phone as a Canadian journalist, working for a Canadian newspaper. Years later, when Durazo had become a fugitive from Mexican justice, it would transpire that Canada was among the countries where he had tried hardest, if finally in vain, to establish a safe haven for himself. It seemed his wife often went shopping in Montreal; she even owned a house there.

Anyway, on the following day, at the appointed time, I showed up at the Federal District police headquarters for my interview with the General. After a short wait, I was ushered into Durazo's office and came face to face with a bull-chested creature of modest height with a somewhat bronze complexion, decked out in a pale-blue uniform that was maybe half a size too small. He had a surfeit of jowls, thinning hair combed across a shining pate, and a gruff gutteral voice. Eli Wallach was made for the part. Also on hand were Durazo's three top police lieutenants. The five of us gathered amid an excessive quantity of fuzzy electric-blue material, whose colour or texture must have held a special attraction for the General. At any rate, the stuff covered almost every available surface in the office — the floor, the walls, and the ceiling. A strange taste in interiors, I thought.

At Durazo's suggestion, we arranged ourselves upon a cluster of sofas and chairs across the blue-carpeted floor from his capacious desk. A row of picture windows ran along one wall, overlooking the grey smoky conglomeration that was Mexico City in the 1980s, smothered in its customary haze. I set about trying to conduct an interview, but rather than reply to my questions, Durazo simply chuckled to his aides or shook his head with what seemed to be amusement that anyone, anywhere, could possibly have the effrontery to ask him, of all people, questions about anything.

When he did deign to reply, his responses invariably took the same unsettling form. He glared at me, ground his right fist into the palm of his left, and growled, "¡*Mano dura!*" which meant "Firm hand". That was how he professed to be keeping control of crime, traffic violations, corruption, and just about anything else you'd care to name. The interview — if you could call it one — went on for half an hour or so, and that was the gist of it, Durazo chuckling to his aides or scowling at me, grinding his fist into his palm and barking, "¡*Mano dura!*"

There were, however, a couple of interruptions. At one point, Durazo's secretary entered with some documents that required the general's signature. At once, Durazo's three lieutenants unholstered their pens and raced to thrust them into their boss's grasp. Durazo squeezed the moment for as much suspense as possible before deciding which of the three pens to accept. Once he'd made his choice, though, the effect was immediate. The two spurned officers slunk back to their seats, visibly deflated. They were followed by the now swaggering victor, his face lit with a wide triumphant grin.

Later, a telephone began to ring — one of the half-dozen or so by Durazo's desk — and the chief himself got to his feet and lumbered across the azure wonderland of his office and around behind his desk to answer it. He remained on his feet as he spoke on the phone. While the general was on the line, another of the telephones started to ring. It might as well have been a starter's pistol.

A three-way foot race exploded across the alarming blue floor. Durazo's three lieutenants — who were, remember, three of the most senior police officers in one of the world's largest cities — immediately darted to their feet and raced pell-mell across the fuzzy carpet in a desperate contest to be the fortunate one, the loyal one, the One Who Actually Answered General Durazo's Other Phone. Along the way, one of the three men tripped over a chair and sprawled on the floor. (I saw it with my own eyes.) The man's foot hooked the chair leg. He lurched to the left to keep from falling. The chair toppled sideways. The man's arms went out for protection. He vaulted forward to avoid crashing down on top of the overturned chair. He landed on his hands and knees on the electric-blue floor. Desperately, he scrambled to his feet and made a now hopeless bid to catch up with the others. Too late. He did not manage to answer General Durazo's other phone.

Finally, with both his phone conversations at an end, Durazo returned to his place on the sofa to continue whatever it was we'd been doing — me asking questions that he didn't answer, him grinding his fist into his palm. Eventually, the general decided that this interview nonsense had gone on long enough, and he asked if I would care to join him and his lieutenants for a bite of lunch.

I looked up from my almost empty notebook. Lunch . . . ? Why, yes, I said. Lunch would be very nice. Very generous. *Muy amable. Gracias.* I didn't know what else to say.

It didn't seem to matter. Durazo merely grunted and strode off into an apartment that adjoined his office. When he emerged about ten minutes later, he was in civilian dress with a huge silver-handled pistol stuffed into the waistband of his trousers. We all rode down to the parking garage in Durazo's private elevator. A wood-panelled Ford station-wagon was already waiting, along with a police squad car and two officers on motorcycles.

We climbed into the station-wagon and set off in a convoy, red lights flashing, for the centre of town. We were bound, it turned out, for the Zona Rosa, a toney shopping and restaurant district. At every intersection along the way, the traffic was blocked by motorcycle police, and I had that rarest of Mexico City experiences — the sensation of actually getting somewhere in a car. In amazingly short order, we reached our destination, an English-style steakhouse called Angus, where the manager was waiting out on the curb to usher us upstairs.

During lunch, which was long and loud and blurry in the Mexican fashion, Durazo divided his time between talking in a low voice to a lawyer who had hurried over to join us and flirting in a much louder voice with our waitress, a remarkably attractive young woman who might have been twenty years old. Before the meal was over, Durazo had arranged to have the woman picked up by his driver when she finished work that evening.

After our meal, we returned to Durazo's office in our convoy of vehicles. Back at police headquarters, the police chief invited me upstairs. A photographer was summoned and, in the lobby of his apartment, General Arturo Durazo Moreno — chief of what was possibly the largest urban police force in the world — drew himself up to his modest full height and presented me with an impressive silver police medallion. We held our poses as the photographer captured the moment for posterity.

The following day, at my apartment across town, a motorcycle-borne messenger from Durazo's office delivered an eight-by-ten glossy black-and-white photo of the presentation ceremony. And that was it — the last I ever saw, in person, of General Arturo Durazo Moreno, the most reviled man in Mexico.

A friend of mine — a journalist and an inveterate traveller — once gave me a useful piece of advice. When you write about a foreign country, he said, don't automatically ignore the obvious stories. They're obvious for a reason — write them. In Peru, therefore, you should write about llamas. In Argentina, about gauchos. In New Zealand, about sheep. In northern Nigeria, about sand. And so it was, when I lived in Mexico, that I wrote about Arturo Durazo Moreno, not because I especially wanted to, but because his name had begun to pop up everywhere I turned. One way or another, he was becoming a Mexican icon.

Durazo was a thug, a small-time bully who hit the big time. He'd got his position as the chief of police of Mexico City the usual way that such things took place in Mexico — through patronage and cronyism. He had been in charge of security for José Lopez Portillo during the years before Lopez Portillo became Mexico's president. Once his boss ascended to the top job, in 1976, Durazo was put at the head of the country's largest police department as a reward for services rendered. There was something intrinsically Mexican about the whole arrangement.

Once at the helm of the Mexico City police force, he proceeded to enrich himself by all sorts of means. By the time Lopez Portillo left office, in disgrace in 1982, Durazo had become perhaps the country's leading symbol of corruption and venality at the top. He was known as *el Negro* — the Black One — and he was the most despised member of the outgoing regime, with the possible exception of Lopez Portillo himself. Maybe it was inevitable that people would start crying for his blood. In any case, they did.

Not long after both men went into retirement, a new book hit the stores in Mexico City. It was entitled *Lo Negro del Negro Durazo* (The Blackness of the Black Durazo) and had been written by one José González González, who had served as a Durazo bodyguard during his years as police chief. González described in lurid detail how his former boss had enriched himself while in office. His crimes apparently included graft, extortion, drug smuggling, and white slavery. González himself admitted to having committed some fifty assassinations during his years in the general's employ. Even so, he remained a free man — don't ask me how — and, following the publication of his opus, he was on the promotional circuit, casually granting interviews to Mexican newspapers and magazines.

Naturally, the book got people thinking. Where *was* Durazo anyway? And, given all this heavily publicized evidence of his wrongdoing, why was it that the government hadn't arrested him? Then, early in 1984, Mexico City newspapers started to carry reports about a government investigation of the former police chief. Eventually, federal authorities raided two mansions Durazo had constructed for himself during his heyday. They seized considerable quantities of illegal goods and materials, including a large cache of armaments supposedly reserved for the use of the armed forces.

One of the houses, located between Mexico City and the resort community of Cuernavaca, included among its contents and facilities the following: a nightclub; a gymnasium; a casino; a discotheque with a state-of-the-art sound and light system; a stable of nineteen "very high quality" race horses; a display room stocked with twenty-three automobiles, many of them antiques; several greenhouses; lots of sprawling pastures; a few artificial lakes; an enclosed swimming pool; and much else. The property covered 250 hectares. The main house had a value, not including furniture, equipment, and decorations, pegged at $24 million. Not bad for a cop.

The other Durazo mansion was set on a hillside overlooking the Pacific resort community of Zihuatanejo. A police raid there yielded more contraband and illegal firearms. Known to local residents as the Parthenon-by-the-Pacific, Durazo's vacation house appeared to have been built without proper permits and on federal property. It certainly

violated every known law of esthetics. A pompous mon-
strosity of faux Greek pillars and hulking concrete slabs, the
house jutted out above the three bays of Zihuatanejo,
including what was possibly the loveliest natural harbour in
all Mexico. But Durazo, it seemed, didn't live there any-
more. Chains were looped across the entrance, and local taxi
drivers would wave at the eyesore, shake their heads in dis-
gust, and inform you confidently that *el Negro* Durazo had
fled the country. He was living in Canada, they'd say.

Normally, Mexican public servants had nothing to fear
from the Mexican judicial system. After all, there was an
elaborate and consistent pattern to the exercise of political
power in Mexico. Each president served a total of six years
— *el sexenio*, it was called — and then made way for another
man, whom he personally selected. As the outgoing president withdrew from Los Pinos — the presidential palace —
he was followed by an army of cronies, gofers, yes-men,
hangers-on, and ancillary tyrants, most of them considerably
wealthier now than they had been six years before.

These were men not unlike Arturo Durazo Moreno.
They left their cosy sinecures, pockets bulging, and made way
for the new president and *his* minions. In the traditional operation of Mexican power, they were safe from harm. They had
nothing to answer for. This was the system; these were its
rewards. No one was ever held accountable. Certainly, no
one ever went to jail.

Occasionally, there was *talk* of people going to jail, but it
was just talk. That was a custom in Mexico, too. And so, as
was customary in Mexico, the incoming president — in this
case, Miguel de la Madrid Hurtado — launched his administration with stirring promises to clean up the immoral

excesses of his predecessor. But, in de la Madrid's case, the talk actually seemed to have a hint of substance.

Maybe the corruption under Lopez Portillo had been so horrendous that de la Madrid had to do something tangible to quell public displeasure. Or maybe he was compelled to action by the state of Mexico's authoritarian political system. The same party had held a vice-like grip on power since 1929, and it was beginning to show signs of weakening. Party strategists may well have felt that a few concessions to the popular will would not be entirely ill-advised. In any case, de la Madrid went beyond the usual bromides about the need for honesty in office. Instead, he promised to bring about what he called the "moral renovation" of Mexican society, and his words really seemed to suggest that *some-body's* head would have to roll.

A lot of people guessed immediately that the head in question would belong to the general. After all, *el Negro* was the perfect fall guy. Just about everybody in Mexico hated him. His greed and abuses of power were legendary. On the other hand, he wasn't so high up the political totem pole that his sacrifice would greatly damage the image of the ruling Institutional Revolutionary Party. He was the ideal scapegoat — not too big, not too small. On the cocktail circuit in Mexico City, locals and foreigners alike flung themselves into orgies of speculation. First, why hadn't the new government moved against Durazo already? Second, when would it do so? Third, where the hell *was* Durazo, anyway? Nobody had seen him for months.

Rumours about Durazo's whereabouts swirled through the capital. Some, like the taxi drivers in Zihuatanejo, insisted he was in Canada, possibly living in Outremont. Or maybe he was in California. One rumour put him in Los Angeles, where he was said to be enjoying good health. Another placed him in La Jolla, where he was thought to be receiving medical treatment for an ailment that had paralyzed half of his body — *which* half wasn't clear. For their part, the Canadians insisted that they didn't have him.

Well, if *el Negro* wasn't in Canada, and if he wasn't in Mexico, then where the hell was he? Nobody seemed to know, and the Mexican government wasn't saying, assuming it had any idea. Meanwhile, warrants for Durazo's arrest were finally issued. The charges included tax evasion, smuggling, possession of illegal firearms, and extortion. Mexican authorities launched inquiries to determine whether in fact the general was in the United States (which had an extradition treaty with Mexico) or Canada (which didn't, although an 1866 treaty with Britain might have served). In any case, those inquiries failed to turn up any sign of the designated fall guy in Mexico's campaign of moral renovation.

Still, the search for the general went on, and gossip about his excesses continued to circulate through Mexico City. But a lot of people were cynical. They began to doubt that Durazo would ever be apprehended or brought to trial, or that his apprehension had ever been in the government's plans. But it did seem that something had changed. In June, 1984, the paunchy former police chief of the world's largest city finally did turn up — in San Juan, Puerto Rico. He landed there aboard an aircraft en route from São Paulo, Brazil, and was promptly arrested by US authorities. Of course, a few questions remained. For one thing, why on earth had Durazo taken a plane to *Puerto Rico*, of all places? Surely he must have known that there was a warrant for his arrest outstanding in Mexico, and that Washington had an extradition treaty with Mexico City. So why would he even think of putting a foot down on US territory? One Mexico City businessman merely shook his head. "You seem to be assuming," he said, "that Durazo *knew* that Puerto Rico was part of the United States."

Well, he knew now. The General was transferred to Los Angeles and clamped in prison pending a US judge's ruling on Mexico's bid for his return.

His arrest and detention were victories, surely, for President de la Madrid's campaign of moral renovation. Or so you would have thought. But, with the capture of *el Negro* Durazo, the attention of many Mexicans quickly turned to other unindicted stalwarts of the previous regime. "Where is Hank González?" they wanted to know.

They meant Carlos Hank González, mayor of Mexico City during the Lopez Portillo years. Once, when asked by a particularly intrepid Mexican journalist to explain his conspicuous wealth, Hank González paused briefly to ponder the issue. Then he issued a sage and memorable reply. "I save a lot," he explained, as if to suggest that his prudent pecuniary habits could serve as an example to all Mexicans. Everybody would be better off if only they could save money as diligently as did the mayor of Mexico City. Hank González never did face charges. He was a rich man — and, in the normal run of things, rich men don't.

'But
Only My
Mexico'

IT IS A HAUNTING CHARACTERISTIC of colonial cities in Mexico that they can often be characterized by the hue of their stonework. The churches and arcades of Oaxaca, for example, seem to generate a soft emerald glow, while the colonial buildings of Guadalajara exude a rich, sun-baked dun colour. In Zacatecas, the old stone houses are almost pink.

But it is Morelia that I am concerned with here and, in Morelia, the venerable stone buildings that fill almost the entire central city are uniformly rose-tinted, a subtle earthy hue, rather like damp clay. They look as if they've just been given a good scrubbing and haven't had time to dry properly yet. That's by day. By night, they assume another complexion altogether. Bathed in floodlights against a deepening purple sky, the stone spires of the plateresque cathedral shed their rosiness and radiate a golden light that is almost dazzling.

Protected by sweaters or shawls against the customary evening chill, the good burghers of Morelia stroll in family groups past the porticoed eighteenth-century office buildings that line the Avenida Madero opposite the cathedral and the adjoining Plaza de los Mártires, surely among the loveliest public squares in Mexico.

By night, the square — referred to as the *zócalo* in most Mexican cities — is a sort of community circus. Wandering vendors sell chewing gum or snacks or helium-filled balloons as passers-by crowd around a performance given by a mime troupe, its members in white face with top hats and tails. Women pull ears of corn from burlap sacks and shuck them expertly before plunging them into huge cauldrons of boiling water. Elderly bootblacks in dark blue uniforms wait by their wooden shoeshine stands and call out for customers. The floodlights play against the swaying azalea bushes and jacaranda trees, and the children romp amid the wrought-iron park benches in the glow of antique street lamps perched atop weathered stone pillars.

One Friday in late summer, I drove up to Morelia from Mexico City, a trip of about six hours. The final fifty kilometres were especially memorable — a tangle of paved switchbacks weaving through lush gorges and stately pine forests, with breathtaking views out across a roller-coaster terrain, all tinged with blue. Entering the city at dusk, I drove beneath the floodlit arches — 224 of them — of a winding nineteenth-century aqueduct, past a profusion of gardens and fountains, and then into the colonial centre of the city.

Meanwhile, a friend of mine — a Canadian economist who also lived and worked in Mexico — drove down from Guadalajara. She and I had arranged to spend the weekend together, here in what is surely among Mexico's most romantic cities. We made our rendezvous at an old *posada* near the centre of town. Neither of us had eaten, it turned out, and so here we were in the brightly lit interior of the Restaurante Monterrey.

Towards the end of our meal — grilled freshwater fish with a bottle of decent Mexican white wine — I noticed that a man was watching us. He was evidently Mexican, and he was ensconced on his own in a corner of the restaurant, apparently drifting along on the effects of several after-dinner brandies. He was barrel-chested and beaming and — here was the point — he was beaming straight at us. Or maybe not at *us* exactly. At my friend.

Presently, the man in the corner scrawled something on a serviette and motioned for the waiter. A minute or so later, a pair of brandies appeared at our table, in heavy, tinted goblets, courtesy of our anonymous new admirer. The waiter also delivered the serviette, which bore a message scribbled in what appeared to be English. Unfortunately, it was indecipherable.

Next, two grizzled balladeers turned up at our table, evidently dispatched by the man in the corner. Both carried guitars. They wanted to know what they could play for us. We requested "Página Blanca", followed by "Reloj", both poignant ballads made famous by Los Panchos, Mexico's great romantic trio.

At the conclusion of the second song, we chatted for a time with the musicians. Part of me was wondering whether I should pay them. I needn't have worried. All at once, the man in the corner presented himself in person. With a grand flourish, he announced that compensation for the musical interlude had already been arranged, personally, by none other than himself. He then offered to entertain us with a third song. He himself, personally, would sing the lead vocal.

The man stood back a pace, unleashed a broad, gold-toothed smile, and then produced a fine vibrato tenor. He flung himself into an aching ballad about spurned love, as the two elderly guitarists dutifully strummed along. With his dark eyes trained unshakably upon my friend, the man evidently meant the lyrics to be taken literally — a suitor's lament that the object of his ardour would be leaving with, ahem, the other guy.

And then, without further ceremony or bother, the man bid us *adiós*. He put back his shoulders and strode from the restaurant, out alone into the cool highland darkness, his air of melancholy dignity flowing behind him like a fine old cloak. My friend and I looked at each other. We smiled, shrugged, and shook our heads. Well, this had been a strange experience, strange but also heartening somehow — a whimsical, romantic, and very human encounter in a city that neither of us knew, in a land that wasn't our own.

Welcome to Mexico — a country that has had wretchedly bad press over the years, vastly worse than it deserves. Certainly, there are troubles in this large and complicated land, but there is immense goodness too. And yet, for many on the outside, Mexico remains a collage of unsavory clichés and distortions.

One weekday morning in Mexico City, for example, in the grand sunlit surroundings of the garden café at the Hotel Presidente Chapultepec, an official of the Mexican government snuffed out his Marlboro, took another sip of black coffee, and asked me what my fellow Canadians thought of his country.

Well, I couldn't really lie. I told him that most Canadians probably had only the sketchiest notions about the only other nation in the world that shares a border with the United States. They probably carried around a jumble of Mexican-like images and impressions. I reeled off a few that came to mind — swan-divers in Acapulco, or sombrero-shaded men sleeping it off in the streets, or acres of cactus, or bull-fights, or mariachi bands, or green-looking tourists. I looked up and shrugged. I added, "Or corruption."

He nodded. Who could deny it? It certainly isn't fair to define an entire nation in terms of illicit greed — it wasn't fair for Nigeria, and it isn't fair for Mexico. Still, corruption is what a lot of people think of when they think of Mexico. Perhaps the main reason that images of bribery and graft are so closely identified with the world's idea of Mexico is that they are pretty closely associated with Mexico's idea of itself. A European resident of El Salvador once told me that there are two kinds of corruption in the world. There is ordinary corruption, he said. And then there is *corrupción a la mexicana.*

What he meant, I think, was that corruption in Mexico is not mainly the product of individual initiative, as it is in many countries. Instead it seems to be built into the national ethos — an unwritten article in the Mexican social contract. People *expect* to encounter corruption. They *plan* for it. Corruption is almost a pillar of the Mexican state.

Once you begin to sort them out, the rules of Mexican-style corruption come to seem almost straightforward, their execution, almost benign, even elegant. If you watch carefully as you make your way through the customs hall at the Mexico City airport, for example, you will sometimes witness a miniature but perfectly choreographed drama.

The customs agent appears. He unzips the suitcase of the passenger in front of you and proceeds to rifle through the contents of the bag, pausing almost imperceptibly as he comes across something that is Not Supposed To Be There. Within moments, a glance is exchanged, a bill changes hands, and the traveller is on his way. It all happens so quickly, so smoothly, and with such perfect communion between the briber and the bribed, that it is almost invisible. If you had blinked, you'd have missed it.

But Mexicans don't blink. They don't hesitate either, and they don't haggle. They have it all computed in their minds — the exact exchange rate between one man's desire to resort to bribery and another man's power to exact bribes. They know exactly what to do. Such transactions are commonly referred to as *mordidas* — literally, little bites — an informal system of pay-offs that has nothing to do with the law or with the "official" way of conducting business, but everything to do with the way business actually gets conducted. Mexico's illicit structure of financial favours is so deeply imbedded in the country's political and economic system that it has sometimes been referred to as *corrupción institucionalizada*. For all the talk of moral renovation during the 1980s, a lot of Mexicans still seem less than certain that the system should be uprooted completely or overnight. The reason is simple. Bad as the Mexican system may be, there is nothing immediately on hand to replace it — or at least this is what many people seem to believe.

Any criticism of Mexican-style corruption should probably be tempered by a reservation or two. In the first place, it isn't ubiquitous. True, graft is endemic in Mexico, but that doesn't mean you can't avoid it. I lived in the country for five years, and I can recall doling out a bribe only once — to a policeman who stopped me after I'd made an illegal turn. And, the fact was, I had made an illegal turn. So who was at fault here — the Mexican policeman who was willing to accept a bribe, or the law-breaking foreign motorist who was willing to pay one?

Normally, if you live within the law, you can get by very well in Mexico without worrying about corrupt dealings. Or some people can. I managed to. I suppose it didn't hurt that I was a fair-skinned foreigner from a G-7 country rather than a more readily exploitable Mexican. Still, for all my normal affairs — paying my bills, entering and leaving the country, going about my daily chores — there was no need to pay bribes in order to get things done.

A little corruption may even carry a compensation or two. There must be some explanation for the remarkable social peace that Mexico has enjoyed for more than half a century — not perfect peace, by any means, but amazingly close by Latin American standards. You can probably attribute at least a share of that peace to the country's system of institutionalized corruption, a system from which a considerable number of the country's eighty million people have confidently stood to gain. The Institutional Revolutionary Party — or the PRI, that oxymoronic political octopus that has ruled Mexico for more than six decades — has long had a genius for distributing financial largesse in all the right places, or in just enough of them to keep the lid on a pot that otherwise might easily blow. That genius certainly seems a little shaky now, amid renewed economic troubles and internecine feuding within the highest ranks of the PRI, but once it was a thing to behold.

For decades, the PRI was able to keep a handle on almost everything in Mexico. Even Mexico's political *opposition*

parties — those that were permitted to exist — were traditionally in the pay of the PRI. They were funded by the
party in power, a revenue base that helped to keep them
alive, and even useful, but largely impotent. The PRI leadership divined something that countless authoritarian politicians in other countries never seem to learn — that it is a
good thing to have opposition parties. They act like safety
valves. They help to release the steam of political discontent
that otherwise would build up to intolerable levels and
eventually explode.

Opposition parties also help to keep political adversaries
out in the open, where you can watch them and control
them, rather than forcing them underground, where you
can't. The PRI has long allowed opposition parties to exist,
but at least in the past it kept them docile by the ingenious
tactic of paying them money. If they got too far out of line,
they risked losing those funds — and it certainly wasn't in
the interests of the opposition leaders to do that.

All this is changing now, or so it seems. But in Mexico,
for decades, the system worked. In Mexico, corruption has
been both a lubricant and an adhesive. It served to grease the
wheels of commerce, industry, and the state, but it also
helped to keep things from falling apart. Almost anywhere
you looked, inside any Mexican institution, you'd find a
variation of the same phenomenon, a system of bribes and
kickbacks from which a surprisingly large number of people
stood to gain — people who therefore had a vested interest
in preserving the system even as they detested it.

Take the press. In Mexico, it has long been a thoroughly
corrupt institution. During the 1980s, Mexico City news-
stands bulged each day with the mastheads of more than

thirty different publications. (By contrast, few North American cities have more than two daily newspapers. Many have just one.) Mexico City's excess of newsprint had little to do with straight economics, for few of the papers made money. They owed their existence mainly to corruption. "It's a true scandal," the publisher of one major Mexico City daily told me. "Journalism is one of the institutions most affected by corruption."

Of the thirty-one Mexico City newspapers in existence in the mid-1980s, only two — *Excelsior* and *Unomásuno* — were managed by career journalists. Most of the others were controlled and operated by businessmen or politicians who regularly exploited their publications to promote their particular interests. At least three of the city's papers had been launched by Mexican presidents soon after they'd left office.

Few had a large readership. Apart from the daily sports tabloids, which circulated widely, only four Mexico City newspapers could claim more than 100,000 readers. Still, many of the dailies were energetic and serious-minded. *Excelsior*, which was probably the largest-selling, at one time maintained fourteen full-time foreign news bureaus, a commitment to independent international coverage that placed it in a league with the *Washington Post*, say, or the *Los Angeles Times*, and far ahead of any Canadian newspaper.

In their domestic coverage, many of the papers often had the appearance of being both forthright and vigorously critical of the federal government. But editors and reporters, or those I got to know, all maintained that their apparent freedom to criticize was largely an illusion, carefully manipulated by the state.

For example, the government controlled the only source

of newsprint in Mexico, a state enterprise called Productora e Importadora de Papel S.A. (PIPSA), to which most Mexican newspapers were heavily indebted. Rather than close an offending paper, the government might simply begin shipping it subgrade newsprint or maybe an insufficient supply. One editor told me that other forms of state harassment included cutting off electricity close to deadline; ordering street vendors — all of whom belonged to government-controlled unions — to boycott the targeted publication; or withdrawing lucrative government advertisements, called *gacetillas*, that were an important revenue source for newspapers. A prudent editor tended to exercise restraint — self-censorship, if you like. Generally, the larger a publication, the more careful it had to be.

For most journalists, corruption was simply a matter of course, part of an insidious system used by the PRI to maintain control over the press as it did over other institutions. "Every effort is made to bring you into the system," a reporter friend told me. "I've had them slip envelopes under tablecloths or leave them on chairs." The envelopes contained cash or, as they said in Mexico, *los embutes* — the stuffings. It was a rare journalist who refused to take his or her share. Those who did refuse ran the risk of being ostracized by their colleagues. Or someone from the government would speak to editors about a recalcitrant reporter, and the offender would soon find himself demoted or shunted off to the sidelines.

In some cases, journalists abandoned all pretence of independence from the agencies they were supposed to be covering. Reporters on the police beat in Mexico City typically would be appointed to the police department itself and placed on the payroll as officers. "They *become* policemen, they have the aura of policemen, they are involved in all ways with policemen," one publisher complained. He added that he knew of two journalists on his own staff who were compelled to participate in the torture of prisoners as a means of cementing their solidarity with the police.

I asked the obvious question. "So why don't you get rid of them?"

He simply threw up his arms. He couldn't — the police wouldn't let him.

A senior editor told me that journalists could easily triple their traditionally low salaries just by accepting the envelopes offered them by government agencies. But there were other, more lucrative opportunities. In some cases, journalists sought and received large sums of money in exchange for using their influence with the attorney-general's office, say, to get someone's relative released from jail. Some reporters made a habit of selling their services to companies or politicians who wanted puff pieces written. A brief article of this sort could earn a writer the equivalent of two months' salary. This sort of practice was especially common among columnists, many of whom also worked an even seamier vein of immorality. One publisher told me there were only five respectable newspaper columnists in the entire country. The other five hundred, he said, were *chantajistas* — professional blackmailers who enriched themselves by confronting people with the threat of a negative story. They would then offer to suppress the piece in exchange for cash. Usually, they collected.

In spite of its pervasive control over the press — or perhaps because of it — the government was willing to accept a surprising range of criticism, without imposing dire penalties upon journalists who wrote such stories or publishers who printed them. It was often said in Mexico that there were only three untouchable subjects (*los tres intocables*, as they were known): first, the Virgin of Guadeloupe; second, the incumbent president; and, third, the army. Anything or anybody else was fair game, at least up to a point. And a surprising amount of fine reliable journalism did get committed to paper, in among the rest. No doubt discerning readers could sometimes spot the difference.

All in all, the Mexican system worked better than many. Certainly, it was a lot less violent than some. Most Latin American authoritarian regimes have taken a very different approach. They have relied upon assassination, whether selective or wholesale, as the instrument of first resort in the resolution of political conflict. The PRI was authoritarian and repressive, but it also had a keen talent for sensing political troubles before they provoked violence. That ability hasn't been foolproof — witness the massacre of hundreds of student demonstrators shortly before the Mexico City Olympic Games in 1968 or the startling insurrection in Chiapas by Zapatista rebels in 1994. But, for the most part, the PRI has tended to respond to threats of unrest in a highly effective way — corrupt, of course, but effective. As soon as the leaders of some new dissident group were isolated — workers, maybe, or peasants, or indigenous people, or students — the PRI would try to buy them off, usually successfully.

The PRI has its tentacles everywhere. It maintains control over peasant groups through the National Peasant Confederation, over middle-class sectors through the National Confederation of Popular Organizations, and over some five million labourers through the Confederation of Mexican Workers. It would seem to have a genius for survival. In that respect at least, the PRI embodies something intrinsically Mexican in character, for Mexicans themselves are nothing if not survivors. They seem able to sink down roots in the most forbidding soil and to find nourishment there. For a very long time, the same could be said of the PRI. Just about anywhere that you found Mexicans, you could expect to find evidence of *el Partido Revolucionario Institucional.*

One cool but piercingly sunny afternoon in Mexico City, I ventured out to a place where you wouldn't have expected to find much in the way of national political organizing going on — a sprawling garbage dump called Lago de Texcoco. The dump tumbled across a section of reclaimed marshland near the international airport on the northern outskirts of the capital. In the distance, through the smoke and the dust, a succession of jetliners floated down through the sparkling sky. They might as well have been spaceships landing on another planet, one where the inhabitants didn't have to scrounge a living out of other people's trash.

The scene at the dump was like some bleak futuristic vision of life after the holocaust. Clouds of foul grey smoke spewed from scattered burning pyres, and flames licked their way along a garbage-strewn wasteland. Mongrel dogs, each missing large patches of fur, snouted through the layers of egg shells, cardboard, tin, rubber, and rot, sniffing for discarded delicacies. And portly little figures, more gnomish than human, all bundled in rags, darted among the endless mounds of litter. They would pause now and then to nab something on the ground. They'd tuck another cast-off treasure into the folds of their clothing, then scurry ahead a few more paces and snatch at something else.

I came upon two young women who were huddled out of the wind against a ridge of trash, carefully counting a handful of coins. As soon as I approached, they tucked the silver out of sight and looked away. A cluster of dismal hovels squatted upon a nearby plateau of rubbish. These were built entirely of abandoned bric-a-brac — oil barrels, wooden crates, strips of metal, sheets of plastic, tires, broken bits of furniture, torn blankets. The people who lived here were wary of outsiders. When I came near, they shook their heads, turned, and trundled away. Who could blame them? It was almost dusk, soon it would be dark — this was no time to be dealing with strangers.

They are called *pepenadores*, these people. Garbage-dwellers. Thousands of Mexico City residents survive in much the same way, by rooting through the capital's garbage dumps in search of tin cans, bottles, cardboard cartons, twists of wire — anything they can salvage and sell for a few pesos.

One of the *pepenadores* at Lago de Texcoco was a bit bolder than the rest. He was a thirty-eight-year-old man named Alberto Lopez Martínez, bound in a pair of woollen sweaters and an old cloth coat, with a mouth punctuated by yellowed teeth and with a hand-rolled cigarette tucked above his right ear. He pulled a small green card from his coat pocket to show that he was a member in good standing of the Institutional Revolutionary Party. Even to work as a scavenger in a garbage dump, you had to be a member of the PRI. Lopez explained that all Mexico City's garbage-dwellers had similar cards and worked in the dumps on concessions granted them by the government. You needed such a card, he said, in order to avoid harassment by the police.

He was referring, of course, to the very same police that were once commanded by my old luncheon companion, Arturo Durazo Moreno. It was a bit of a shock to think that the same system that enabled *el Negro* to accumulate tens of millions of dollars, not to mention fleets of antique automobiles, strings of race horses, sprawling mansions, and pretty young waitresses, was the very same system that granted to Alberto Lopez Martínez his soiled PRI card, along with the right to pick through other people's garbage for a discarded bottle here, a bit of wire there. This was *corrupción a la mexicana*, I suppose. Everybody took, everybody gave, and some people took more than the rest. "Who knows how this is going to end?" Lopez asked me. He gestured around with his arm. "How much longer are we going to have a life like this?"

It was not a question that he or I — or anyone else — could easily answer. At the time, Mexicans were undergoing some rapid and wrenching changes. For one thing, they were fast becoming an urban society. In 1940, only twenty per cent of Mexicans lived in cities. By the mid-1980s, at least sixty per cent of Mexico's eighty million people were city-dwellers — of a kind. They mostly made their homes in vast and burgeoning squatter settlements and eked out meagre livelihoods as bootblacks, strolling vendors, street-sweepers, professional beggars, watchmen, or *pepenadores*.

Near the fancy sidewalk cafés in Mexico City's Zona Rosa, for example, you'd often find a gaggle of young boys pounding sticks against empty shoe-polish tins while wailing out a *ranchera* in hard and cracking voices. They weren't fooling anyone, least of all themselves. This wasn't entertainment. The boys simply refused to stop that awful noise until you paid them. You can call it extortion. Or you can think of it as a good hard sell.

At downtown intersections, particularly during rush hour when the traffic barely moved, hordes of ill-clothed boys armed with grubby rags would hop onto the hoods of vehicles and make a show of wiping the windshields. In fact, they were deliberately soiling the glass, so that their colleagues at the next intersection could collect a few pesos by restoring the windshields to their original state.

At many intersections, you'd find *tragafuegos* — boys who fill their mouths with kerosene and spray the stuff through a flaming torch clutched at arm's length. Joaquín Mendez was one of these. Just seventeen years old, he headed out each weekday afternoon to take up his post near the base of Mexico City's soaring monument to the 1910 Revolution. There he stood, a slim shirtless fellow with badly singed brown hair. In one hand, he carried a dingy plastic container of fuel oil, in the other, a makeshift torch made of clotheshanger wire tipped with a wad of burning cloth. When the traffic light at his corner turned red, Mendez promptly took a swig of oil, strode out into the middle of the street, and with a melodramatic flourish, raised the burning torch to his mouth and spat through it. A six-foot plume of flames would flash into the evening air.

After performing this feat several times, Mendez would stroll through the lanes of traffic, accepting the occasional coins or small bills proffered by motorists. He then stepped aside, let the traffic go, and waited for the next light. "I do it only to eat," he told me. "It's just that there's no work." In exchange for an hour or so of breathing fire, which was about all he could tolerate in a day, Mendez earned the equivalent of $2. He added those earnings to the equally trifling amount he garnered in his normal line of work — selling balloons in the street — and, on that, he got by.

It sometimes seemed that anybody in Mexico who had anything to sell, sold. The capital was riddled with dowdy old streets lined by three-story grey plaster buildings, their ground floors indented by entrances to miniscule, one-room shops — a plumber, a key-cutter, a man who bought old newspapers, a woman who made *ricas tortas* ('delicious sandwiches'), a shop that sold only eggs, or only disposable diapers, or that only made photocopies. Most common of all were the countless dark and cramped stalls where millions of Mexico City residents did most of their grocery shopping and where the limited stock typically consisted of a few soft drinks, some bottled beer, a smattering of tinned goods, packaged sweet rolls, and maybe a few tomatoes or eggs. Somehow, such marginal enterprises managed to survive.

Bernarda Morales, for example, had been running the same microscopic grocery store at the corner of Nilo and Nazas streets in downtown Mexico City for twenty-seven years. Now sixty years old, she was out sweeping the street in front of her shop one afternoon, following a short but drenching rainstorm. She wore a green-and-yellow sweater, a blue skirt, and a brown-checkered apron, and her dense grey hair was tied back. Inside, she had for sale some soft drinks in a basin of galvanized tin, a smattering of melons, onions, and tomatoes, as well as a selection of chocolate bars and cigarettes. The dozens of parakeets in their golden cages were not, however, for sale. Bernarda told me that her husband was dead now and her children had moved away, but still she worked seven days a week, from eight in the morning until nine at night.

I asked, "How much do you earn?"

"Very little," she said. Then she brightened. "But I lack for nothing." She gave a grand all-encompassing sweep of her arm, a gesture that seemed to include not only her street or her city but the entire surrounding land and its eighty million people. She straightened up and assumed an air of moment and solemnity. "I don't esteem any other country," she announced, "but only my Mexico."

And I thought, as I walked away along Río Nilo, that you'd have the devil of a time explaining a woman like Bernarda Morales to a man like Arturo Durazo Moreno. In fact, you'd be crazy to try. But there was a barrel-chested tenor in the highland city of Morelia who, I'm pretty sure, would understand both the woman and her sentiments, from the bottom of his Mexican soul.

Somewhere on Lake Titicaca

I ONCE FOUND MYSELF watching a sports programme on Bolivian television when a reporter came on to conduct a series of man-in-the-street interviews about the state of the national soccer squad — the *disastrous* state of the national soccer squad. The team had just lost three consecutive exhibition matches against neighbouring countries, surrendering no fewer than eleven goals and scoring a grand total of — well, let's not beat about the bush — *none*. One rather portly mustachioed gentleman came on the screen. He wore a grey double-breasted suit and seemed quite confident that he knew exactly what it was that Bolivia's top soccer players were lacking. No, not coaching. Not experience. Not conditioning. Not even money. No — they were lacking *"amor de la Patria"*.

Love of the Fatherland.

Well, this was a rather stirring notion in a country that had endured 180 coups or revolts and 190 governments in just 160 years. It would be hard to say exactly what role love of the Fatherland had played in Bolivian history. Was it love of the Fatherland that induced a mob of peasants, one day in

July, 1946, to raid the presidential palace on the Plaza Murillo in La Paz? They set upon the president of the day, one Gualberto Villarroel, dragged him from his office, and hanged him to death from a convenient lamp post — a stark reminder for national presidents the world over that there are at least two kinds of executive power.

A European acquaintance of mine, a long-time resident of La Paz, summed Bolivia up with a broad cultural observation. Bolivians, he said, are basically an anarchical people. "They don't like governments for any length of time."

Evidently not. On the other hand, for much of the country's history, it hasn't really mattered what most Bolivians have thought of their governments — because nobody ever asked them. It was as if the government and the governed dwelled in two different centuries — which, in a way, they did. From the steep crowded streets of La Paz, it is a simple matter to journey far back in Bolivian time simply by boarding a cross-country bus.

All around the capital soars the *altiplano*, the high Andean plain — a barren, windblown sweep of land hemmed in by the eastern and western ranges of the Andes and home to most of the country's five million inhabitants. For the most part, these are deeply marginalized people. The more accessible of their villages are scattered along the few paved roads that criss-cross the *altiplano* — lonely, treeless communities of mud-grey adobe brick, set amid a stern climate and a spooky terrain under a massive dome of deoxygenated air, some four thousand metres above the distant, invisible sea.

These people speak little Spanish — Aymará and Quechua are their languages — and they mostly live outside the modern economy, such as it is. They subsist by tending their flocks of sheep, llamas, and alpacas, and by cultivating the few hardy plants — potatoes, millet, corn — that will grow here. In all, between fifty and seventy per cent of the country's people are thought to be pure Indian, which puts Bolivia up there with Guatemala as the two Latin American nations with the largest proportion of indigenous people.

Pablo Ramos Sanchez, former rector of the San Andres University in La Paz, once told me that only about one Bolivian in twenty belongs to the country's modern, educated society and only between 100,000 and 200,000 could be called fully-fledged citizens in the North American sense. The ruling class and the opinion-makers number maybe two thousand to three thousand people — in a nation of five million. Ramos Sanchez shrugged. "You can appreciate the difficulty of forming a cabinet."

You can appreciate the difficulty of a lot of things, including the challenge of developing a democratic state based on modern notions of individual rights and liberties. Like other South American countries, Bolivia has long had a shaky record on that score. More often than not, the military has shouldered the task of running the country, and it has done this the same way the military does most things anywhere in the world — with a lot of noise, a clamour of medals, and a preponderance of sheer physical strength.

On the other hand, the Bolivian armed forces have never proved themselves especially adept at what is nominally their main line of work — fighting wars. The country was badly humiliated in both of the international conflicts that it has got itself mixed up in. In one instance, Bolivia lost the Chaco, a huge expanse of territory that now makes its home in Paraguay. In the other, it surrendered its access to the sea.

What was once the Pacific coast of Bolivia now constitutes a goodish chunk of northern Chile.

Despite their failures on the international front, the Bolivian armed forces have regularly seized and held political power at home — basically, whenever another colonel or general saw the need to return the country to what was typically referred to as a regimen of "law, order, and discipline". In fact, coups soon became something of a Bolivian specialty. "When you get an appointment to the military academy," a foreign resident of La Paz told me, "the thought flashes in front of your eyes — 'I could be president'." And it was true — you really could. All you needed was a pistol, a pair of sunglasses, and a really big moustache.

But it wasn't pistols or sunglasses or even moustaches that I was looking for, one weekday afternoon, when I headed around to the La Paz headquarters of *la Armada Boliviana* — the Bolivian Navy. What I wanted to know was, what on earth was Bolivia doing with a navy? After all, it has been more than a century — 112 years, to be precise — since Bolivian soil has last felt the bracing splash of salt water. As it turns out, however, it takes a lot more than the absence of an ocean to keep a South American navy down. The men in sunglasses at the Navy General Command in La Paz seemed delighted to make my acquaintance, and a few days later I was out on patrol with the Bolivian Navy, high in the mountains of a land-locked country, somewhere in South America.

The uncovered inboard engine rhythmically punches out its full thirty-six horses of thrust, propelling Navy Patrol Launch No. 2 through the Strait of Tiquina and out onto the shimmering waters of Lake Titicaca, loftiest navigable lake in the world. At the helm, Lieutenant Franz Wilson Vera Barka peers through the shattered windshield of the eight-metre wooden launch and expertly sets his course — north by northwest.

In the stern, Lieutenant Gonzalo Helguero Viñas relaxes by a faded Bolivian flag. He is acting commander of the naval base at Tiquina. Now, he squints through the afternoon glare, across the lake's broad blue sweep towards the hazy islands of the Moon and Sun, mythical birthplace of the ancient Inca civilization. Like Lieutenant Wilson, he wears a green camouflage uniform. Just now, he is telling me about the smugglers who use Lake Titicaca as a route to sneak contraband across the border into Peru, providing plenty of work for the Bolivian Navy here in the country's Fourth Naval District. "It's a big problem," he says.

The other passengers on board LP-02 for the afternoon voyage include: two black-sweatered able seamen; Lieutenant Amado Jerez Mendoza, the base's medical officer; Lieutenant Helguero's young wife and their two infant sons; his two sisters-in-law; his mother-in-law; their nanny; and me. The launch ploughs defiantly ahead through the placid waters of Lake Titicaca, bearing towards its as yet undisclosed destination. Our mission? Well, I'm not exactly sure.

During the long dry years since 1883 when Bolivia lost its maritime real estate to Chile, it has never renounced its claim to the sea, and more recently has sought redress in such international forums as the United Nations General Assembly and the Organization of American States — so far, without success. For now, the Bolivian Navy is severely restricted in its access to the sea. But rivers are not without their virtues. And Lake Titicaca, which Bolivia shares with Peru, contains a considerable quantity of water.

After taking a serpentine course across the middle of the lake, Lieutenant Wilson wheels LP-02 towards a sheltered pebbly cove on the large Copacabana Promontory of Titicaca's southwestern shore. With expert skill, he beaches the craft against Bolivian soil, and the two able seamen lower a small ladder from the bow. Our landing party climbs ashore.

Before long, a skinny black dog — our first direct contact with a local inhabitant — trots up to greet us. He appears to be friendly and accompanies our party as we continue our reconnaissance of the coast.

Numbering about two thousand men and women, divided into six under-strength marine battalions, the Bolivian Navy has called itself by that name only since 1981 and has existed as an independent military force only since 1963. Before that, whatever naval capacity that Bolivia could muster was administered directly by the army. In 1963, however, the *Fuerzas Fluviales y Lacustres* — the River and Lake Forces — were established as a separate institution. Three years later, the name was changed to the Bolivian Naval Force. Then, in 1981, Bolivia finally got itself a Navy.

Sort of. There was still something of an equipment problem. I spoke about this to someone in La Paz who said he wanted to be identified only as "a foreign military analyst", which was more or less what he was. He said, "If you exclude rowboats and canoes, they have about twenty things we would consider vessels, all in a state of disrepair."

At the Tiquina base on Lake Titicaca, for example, the Bolivian Navy had five small patrol boats, only two of which worked, plus an old wooden barge-ferry that was out of service for lack of parts. The pride of the base was the *Julian Apaz*, a twenty-eight-metre-long hospital boat equipped with a dentist's office, a small operating room, a basic laboratory, and X-ray facilities. One of two hospital boats in the fleet of the Bolivian Navy, the *Julian Apaz* was used to make monthly rounds of the Indian villages that dot the lakeshore. Owing to a lack of funds, however, the vessel had not gone anywhere for almost three months — and no one could say when its voyages would be resumed.

Meanwhile, the crowning glory of the Bolivian Navy was to be found in another land entirely — in Argentina. The port of Rosario, northwest of Buenos Aires, was home to the the 122-metre *Libertador Bolívar*, a somewhat elderly merchant vessel donated to Bolivia in 1978 by Venezuela. The *Libertador Bolívar* could carry a complement of more than two hundred sailors and was now used by Bolivia as a training ship. "There's a hell of a lot of prestige in the Bolivian Navy to have captained that blue-water vessel," said my friend, the foreign military analyst.

Bolivia also sends its naval officers away for training in foreign lands, just about any place that has a seacoast — to Argentina, Peru, Colombia, Venezuela, and the United States. *But not Chile.* It also participates in South America's annual Unitas naval exercises, albeit aboard other countries' vessels. I had already spoken to Captain Gaston Unzueta at the Navy's General Command in La Paz about the purpose of all this training in a country that, not to put too fine a point on it, fails to coincide with the sea. He explained that Bolivia wanted to have seamen and officers capable of sailing everything from submarines to frigates to destroyers, so that they will be prepared to go to sea on that great if admittedly somewhat uncertain future day when Bolivia has a sea to go to. "The minute we have a submarine, the people will be there, ready to take up their posts," he said.

Right now, however, there is only a lake, a lakeshore, and a landing party. The landing party makes its way to the yard outside a small trout hatchery by the edge of Lake Titicaca. Near a footpath above the hatchery, we come upon a woman of advanced years with her hair in long greying braids. She identifies herself as one Beti Navajas and informs us that, along with her husband, she owns the hatchery and the adjoining gardens. She proceeds to complain to the medical officer, Lieutenant Jerez, about a toothache that has been bothering her now for quite some time. He recommends that she come around to the base the next day so that the dentist there can have a look.

With that, we dispatch Lieutenant Wilson to head back on his own to the pebbly cove in order to bring the launch around to the hatchery and to pick up the rest of the landing party there. He follows his instructions to the letter. In short order, LP-02 heaves into view and rounds the Copacabana Promontory en route to the hatchery. We stroll down to meet the vessel. Along the way, the officers and gentlemen from the Tiquina Naval Base assist Lieutenant Helguero's wife, their two infant sons, his mother-in-law, his two sisters-in-law, and the nanny to climb over a forbidding field-stone fence. We then make our way to the lake and clamber aboard the launch for the voyage back to base where — our mission accomplished — we plan to fortify ourselves with coffee and sandwiches at Lieutenant Helguero's house. As they say in Bolivia, Long Live the Fatherland.

4

FROM
EQUATORIAL
GUINEA
TO
ZIMBABWE

'The Worst
Country in
the World'

D URING A TRIP to West Africa in 1989, I took some time off one day in Douala in order to pay a visit to the consulate of Equatorial Guinea. I wanted to apply for a visa to the Worst Country in the World.

The commercial capital of Cameroon, Douala swelters on the humid, marsh-bound West African coast, where lizards scale the fading colonial façades and even the dense, waxy-leaved guava trees seem to sag in the vapour-laden air. This is the torrid zone, at sea level, on the equator; the heat and the humidity seem to weigh down upon you with about twice the force of gravity. You do not go out for a stroll here. You go out for a lurch, a stagger, a slump. Douala also happens to be the ideal African staging point for a journey to Equatorial Guinea, a country with a reputation.

Diplomats and foreign-aid officials had long considered Equatorial Guinea to be as bad as a country on this particular planet could get — the last place on earth where any self-respecting diplomat would want to be posted, which is not to say that very many of them ever were. It was a small place, after all, and you could probably entertain the local diplomatic representation in a single restaurant booth. Still, for the diplomatic corps of the globe, Equatorial Guinea had somehow managed to become the standard for national ghastliness. It was the Worst Country in the World.

Even now, Equatorial Guinea is among the poorest countries in Africa and absolutely the smallest. It consists of a smattering of islands off the steamy coast of West Africa and a miniscule chunk of soil on the African mainland, sandwiched between Cameroon and Gabon. It has a population of 420,000 or so and survives on a spotty trade in unremarkable tropical exports — cocoa, coffee, bananas, palm oil.

Because of its name, Equatorial Guinea is easily confused with Guinea or Guinea-Bissau — two rather larger African states — but it is actually a separate and distinct nation. Despite its size and its obscurity, Equatorial Guinea does have a few noteworthy aspects. For example, it was in Malabo, the Equato-Guinean capital, that thriller writer Frederick Forsyth lived while he worked on his novel, *The Dogs of War*. Equatorial Guinea also happens to be the only country in Africa with Spanish as its official language. Unfortunately, the proud Castillian tongue merely serves as another source of isolation, because all of Equatorial Guinea's neighbours are former colonies of Britain, Portugal, or France, the big three among the European imperial powers in Africa. Spain was never much of a presence on the continent, and Equatorial Guinea was all that Madrid left behind in sub-Saharan Africa when the colonial era stumbled to a close in the 1960s. At first glance — *pace* Mr. Forsyth — there isn't a lot about Equatorial Guinea that would interest an outsider.

But I was interested all the same. For one thing, I wanted to know how the Worst Country in the World was making out in the aftermath of a long reign of terror inflicted upon its people by the previous president, uncle of the current ruler. And I had heard some weird rumours about South African agents operating there with a view to destabilizing neighbouring Nigeria. I suppose I also wanted a chance to practise my Spanish.

For travellers to Equatorial Guinea — never what you would call a vast and burgeoning horde — Douala is the favoured jumping-off point. From here, the flight to Bioko Island (where the Equato-Guinean capital is located) is just a twenty-five-minute hop across the Gulf of Guinea, in theory at least. In practice, it can take a bit longer.

Or, as in my case, a lot longer. After my Cameroon Airlines Avro-748 took off from the Douala airport, I remained in my window seat for nearly an hour — reading an article in ¡Hola! about the Spanish royal family and peering down at patches of the sea through herds of bloated, bovine clouds — before the craft finally began its descent. Soon, a rather large city swelled into view, a surprisingly impressive city, with several tall, sparkling office towers that overlooked what seemed to be passably bustling streets. I hadn't expected Malabo to be nearly so substantial a place. Its population, after all, was only about fifty thousand. It was supposed to be a backwater, a mean little settlement with a haunted past. Where would it get skyscrapers?

Just then, a voice crackled over the aircraft's public-address system. It announced, a tad late, that the plane had been denied permission to land at Malabo — "because of a presidential activity" — and had been forced to return to

Douala. So this explained the skyscrapers in Malabo. They *weren't* in Malabo. They were in Douala. We'd come full circle, back to Cameroon.

The plane landed and taxied up to the impressively modern but already decaying Douala airport. The other passengers and I trooped across the steaming tarmac, climbed a set of stairs, and filed into a small lounge where, it so happened, the air-conditioning was working. It was time once more for that familiar African pastime — another long wait. From my knapsack, I withdrew the book I was reading — *A Bend in the River*, by V. S. Naipaul, an unnerving portrait of Africa in turmoil — and I settled in for the afternoon.

The delay also gave me time to reflect on the country I was intent on visiting — the Worst Country in the World. The president of Equatorial Guinea was then, as he is now, a man called Teodoro Nguema, or Obiang Nguema Mbasogo, the African name by which he prefers to be known. He was and is the nephew of the former president — one Francisco Macias Nguema, a true African despot. In fact, the current president served as interior minister in the Macias government. His job in those days included responsibility for domestic security, which likely meant he was no angel. But it was his uncle, the former president, who earned for Equatorial Guinea its reputation as the Worst Country in the World.

During his eleven years in power, from 1968 to 1979, Macias presided over a regime of astonishing brutality. Through a combination of exile and murder, he managed to reduce his country's population by a third. He was one of those blood-chilling but still very human monstrosities that slouch onto the world's stage every once in a while. They are certainly not the sole preserve of Africa. But Africa has produced its share, and Francisco Macias Nguema was one.

In his early adulthood, Macias had been an employee of the Spanish colonial administration in Malabo. When Madrid granted independence to its only African territory, in October, 1968, Macias became the first president of Equatorial Guinea. The horrors commenced within months. First, Macias got embroiled in a dispute with Spain over timber contracts. When two of his senior officials — foreign minister Atanasio Ndongo and UN ambassador Saturnino Ibongo — tried to mediate the conflict, Macias had them arrested and executed. Thus was the post-colonial pattern set.

During the ensuing ten years, Macias presided over a spiralling campaign of terror against his own people. He or his henchmen butchered or bundled into exile anybody who could conceivably pose a challenge to his own power or to that of his clan, a branch of the rather unfortunately named Fang tribe. Foreign priests were deemed a threat, so they were detained, imprisoned, or expelled. The churches were boarded up, which marked the end of organized Western religion for Equato-Guineans. Mission-run schools were seen as breeding grounds for dissent, so they were shut down, too. Goodbye, formal education.

When Equato-Guineans began taking to boats in desperate efforts to flee Bioko Island, Macias ordered all the island's boats to be sunk. No more fishing industry. When his people would no longer work for so murderous a regime, Macias brought in some twenty thousand contract labourers from Nigeria and proceeded to treat them in predictably brutal fashion. Predictably, they rebelled, and Macias unleashed his army and the police. Nigerian diplomats protested, so Macias ordered his youth movement to attack the diplomats and to beat *them* up. Although it didn't invade Bioko Island — as it threatened to do — Nigeria did repatriate its abused workers. Equatorial Guinea was left without an agricultural labour force. Spain broke off diplomatic ties.

During his decade in power, Macias hunted his people down with a maniacal ferocity and an admirable lack of prejudice. He was willing to kill just about anyone — politicians, intellectuals, people with technical skills, people without technical skills, and just plain folks who somehow stumbled into the widening gyre of bloodshed. In the jails of Malabo, Equato-Guineans were tortured by the thousands, and by the thousands they were killed. Eventually, some 28,000 people — or about one-tenth of the country's population at the time — were put in forced-labour camps, mostly on the mainland territory of Río Muni, where they were starved, abused, or beaten to death. As the years staggered by, the terrors only got worse.

It was early on in Macias's rule, when the whirlwind of violence was just beginning to spin, that a signal event took place, one that probably did more than anything else to garner for Equatorial Guinea its one brief and unhappy footnote in the annals of international diplomacy. This particular horror took place on a typically hot, sticky night in 1971. Some combination of the torrid tropical climate, the grinding isolation, and the screams of the torture victims — twisting up from the bowels of the presidential palace just across the plaza — finally conspired to unhinge one of two US diplomats posted to the American consulate in Malabo. The man went nuts. He grabbed a pair of scissors, set upon his only American colleague, and stabbed him to death.

Soon after that episode, Washington closed the consulate down, as much in response to the deteriorating political conditions as in specific reaction to the diplomat's death. Still, this was a stunning event, the kind of incident that triggered the imagination of those who heard about it and seemed to encapsulate the surrounding horror. A tyrant murdering his people wholesale — that is almost incomprehensible. But one man going berserk and having at another — everyone can probably manage to envision that. The killing of the American by his colleague soon became notorious among the diplomatic services of the globe, securing for Equatorial Guinea its reputation as the Worst Country in the World.

Meanwhile, the bloodshed and the terror raged on. Before he was finally forced from power, Macias managed to kill or exile approximately 100,000 people, or a third of all Equato-Guineans. Finally, in 1979, he was overthrown in a coup led by his nephew. The old tyrant tried to flee but was caught in Río Muni, apparently trying to escape into Gabon along with whatever plunder he'd managed to lay his hands on. He was quickly executed, along with his chief bodyguard and a handful of cronies, and his nephew assumed what amounted to the Equato-Guinean throne.

The old dictator was dead, but Equatorial Guinea was not suddenly transformed. Things are rarely so simple. Still, some aspects of life in the country did improve. Restrictions on the Catholic Church were lifted. Diplomatic ties were restored with Madrid, Washington, and other capitals. Exiled dissidents were encouraged to return, and some even did so. But clan and tribal hostilities persisted, and political freedom remained little more than a couple of words you

could look up in a dictionary. Although there was vastly less
bloodshed than before, repression was still a fact of Equato-
Guinean life. The country continued to be desperately poor.

On the positive side, at the time of my trip, Equato-
Guineans were preparing to vote in their first presidential
elections since the 1979 coup. Unfortunately, there was to
be just one candidate — President Nguema himself. Maybe,
in the Worst Country in the World, this was the sort of
thing that qualified as progress. With any luck, I'd find out
soon enough.

I turned back to my book at the airport in Douala. The
afternoon wore on until, three hours after our forced return
to Cameroon, we were all finally ushered out to the plane
and welcomed back on board. This time, the flight went
smoothly, without interruption, and the chubby little Avro-
748 landed half an hour later at the airport in Malabo, capital
of Equatorial Guinea. The craft drew up in front of a small
concrete shed poking out of the tropical forest and the pilot
cut the engines. I almost expected a banner: Welcome to the
Worst Country in the World. But there was no such sign.
There was only the customary riot of raised voices, curdling
sweat, and general bedlam that greets any traveller venturing
into the arrivals area at almost any West African airport.

It was morbidly hot. Everyone's clothes were soon
wringing wet, and I was quickly reduced to that slumping
stance and bleary aspect — a melting vanilla ice-cream cone
— that constitutes the standard Caucasian response to the
deadening torpor of the tropics. I did not have an easy passage through the arrivals hall. The immigration official at
first refused to admit me into the country, although I had a
perfectly valid visa in my passport. I didn't panic. You can

sometimes outlast an official in search of a bribe simply by looking sufficiently bewildered. Time is money, after all, and so he may just give up and try somebody else. Eventually, I got my passport stamped and was allowed into the country.

Next, the customs officials insisted on seizing my equipment — a laptop computer, a tape recorder, some spare batteries, a short-wave radio, and a camera with a supply of film. After some pleading and coaxing, I persuaded them to accept a list of serial numbers instead, plus one of my business cards. And so I sagged outside into the late-afternoon sunshine and heaved my bags into the trunk of a waiting taxi. I climbed into the passenger seat in front. Immediately, a policeman appeared at my window and announced that he would like to receive a little something on account of this being Saturday.

"Saturday . . . ?" I said.

He nodded. It was all he could think of, I guess.

I shook my head and let my face dissolve into that addled look I'd already used with the immigration officer, a combination of acute suffering, befuddlement, and benevolence — an expression that was meant to say, "It pains me that I do not speak your beautiful language, *Señor*, but if only I did I am sure we would make the most excellent and sublime poetry together." In time, the policeman gave up. He shrugged and went away.

Salvando, my driver, just laughed and shook his head. "Those policemen," he said. "They're all like that."

We drove to the only good hotel in the city, the Impala, on Calle de Enrique Nvo near the intersection with la Carretera del Aeropuerto. I trudged inside, leaving a small river of perspiration in my wake, and shuffled up to the counter. The receptionist, a gentle-voiced young man, informed me that there were no rooms.

I found this hard to believe. Equatorial Guinea was not exactly a tourist mecca. In fact, almost nobody from the outside world ever came here. Who could be filling all the rooms?

Well, said the receptionist, in fact, there *were* vacant rooms —

"Well, then — "

The man put up his hand. Yes, there were vacant rooms. This was technically so. But, unfortunately, all of them were booked. The people who'd reserved them, he explained, would be turning up, oh — he glanced down at his cheap digital watch — in, approximately, sometime, later. He wasn't exactly sure when.

"Oh," I said. I tried to look both bewildered and benign. It didn't seem to be working. And so I had another idea. An old Africa hand I used to know had once entrusted me with a piece of advice I've never forgotten. He said that it had been handed down to him by a wise old reporter near the end of his career. My friend said he was now passing it along to me, rather as some grey-headed tribal elder might do with a secret, well-burnished charm. In difficult circumstances in Africa, he said, it is best not to become belligerent. Instead, when nothing else works, do this: take your antagonist's hand in your own; cradle his elbow in your free palm; and appeal to him on that most primordial level, as a fellow member of the human race, another resident of this planet, our Earth. Say to him, "Brother, there must be a way." I decided to give it a try.

I must have done it wrong because the receptionist

stepped smartly back and announced that there was nothing he could do to help me. I was welcome to stick around just in case some of the expected legions of guests failed to show up. He wasn't optimistic, but you never knew. He went back about his business.

"All right," I said.

Salvando announced that he would wait, too. I flopped down with my bags in the vacant lounge near the reception desk. So much for the folk wisdom of venerable foreign correspondents. I took out my book and started to read. It was Saturday. I could wait.

An hour later, Salvando sauntered back over to my chair, hunched down, and whispered that things seemed to be looking up. The receptionist, it turned out, was his brother — an imprecise term in Africa — and was willing to risk letting one of the rooms go. This was a huge favour, however, and so . . .

By this time, I'd reached my bribe-resistance limit for the day, so I paid a considerable sum under the table — rather less, I tried to reassure myself, than I would have done if I'd offered the money straight off — and I was given the key to room 104 just up the stairs. It commanded a fine view of a gas station and the modest Malabo harbour. At night, giant fruit bats thunked down from the hotel attic and coasted off into the darkness like so many miniature, articulated stealth bombers — and none of the promised guests ever did show up to claim their rooms.

Klieg
Lights and a
Tweed Coat

I HAD NOT COME to the Worst Country in the World in order to interview the president. But it soon became clear that I was not going to *leave* Equatorial Guinea unless I agreed to talk to His Excellency Obiang Nguema Mbasogo. So I did. I didn't have a choice.

After all, President Nguema seemed firmly in control of the place. For example, he had recently transformed Equatorial Guinea — the only Spanish-speaking country in Africa — into a French-speaking nation, which takes a certain degree of authority. In fact, I learned that this "presidential activity" — the one that had sent my Cameroon Airlines flight back to Douala — had been the President's return in triumph from Dakar, Senegal. While there, he had attended a summit meeting of la Francophonie, a sort of congress of the world's French-speaking countries — essentially, France plus its overseas territories and former colonies.

Whatever you thought of his politics or of his choice in uncles, President Nguema was no fool. He could read a map. With the huge exception of Nigeria, almost all of Equatorial Guinea's neighbours are former *French* colonies, and Paris — unlike Madrid — remains a formidable presence in West Africa. The Portuguese were kicked out of Africa, the Spanish were never really there, and the British withdrew, more or less voluntarily. But the French — *mais non*. They just stayed put. They now play a kind of proconsular role in their former African colonies.

Here is a small illustration of France's continuing involvement. When I lived in Africa, I was based in Zimbabwe, which is a former British colony in southern Africa. At one point, I was planning a trip to West Africa and wanted a visa to visit the Ivory Coast, a former French colony. But there was no Ivorian embassy in Harare, the Zimbabwean capital. So I went straight to the French Embassy and applied for a visa there. It took a day or so. And the visa they gave me didn't even say Côte d'Ivoire on it. It said République Française. Later, when I landed in Abidjan, the main Ivorian city, the immigration officials didn't dither. *Pas de problème, Monsieur.* They just stamped the thing and let me in.

The influence France still exerts in its former African colonies may not be an unadulterated good, but it certainly has had its benefits. In French West Africa, for example, most of Paris's former colonies participate in a joint monetary agreement — the CFA franc zone — which is linked to the French franc and has provided the region with a degree of monetary stability unusual in Africa. Besides, Paris pumps a considerable amount of cash into its one-time African possessions.

Knowing all this, President Nguema of poor, isolated Equatorial Guinea probably felt a bit neglected. Although it is the only Spanish-speaking country in Africa, Equatorial Guinea isn't exactly showered with attention from Spain.

Apart from a weekly Iberia flight between Malabo and Madrid, a sprinkling of foreign aid, a few Spanish missionaries, and a Spanish embassy whose chancery was an aging clump of prefab office modules dumped in an overgrown field at the edge of Malabo, there is not a lot of Spanish munificence on display in Equatorial Guinea. Being a former Spanish colony in Africa doesn't seem to count for much.

Far better to be a former *French* colony, but Equatorial Guinea wasn't one. So Nguema did the next best thing. In fact, he did three ingenious things. First, he lobbied to join the CFA franc zone — and succeeded. Now the country had a convertible currency, enabling it to trade more easily with its French-speaking neighbours, and paving the way for loans and new credit facilities from the International Monetary Fund and the World Bank. Then the President took the kind of action that makes dictatorship seem a pretty sensible way to run a country. He decreed that henceforth French would be one of the two national languages of Equatorial Guinea, to be taught in all of its schools. Just like that, the country became a French-speaking territory, in name if not in fact. And third, incredibly, he applied, with partial success, to have his country join *la Francophonie.*

Equatorial Guinea was not admitted as a full member, but was nonetheless granted observer status. This explained President Nguema's presence at the 1989 summit of la Francophonie in Dakar, Senegal, and his subsequent return in triumph to his own country. Equatorial Guinea was now a French-speaking nation.

Coincidentally, soon after his return, the president learned — this being a small country, not much frequented by *les étrangers* — that there was a foreign journalist wandering around the rolling streets of Malabo, an almost unheard-of occurrence. What was more, the journalist was — Canadian! Canada, mused the president, was a French-speaking country, too. It belonged to la Francophonie and was a member of the exalted Group of Seven major Western industrialized powers to boot. It donated lots of overseas development money to French-speaking countries in Africa. So, the President instructed his people to track down this foreign journalist and see about arranging an interview.

At the time, I was well outside the palace gates, going about my business in the capital of Equatorial Guinea, a modest but surprisingly charming city that spills down to the sea in the shadow of Mount Malabo, a huge, green volcanic pyramid, now extinct.

I had quickly reconnoitered the terrain. I had already established that there was a goodish bar-restaurant called the Beiruthi on la Calle de Kenya, and, a little farther up the hill, I'd located a noisy, rustic spot owned by Pedro, a gruff Andalusian seafarer, now retired. This was where almost everybody who was anybody — Equato-Guineans and a smattering of expats — came to drink, eat, drink, and gaze down over the city and the flowering trees toward the sea.

I also discovered that there were quite a lot of Moroccan soldiers around, although they kept very much to themselves. Their presence seemed odd at first, but there was a reason for it. They were the elite presidential guard, barracked in the centre of town, separately from the local forces. It seemed that President Nguema had decided to rent his personal guard from Morocco, on the sensible premise — by no means unprecedented in Africa — that as foreign mercenaries they were less likely to get mixed up in partisan or tribal disputes.

The other remarkable thing about Malabo, apart from its commendable cleanliness — a recent phenomenon, apparently — and the lovely tiles decorating the plaza near the Presidential Palace Area ("Closed to the Public"), was the impressive and very frequent image of the US ambassador's four-wheel-drive truck roaring through town, to and from the harbour, hauling a huge powerboat on a trailer. The craft looked big enough to take on the entire Equato-Guinean navy, assuming there was such a thing, but it was outfitted for sport-fishing, not business. Almost two decades after that ugly business with scissors, the Americans were back in Equatorial Guinea.

Meanwhile the word was out that the South Africans were here too. Rumour had it that President Nguema had been permitting South African agents to use his country's territory to spy on neighbouring Nigeria, the most populous and powerful country in black Africa. I'd heard accusations that the South Africans were even constructing some kind of military base on Bioko, with a view to invading Nigeria. This was potentially important news, of course, although nobody who spoke of such things — always in voices of darkest foreboding — was ever able to explain to me exactly why it was that South Africa would *want* to invade Nigeria.

Still, in the months prior to my visit, the rumours had become sufficiently rife that Nigeria finally demanded that Equatorial Guinea expel these nefarious South Africans, threatening various unspecified but unpleasant consequences if this demand went unheeded. So, the South Africans were rounded up and expelled. There were four of them, it turned out. Cattle farmers.

That should have been the end of it. But I'd heard that the South Africans had in fact *returned* to Equatorial Guinea, this time carrying passports of various different nationalities — some combination of Botswanan, British, and Irish. This was quite possibly true and perhaps even legitimate: many South Africans hold dual citizenship and carry more than one passport. If the South Africans were indeed back on Bioko, however, it probably wouldn't be long before Nigeria got wind of the news and turned angry once again.

This was the story that I was in Equatorial Guinea to pursue. But the country was a dictatorship, and it seemed that the dictator had other ideas. One morning, after I'd been in Malabo for only a few days, a pair of palace aides showed up at my hotel to speak to me about my upcoming interview with the president.

"Interview . . . ?" I said. "President . . . ?" I hadn't requested any such interview.

"Yes," they said. "It has been scheduled for next Tuesday."

Well, this was news — an interview with the president. My editors would likely be pleased. Like train wrecks and mining disasters, presidential interviews are more or less guaranteed front-page treatment, regardless of what country the president in question is president of, or how he got there, or even what he said in the interview.

Unfortunately, I had a problem. I was just about broke. It turned out that I had badly underestimated how much cash I would need in Equatorial Guinea. I was accustomed to using a credit card for most basic expenses, such as hotels and so on—something that had turned out to be impossible in Equatorial Guinea — and I was now dangerously low on funds. For financial reasons, if nothing else, I planned to head back to Cameroon on the weekend. It would not be possible for me to remain until the following Tuesday. I looked at the presidential aides. I explained, without going into details, that I had to leave the country before then. Couldn't the interview be moved up a few days? How about this Friday?

They were doubtful but said they would check.

I made the rounds of local banks trying to drum up some cash in a hurry. In most countries, there's usually some way of turning a valid credit card into paper currency — but not, it turned out, in Equatorial Guinea. Nonetheless, I knocked out a list of written questions for the president — something I'd been requested to do — and delivered them to the palace. I was informed that the interview could not be rescheduled. Next Tuesday was the day. I was told that I would simply have to make arrangements to extend my visit.

I now had no choice but to explain my problem. It was pretty humiliating — the correspondent for a big North American newspaper, penniless, in one of the world's poorest countries. The aides thought about the situation for a while and then offered to pay any expenses I incurred during the extra time I would have to remain in their country. I shook my head — that was definitely out. My employers had firm rules that prohibited me from even considering any such arrangement. Besides, it was just too galling to contemplate; my being on the dole in a country where most people dwelled in thudding poverty. I was firm. "I have to pay my own way."

"But you have no money."

True. There was that. Well, I said brightly, I would see what I could do. And, in the end, I managed to make a private and unorthodox but quite legal financial arrangement with a representative in Equatorial Guinea of a certain third country. It meant I could remain for the interview, which promptly presented a new problem. I had brought nothing to wear.

"Suit and tie," the presidential aides informed me. "No exceptions. He is the president."

I remembered a man I'd met a few days earlier. His name was Ronald Migneron, and he was about my size. He was also the only other Canadian in Equatorial Guinea. Possibly he had a suit. I left the palace and headed off to look for him. Migneron had wound up in the country pretty much by mistake. Something about the name. He'd been under the impression all along that he was travelling to French Guyane, which is in South America, just north of Brazil. It was only on the day before he left Montreal that he found out where he was really headed. He'd gone around to pick up his tickets and they told him he was travelling via Belgium.

"Via *Belgium* . . . ?" he said. "Why do I go through Belgium to get to South America?"

"Because you're not *going* to South America," they said. "You're going to Africa."

He looked at them as if they were crazy. *Mais non*, he protested. Guyane wasn't in *Africa*.

Eyes rolled. Not *Guyane*, they said. *Guinea*. Equatorial *Guinea*. Spanish-speaking place. Somewhere near Nigeria.

"So that's why I'm here," Migneron had told me over a beer up at Pedro's, a year after his arrival. He shrugged and gave me a wrinkled, sad-dog smile. "If I hadn't asked that last day, I'd never have known I was coming to Africa."

Migneron explained that he was here in Africa — Equatorial Guinea, to be precise — on a contract with a Montreal-based foreign-aid agency, le Centre Canadien des Études et de Coopération. His mission — to fix the schools. They'd all been ravaged by the president's uncle, and not much had been done to repair them in the ten years since the tyrant's death. They were in miserable shape.

"Some of them had chickens in them," Migneron said. "When the Church finally received permission to come back, they had no money to rebuild."

But they were getting around to it now. Migneron's contract was for two years, with a budget of $185,000. He worked so quickly, however, that he'd managed to fix all the schools in half the time. Rather than go home early, he decided to stay on and see about restoring the churches. Under Macias, they'd also been banged around pretty badly. The money for the work was showing up in dribs and drabs, mainly from private donors in West Germany and Spain. Migneron took me around to show me the projects he was working on — the rambling Seminario de Nuestra Señora del Pilar just outside town (built in 1912 and the oldest concrete structure in Equatorial Guinea), plus the handsome but crumbling Catedral Santa Isabel on the city's main plaza.

Forty-seven at the time, with a wheat sheaf of straight blond hair, Migneron struck me as a bit of a lost soul, one of those modern-day misfits that you find tramping around the tropics — goners, someone once called them. In both Latin America and Africa, I'd met quite a number — backwards refugees, going against the grain, always in flight from the comfort and security of the First World.

Migneron had left behind an ex-wife and two daughters in Montreal and had spent years knocking around the Caribbean and Central America before pitching up in Africa, drawn by the rough edges and easy fraternity of what a West Indian friend of mine once called "the Afro-Latin outdoor culture." Migneron had made a good life for himself by some lights — a steady supply of European cigarettes and certain other amenities, not to mention a comely Equato-Guinean girlfriend who owned a local bar (bar-ownership being, by a wide margin, the leading professional ambition of upwardly mobile Equato-Guineans). It didn't seem likely that Migneron would ever return to settle in Canada. "I've almost lost my culture," he told me. "I get lost in the cities now."

The first place I went to look for Migneron after I left the palace — the first place I'd look for just about anybody in Malabo — was up at Pedro's. And I was in luck. He was there. Even better, he *did* have a business suit. That was the good news. The bad news was that the suit was a heavy brown tweed, the same suit he wore in the *winter* in *Montreal*. I happened to know a little something about Montreal in winter and about the sort of clothing that Montrealers in winter are compelled to wear. Still, this seemed to be my only option, the only business suit in Equatorial Guinea that was more or less my size and that I could easily get my hands on. Fine, I said. It would have to do.

And so, at the appointed hour on Tuesday morning I stood, slowly melting in the hotel lobby, obediently turned out in Migneron's suffocating tweed. I was waiting for the presidential aides to pick me up. They appeared right on schedule, and we set off in a government jeep for the presidential palace. Once inside the palace compound, I was ushered upstairs into a dark, air-conditioned anteroom with a mossy green carpet. I waited there, perched on a swivel chair, for about half an hour while one of the aides slumped on a sofa in front of me and scratched his nether regions. I worked on getting my metabolic rate back down to normal in order to avoid any hint of perspiration.

I should mention here that I possess a somewhat nervous disposition in general and sometimes have to contend with a severe nervous-perspiration problem. When I get flustered, I start to sweat. This has long been the bane of my existence. Once, some years ago, I was running late on my way to a job interview in Toronto. I arrived on time but in a somewhat overheated condition. As is usual with me, I was also a bit keyed up. I started to perspire. The job interview began — and it proceeded badly. I became more nervous, and so I started to perspire more, which made me yet more nervous. This familiar spiral of nerves and sweat continued until the interviewer stopped speaking and simply stared at me. "Is it just hot in here?" he asked. "Or do you have malaria?"

Well, I didn't have either malaria or the job. But I was now facing an interview with the president of Equatorial Guinea. Eventually, the palace aide led me down a corridor into a rather large, sparsely appointed room, which was where the interview was to take place. The room was already crammed with palace staff who had gathered to observe the grand spectacle of their president being interviewed by a foreign journalist. A local television crew was setting up its equipment — which seemed odd, there being no TV service in Equatorial Guinea. It turned out that this was President Nguema's personal video crew. He liked to be able to watch himself on TV after important presidential activities, even if no one else in the country was able to.

I was instructed to sit down in a plush upholstered chair at one end of the room, beside a coffee table and cater-corner to a matching chesterfield. There was a microphone on the table. I checked my tape recorder to make sure it was properly set, and I placed it on the table beside the mike. Then I proceeded to await the president. In Migneron's crinkly tweed suit, which was maybe a half-size too small, I felt like an overdressed sheep. I tested my forehead. Damp — that was all. Good. Maybe I'd be all right.

The TV people started to fidget with their equipment. They set up the klieg lights and switched them on. Klieg lights are extremely *hot.* My neck started to itch, and I soon began to perspire. Not too badly, though. Thank God for the air-conditioning. I felt I had the situation under control. All I needed to do was take deep breaths and concentrate on staying calm.

Then the TV people began to make a fuss. It seemed the air-conditioner was making too much noise. It was interfering with the sound level on their recording equipment. "Turn it off," they demanded.

What were they saying? Turn off the air-conditioning? Were they crazy? And yet someone complied. Almost immediately, the room transformed itself into a sauna bath. With the windows closed, there was no circulation at all. The klieg lights burned, and the ponderous equatorial air grew steadily hotter and damper. The stiff tweed fibres of my borrowed suit seemed to quiver and snap, like the mandibles of a million carniverous insects. I ran a hand across my brow.

Drenched. Hot globules of water now started to run down my neck, sopping my shirt and proceeding down my back. Steam drifted up from my collar.

Well, this was rather embarrassing. And so, inevitably, I felt myself becoming rather *nervous*. I glanced at my list of questions for the president. They were typed on a sheet of heat-sensitive thermal paper. I had to blink in order to see the page. Not that it mattered — the paper was already thickly splattered with perspiration, and the print was starting to blur.

"Open the windows!" someone shouted.

It seemed we were all about to suffocate. People climbed over each other to get to the windows and throw them open. Thin currents of air soon began to trickle through the room. They felt like a healing balm, miraculous properties, like water in the desert, or the touch of a cool and comforting hand at the end of a terrible dream. I felt confident that I could get things under control now. I concentrated on my breathing, tried to take slow breaths. I willed my sweat pores to close. I felt I was getting things under —

"Close the windows!" shouted the TV crew. "Close the windows now!"

What? Again? But they'd just been opened!

Unfortunately, it seemed the ambient noise from outdoors was the problem now. It interfered with the sound level inside the palace. And so the windows were all slammed shut once more. This was an authoritarian state, after all. And I was soon transformed back into my vaporous alter-ego — the Human Steam Kettle. Pretty soon, I'd wind up in a puddle of liquid and tweed fibres on the floor, like something out of *The Wizard of Oz*.

Finally, there was a commotion at the door, and the president strode into the sweltering room — a cool and rather scholarly looking gentleman of medium height and middling age, the same man who'd had his genocidal uncle put to death. I struggled to my feet, thrust out my hand, and apologised for this excessively aqueous display. President Nguema merely shrugged. Perhaps he was not unaccustomed to seeing people sweat. He wore a stylish dark business suit and heavy-framed glasses. His complexion was jet-black, almost bluish in its darkness. His grip was perfectly dry. There was not even a sheen of dampness on his brow.

We sat down, and the interview began. The president insisted that the four South Africans in the country really were nothing but farmers (a claim that I'd already discovered to be true). He denied that there were serious human-rights problems in his country any longer — a much more debatable point. And he spoke quite eloquently about the difficulty of governing an impoverished African nation the same way you might run Sweden (which often seems to be what North Americans or Europeans expect Africa's leaders to do).

He used the same kind of argument to defend the shortage—in fact, the complete absence — of opposition candidates in the upcoming presidential elections. Equatorial Guinea, he said, wasn't yet ready, wasn't yet "mature" enough, for more democracy than a single-candidate election would allow. He may have had something of a point there, but his line of argument would have washed a good deal better if government largesse and political power were not still so heavily concentrated among members of the president's own clan.

Towards the end of the interview, President Nguema denied persistent rumours that a distant, uninhabited Equato-Guinean island called Pagalu was being used as a dumping site for toxic waste from Europe. I was never able to determine whether he could be believed on this point or not. The president then wound up by issuing a plea for development assistance from Canada.

It was, on the whole, an impressive performance. Nguema was articulate and thoughtful — and in at least two languages. He spoke excellent Spanish, of course. And, when we switched to French, he proved to be perfectly fluent. For the umpteenth time, I marvelled at the astonishing linguistic facility of Africans, a virtue that is surely one of the continent's most remarkable but least advertised wonders. Even more amazing, the president conducted the entire interview without emitting so much as a droplet of perspiration.

I, of course, disgorged a flood. But, unlike my job-interviewer years ago in Toronto, the president of Equatorial Guinea did not slip into his most sarcastic voice to inquire whether I was suffering from malaria. He didn't seem to notice at all or to care.

That evening, after I had returned his now somewhat bedraggled tweed suit, I stood my new friend Ronald Migneron to dinner at the Restaurant Beiruthi, where we did a good job of replenishing our bodily fluids. Later, back at my hotel, I drifted off to sleep, listening to the fruit bats scamper down from the attic to sway out over the dark Atlantic coast of what may have been once — but now probably wasn't quite — the Worst Country in the World.

Why I
Went to
Madagascar

I LEFT MY HOTEL one fine Friday morning in Madagascar
and ventured out to see the Zoma. I had been warned
about the Zoma, but I decided to ignore the warnings.
The Zoma was one of the reasons I had come to Madagascar.

In Malgache, the main language spoken in Madagascar,
Zoma is the word for Friday, and Friday is the day for shopping. It's the main market day. In Madagascar, these two
concepts — Friday and market — have become inextricably
linked. They have merged into that one eponymous word,
Zoma. Until you have experienced market day in Antananarivo, the capital of Madagascar, you have not experienced commerce.

On any day of the week, but especially on Fridays, the
result seems to overcome Antananarivo. The Zoma fills the
maze of cobbled alleys and staircases northwest of l'Avenue
de l'Indépendance and spills out to overflow almost the
entire central area of this topsy-turvy city. The result is both
a triumph of the mercantilist spirit and a heaving, sentient
monument to chaos. Automobiles barely move at all, and
pedestrians can do little better than inch their way painfully

ahead, groping for purchase — either kind — amid the dense clusters of market stalls and the crush of shoppers, vendors, beggars, pickpockets, cripples, and ragged, wild-haired urchins who crowd the city from just below the Ritz Cinema all the way down to la Gare de Soarano—a good long way.

For the length of that route, the streets are crammed with a maze of canvas awnings or octagonal cotton parasols, each sheltering another table or mat piled high with merchandise of every possible description, from parrots in cages to cartons of Gauloise cigarettes, from boxes of Chinese "Double Happiness" wooden matches to loaves of *koba*, a Malagasy delicacy made of pistachio and peanut paste, wrapped in green banana leaves. If you wish, you can pick up a strange stringed instrument fashioned from intricately carved bamboo. Unique to Madagascar, it yields a rich, happy tone and is called a *valiha*.

Or you can buy groceries. There is no shortage of food. As I pushed my way through the Zoma that Friday morning, a stocky woman poked her head from a dark butcher's stall. "*Venez!*" she cried. "*Achetez!*" She slid her bare arms into a mass of unspeakable viscera and raised the conglomeration aloft — fresh, pliant tentacles of blood-red tripe. The stuff dripped its odiferous richness onto the sopping cobbles, very near a pair of immediately familiar shoes. I took a quick step backwards. "*Achetez!*" the woman repeated.

I replied with a polite but firm "*Non, merci.*"

She shrugged and let her wares fall back onto the brick counter, where they settled into a spongy mass amid the bound pairs of pig's feet, the strings of plump *saucisses fraîches*, and the fuzzy goats' heads, whose gooey grey eyes gazed dreamily off into the remotest metaphysical distance imaginable. I waded on through the curdling aromas of fried fish, mammalian tripe, and who knew what else. I wasn't here to shop. I was here to explore.

In Madagascar, there was no end of exploring to do. Nothing I had seen in Africa — nothing I had seen in the world — quite prepared me for the human and geographical maze of Madagascar. To be sure, the country is not exactly Africa, at least not in the physical sense. Some 165 million years ago, what we now call Madagascar wrenched itself loose from the eastern coast of its mother continent and gradually drifted to its current address, brooding above the Indian Ocean about five hundred kilometres across the Mozambique Channel from Mozambique.

Madagascar had become an island — the fourth largest on the globe — and the ensuing eons of isolation have done their work. A world of difference separates Madagascar from just about anywhere else on earth. The island is resolutely *sui generis*, virtually a continent unto itself.

The differences became apparent the moment I arrived in the capital, Antananarivo, or Tanarive, or simply Tana. True, Tana is a poor city, which hardly distinguishes it from the general run of African towns. But it is about the grandest and most intricate poor city imaginable. It is impossibly convoluted — a labyrinth of brick and stucco façades, church spires, stone stairways, dark tunnels, cobbled lanes, rows of jacaranda, and scattered belvederes, all clinging like mottled honeycomb to a range of hills that looms above the checkered rice paddies of the surrounding plateaux. The place reminded me of nothing so much as a three-dimensional game of Snakes and Ladders.

The city has an impressive array of excellent restaurants — French, Chinese, and Vietnamese — and much stunning architecture. Handsome colonial buildings, mostly in reddish brick, seem to tumble down the slopes of precipitous hills, whose summits afford dazzling vistas across the highland plains. Here is a city you could stroll in and climb through for days, if not weeks.

Antananarivo really does exude a kind of magic, but that strange quality — at once eerie and fabulous — is not equally shared by all its residents. On the stairways leading down to l'Avenue de l'Indépendance or on the twisting streets near the Hôtel Colbert, the full force of Malagasy poverty is on constant display: the street children, like wild spectres; the beggars; the cripples; the blind. They huddle at street corners or at the edges of stone staircases, balefully seeking alms. The children attach themselves to the pant legs or skirts of passersby and do not let go.

Not many foreign travellers came to Madagascar in those days, and those who did come were not inclined to tarry long in the capital. They mostly had a common purpose. Almost as soon as they arrived at the international airport in Tana, they boarded an Air Madagascar Boeing 737 for the flight north to Nosy Be, a miniscule spice island bobbing above the sea just off Madagascar's northwestern tip. It is a compact and mountainous paradise of utterly deserted beaches, coral-encrusted islets, sunken volcanic lakes, sleepy fishing hamlets, and rambling plantations of sugar cane, ylang-ylang, vanilla, and cloves. Several sheltered and dreamy seaside hotels are tucked by the sand near gentle, variegated bays and palm groves, where the seafood is sumptuous and where the rose-and-scarlet sunsets—filtered through the fiery haze drifting over a distant, invisible Africa — are simply miraculous.

But the greatest single discovery of my time in Madagascar was a place called Antsiranana, or, if you prefer, Diego-Suarez. Like many Malagasy cities, Antsiranana has two names, one of them Malagasy and the other European. Antsiranana was a true revelation, the sort of destination that inveterate travellers might spend their whole lives seeking but yet never manage to find.

Imagine Rio de Janeiro — the precipitous mountain setting, the linked sea bays washing the successive arcs of sand. Picture the sugar-loaf island, the vaulting skies, and the mothering sun. Now, take away the muddy miserable *favelas*, the smog, the roaring buses, the homicidal taxis, the skyscrapers, and the general crush of humanity. Replace them with a modest French colonial town, settled and tidy, perched upon a low ridge jutting above the sea, a place I suspect Ernest Hemingway would have especially loved, if only he had discovered it.

I stayed at the twenty-eight-room Hôtel de la Poste — in its way, a perfect hostelry. True, it had cockroaches. Lots of them. Big ones. They scurried out at night, reached critical mass, and suddenly, as one, the entire hotel staff would yank off their footwear and go banging about the bar and the restaurant, clobbering the things with their shoes. It was a thoroughly messy business, but to my mind this nightly performance also served to imbue the place with a certain rustic charm. The bar itself was a fine affair, with a great crocodile hide mounted on one palm-matted wall beneath a lofty ceiling where fans whirled in discreet silence.

Outside, by day, a sunlit sidewalk terrace overlooked a

spreading banardi tree, a blue-green streak of the bay, and the distant dun-and-olive hills. If I were Ernest Hemingway, this is where I would have lived while completing my — let's see — my *seventh* novel. I would take Room 11, on the second floor in the corner, whose windows, with the louvred shutters thrown open, afford a superb prospect of a jade sea surging landward beyond a small green park and a white wrought-iron bandstand, its paint chipped and peeling. I would write well and truly all day and dine on grilled lobster and Three Horses beer at the Hotel Valiha every night.

But I am not Ernest Hemingway, and so I left Diego-Suarez empty-handed — or at least without having completed the first draft of anything — and headed back to the capital. There, one Friday afternoon, I somehow managed to insinuate my way through the Zoma and caught a train for a four-hour rail journey south to a mountain town called Antsirabe.

The sole first-class car on that train was jammed with dark, fine-featured men — almost Amerindian in appearance — with grey fedoras atop their heads and sombre expressions on their lined and weathered faces. They neither spoke nor smiled. The French-built diesel engine broke down along the way, and a replacement had to be rushed out from the capital — well, not *rushed* exactly — to propel us the rest of the way. Still, we got to Antsirabe in the end.

It was well after dark when we arrived, and I was greeted by rain, a misty mountain chill and dozens of small, eager men crying "*Moi! Moi!*" in an urgent spectacle that to the uninitiated — in this case, *moi* — made no sense at all. I let one of the men hustle me through the station and out onto the dark and glistening street where hundreds of rickshaws were assembled in the rain. I heaved my haversack onto a pair of wooden struts and climbed in. The man tucked a plastic sheet around me up to my chin, like a floor-length bib, and we set off through the rain, bound for an Antsirabe institution — the Hôtel des Thermes.

Built in 1885, the hotel is a three-story palace of cupolas and gingerbread, balconies and pillars, dormered windows and gabled roofs. It has sprawling private gardens and forty-two vast rooms, and it was here, in 1955, that King Mohammed V of Morocco whiled away his time in political exile. When I got there, however, the place was almost empty and had a rather lost and lonely air. After two nights amid these corridors, I was feeling a little lost and lonely myself. So I decided it was time at last to set out on the road trip south to Fianarantsoa, where I had two things I especially wanted to do. I wanted to climb into the rain forest above Ranomafana to search for golden bamboo lemurs, and I wanted to sample the fare at a fabled Malagasy restaurant called Chez Papillon, renowned across the Indian Ocean, especially for its seafood.

I rolled into Fianarantsoa late in the afternoon. Overhead, a huge rain-storm sky was scattered with smaller, lower clouds, scalloped and glowing white, like seashells spread against a sprawling beach of pewter grey. I headed straight for Chez Papillon, which squatted in a rather dreary section of an undistinguished street, right beside a car-repair shop. It looked like a good place to have bad fish-and-chips. Still, I walked inside and asked to see the menu. It was the right thing to do.

On a cloudy Malagasy morning, several memorable

meals later, I invited the proprietor and *chef-de-cuisine* of the
country's leading culinary shrine to join me on the patio for
a coffee. Before long, Louis Papillon, a transplanted
Frenchman from Lyon, settled himself at a table on the sidewalk outside his restaurant. He toyed with an unlit cigarette
for a time and then proceeded to reminisce about several
decades spent a very long way from any place you were
likely to find mentioned in the *Guide Michelin*. Yet, here in
Madagascar, Papillon was a celebrated name. "I'm well-
known," he conceded. "All the people on the road between
Antananarivo and Tuléar stop and eat here."

It was largely thanks to the crayfish that they came — *au
gratin, américaine, flambée,* or *grillée.* All were Papillon special-
ties. Meanwhile, Papillon's rich and pungent *bisque
d'écrevisses au crouton* was renowned across the length and
breadth of the republic. The same went for his shrimp
sautéed in whisky sauce, or his recipes for black bass, trout,
oysters, and lobster. In fact, just about everything that origi-
nated in the kitchen of Louis Papillon, but especially the
seafood, was worth a longish trip — say, five or six time
zones.

A small round man with wavy grey hair and a square,
liver-spotted face, Papillon was a vigorous seventy-two
when I met him. He had been operating his restaurant since
1959 and personally awarded it the equivalent of four
Michelin stars. A twelve-room hotel adjoined the place. I
had already taken a room there; it was spartan accommoda-
tion without much of a view, but it was convenient to the
restaurant.

For three decades, Papillon had resisted the repeated
entreaties of Malagasy *gourmands* who urged him to abandon

his location in Fianarantsoa and move to the capital, so that they could savour the *fruits-de-mer* of his labours more often and at greater leisure. I asked Papillon why an accomplished French chef — once the private cook of the American ambassador in Paris — would decide to establish and operate a four-star restaurant in, of all places, Madagascar. And, having decided to do that, why on earth would he choose to put it in Fianarantsoa?

Papillon shrugged. "Everyone tells me I should be in Antananarivo," he said. "But it's no easy thing to establish a new business. Anyway, I feel I'm doing pretty well here."

He explained that he first came out to Madagascar in 1953, when it was still a French colony. At the time, he'd had an offer to run a restaurant at a new hotel that was opening in Fianarantsoa. After a year or so, some personal problems arose, and he returned to Paris for three years. But his old employer in Madagascar pleaded with him to return — memories of the *bisque d'écrevisse*, perhaps? — and Papillon complied. The employer, however, promptly went bankrupt. That was in 1957. Reluctant to leave Madagascar yet again, Papillon and his wife set up their own hotel and restaurant in 1959. And they flourished — Papillon in the kitchen and his wife in the business office.

Still, it is no easy matter to run a first-rate restaurant in a humble city in a dirt-poor developing country — especially a restaurant that specializes in seafood while hovering on a plateau 1,300 metres above sea level. Papillon told me that most of his crustaceans were flown in from points along the Malagasy coasts — green oysters from Morondava, lobster and shrimp from Port Dauphin, white oysters from Manakara.

Papillon raised trout and black bass at his own farm high in the mountains, twenty-seven kilometres outside Fianarantsoa, where he also grazed beef cattle. The local highland streams provided the restaurant's fabled red crayfish. The wine list included both imports and surprisingly agreeable domestics, thanks to a local Swiss-run vineyard that produced reds and whites of fine quality, and a particularly good rosé.

By six p.m. it is almost dark, and Papillon's restaurant becomes a cosy inner sanctum of golden tablecloths, dun curtains, and polished wooden panels. Clad in a burgundy jacket, grey flannels, and sandals, headwaiter Emile Rasolofon, a twenty-year veteran, ushers me to my table with an austere grace. My order appears to meet with his approval: *soupe de poisson à la Marseilleise* and *filet de Capitain avec crevettes, sauce d'Antin*, followed by *coupe Jamaïque* and black coffee. Emile produces a half-bottle of dry white *Lazan'i Betsileo*, and another memorable dinner, chez Papillon, has begun.

In Search
of the Golden
Bamboo Lemur

T HERE is just one place in Madagascar to find golden
bamboo lemurs. In fact, there is just one place in
the world. High in the central Malagasy massif, the
village of Ranomafana is cradled in a slender valley flanked
by sudden green walls, and it is here that the last golden
bamboo lemurs on earth are living out what well may be the
final days of their kind.

On the precipitous slopes above the village, a narrow
range of cloud forest is home to untold species of flora and
fauna, many of them unique not only to Madagascar but to
the world. The golden bamboo lemur was sighted for the
first time — discovered, if you like — in 1987, only a year
before my visit. In a stand of cloud forest no more than thirty
kilometres wide, and shrinking all the time, the last golden
bamboo lemurs in existence dwelled on the machete's edge
of extinction. There may have been twenty-five of them left
at the time, at most fifty. I wanted to see at least one.

I made some inquiries around Fianarantsoa and soon
managed to hook up with an apparently trustworthy fellow
whose name was Benjamin Hery. He was twenty-six years

old and temporarily unemployed but hoping for a job in banking, and he agreed to drive me up into the mountains in his father's white 1963 Peugeot 403. He said he would wait for me up there as long as necessary and then chauffeur me back down

We left Fianarantsoa bright and early one morning, drove farther and farther up into the mountains until we could go no higher, and then we started to drive down the other side. Eventually, we arrived at Ranomafana. (That, as it turned out, was the easy part. It was the return portion of the journey that would cause all the problems.) Immediately, I was struck by what now seemed the obvious stupidity of my plan. Here I was, preparing to climb up into unfamiliar mountain terrain, looking for a creature that had been formally discovered only a year earlier, an animal that no more than a handful of human beings had ever laid eyes on before, and one that was essentially unrecognizable to me.

But I was in luck. No sooner had I climbed out of Benjamin's car following our arrival at Ranomafana than I bumped into a pair of US naturalists from Duke University in North Carolina. They were getting into a truck in order to drive down to Fianarantsoa, but they were willing to stop and talk habitat for a time.

"We've found, just literally in the last three weeks, four species of butterflies that are known to be rare," said one of the naturalists, Claire Kremen, a lepidopterist. "We've found one species that has only been recorded in one other part of Madagascar. Plants — I don't think we've even begun to tap what there is."

I already knew that Madagascar sheltered a greater variety of unique species of plant and animal life than any other part of the world, more even than the Galápagos. The forest that still clung to the mountains' slopes around Ranomafana was among the few remaining refuges for the island's natural riches, but the forest was disappearing fast. Once, a vast jungle of trees, mosses, ferns, and vines had been draped over the huge central massif. But the cloud forest of Ranomana had been steadily whittled away over the generations. Now its retreat was accelerating dramatically, thanks to thirteen licenced lumbering outfits that were harvesting the trees for short-term gain and long-term ruin. Meanwhile, local peasants had cleared much of the forest for crops, thereby inviting — for their culture and for much of their country — a slow death by ecological suicide. The slender layer of topsoil that the cultivators left behind was soon washed away in the driving summer rains, explosing a red clay on which nothing would grow.

It was the same story throughout Madagascar. Only about ten per cent of the country's original forest cover remained. The World Wildlife Fund had already declared the island to be the most seriously eroded region on earth. And yet Madagascar was also considered "a naturalist's promised land." Eighty per cent of the country's eight-thousand flowering plants were endemic — that is, unique to Madagascar. So were half of the more than two-hundred bird species, ninety-five per cent of the reptiles (including two-thirds of the chameleons), almost all of the two-hundred-fifty kinds of frogs, ninety-seven per cent of the three-thousand varieties of butterflies and moths, and almost all of the native mammals.

After wrenching itself loose from continental Africa millions of years ago, Madagascar had gone off on an evolutionary journey of its own. Continental Africa, for example, has just one species of baobab tree, a portly giant that looks as though it was planted upside down. Madagascar has eight. Many of Madagascar's endemic plants and animals have already died out, including more than a dozen species of lemur, a monkey-like family of primates that evolved in Madagascar and nowhere else (except, possibly, the Comoros Islands).

Lemurs flourished in Madagascar precisely because there were few competing mammals — and no monkeys, which are more intelligent and more dextrous. Although they evolved in Africa, monkeys never emerged in Madagascar, and that opened a niche in which lemurs were able to thrive. Man didn't evolve here either, but he showed up all the same. For the past 1,500 years, lemurs have had to compete with the most destructive primate of all. They are losing. Now, just twenty-eight known species of lemur survive, ranging from tiny mouse lemurs to nimble tree-dwelling creatures the size of large monkeys. All the surviving lemurs are engangered, some tottering on the verge of extinction, with nowhere to hide.

At least twelve of the remaining lemur species continue to dwell in the remnants of the southern rain forest, now piled like a heap of damp woollen sweaters atop the spine-like mountains that soar and plunge above Ranomafana. They include the few remaining golden bamboo lemurs, nourishing themselves on shoots of bamboo as they await their version of the apocalypse.

In 1986, in an effort to delay or avert that day of reckoning, a team of naturalists from Duke University first proposed establishing a national park here. It was simply a question of survival. "We realized that we were going to have to do something major, if we weren't going to lose our study site," said Patrick Daniels. He was the co-ordinator of the university's project at Ranomafana and one of the two US researchers I met on my arrival.

The Malagasy government eventually agreed to the park proposal, and plans were approved for a 45,000-hectare forest reserve. While important, the move was no panacea. Madagascar already had about thirty-six official parks or reserves, which sounds fairly impressive. Unfortunately, to operate them, the Malagasy Department of Waters and Forests was allocated an annual budget of roughly $1,200. Daniels said that he and others were seeking outside funds to help ensure that the Ranomafana park would fare better than others had done. The money would be used in part to provide services and employment opportunities for local peasants, to help compensate them for their loss of access to the forest. Was he optimistic? "Well," he said. "We're hoping."

Daniels and Kremen gave me directions to their research station higher up in the mountains. Then they climbed into their truck and rumbled along the winding road and away. I left Benjamin behind to watch over his father's Peugeot and set off on my own on foot, in quest of the elusive golden bamboo lemur. After a modest climb, I managed to find the project station operated by the Duke University team — a cluster of tents perched on a forested ridgetop — and a resourceful young man named Roger Randalana.

Roger was a student at the *lycée* in Fianarantsoa who worked up here in the forest on his vacations, acting as a guide for the very occasional visitors who, like me, clambered up from Ranomafana. I explained that I wanted to find a golden bamboo lemur, probably the rarest inhabitant of this forest. Roger merely shrugged and smiled and said he'd see what he could do. The whole enterprise turned out to be almost absurdly easy.

The two of us slogged through the forest together for a half hour or so, and then Roger suddenly put up his hand. "*Voila!*" he whispered. He pointed up through the dense green foliage. I eased my way alongside him, shifting past the clustered trunks of harongana trees and bamboo. Following the direction of Roger's outstetched arm, I gazed up into the translucent fretwork canopy of the rain forest — and I saw.

There he was, a golden bamboo lemur, perched on a bowed bamboo limb. He was a small male, maybe thirty centimetres in height, with his tail adding another thirty or so as it dangled beneath him. He was light brown and he made faint interrogative grunting sounds — whoo, whoo — like an owl with a chest cold. Keeping perfectly silent, Roger and I watched him as he busily stripped away the tiny green bamboo shoots with his long fingers, munching them like barbecued spareribs. He made discreet chewing sounds clearly audible from the ground below. He glanced about nonchalantly now and then as he tossed the leaves away — the very picture of existential confidence.

Muted by the forest cover, the late-afternoon sunshine spilled through the trees like an oleaginous liquid, streaking the tangle of leaves, vines, and mosses with pools of hazy gold. Overhead, the smaller branches shifted in the breeze. Somewhere in the distance, birds were singing. Suddenly, the creature's head shot up. In an instant, he was gone, bursting away through the branches like a fur-covered spring. A smattering of leaves fluttered to the ground, marking his flight. Still, I undoubtedly saw him — a golden bamboo lemur.

"*Il est vite*," marvelled Roger, as the creature fled deeper into the forest.

Our mission accomplished, we headed back to the research station, where I chatted briefly with Judy Rosenthal, a young woman from California who kept a large brown but unidentified snake coiled snugly around her neck as she spoke. She and the other researchers seemed unfazed by my intrusion. Just the opposite, in fact. Up here, they didn't get a lot of foreign visitors. "It's not a problem," she said. "The more people who come to see the park, the more support the park gets."

What the park seemed most likely to get just now, however, was an immense amount of rain, for the weather had suddenly changed. It was also growing late, so I said my goodbyes and began the return trek down to Ranomafana on my own. Eventually, I found a shaky wooden footbridge that swayed across a churning stream, and I emerged onto a narrow road that snaked down to Ranomafana.

As great grey clouds impaled themselves upon the surrounding mountaintops, I hurried on foot through a rainless serpentine corridor, hoping to reach Ranomafana without drowning first. Thanks to an obliging truck driver, I did — but Benjamin was nowhere to be found. Meanwhile, overhead, the dark overburdened clouds suddenly seemed to explode. In an instant, the world turned to water.

In spite of the rain, I kept looking for Benjamin. I asked everywhere, but the answer was always the same. Nobody had any word of my driver. It was as if he'd disappeared. Still, I kept looking. I plodded like an idiot through the driving rain. I sloshed from house to house. I picked my way through the mud outside a succession of rickety wooden stalls where the people huddled sensibly inside. I dripped water all over the floor of a small dark restaurant where the patrons crouched in the shadows by a smoking fire. I called in at Ranomafana's only hotel. But nobody had seen Benjamin Hery.

Finally, after about forty minutes of fruitless search, I received a promising tip. A stranger emerged through the veils of rain to tell me he had seen a car, a Peugeot, parked at the edge of a field on the outskirts of town. Could it be . . . ?

It was. Benjamin and three newfound companions had crowded out of the rain and into the Peugeot, along with what had started out as a copious supply of Malagasy rum. When a sopping wet, very muddy, and somewhat angry Canadian journalist suddenly materialized outside his window to announce that it was time to drive back down to Fianarantsoa, Benjamin could not conceal his dismay. It turned out that he had planned a nocturnal excursion to a local cockfight and had amorous designs on a young Ranomafana woman who had returned his smile.

"*Maintenant* . . . ?" he moaned, as his three acquaintances fled on silent feet into the pelting downpour. In the first place, he protested, it was getting dark. In the second place, the lofty route over the mountains — treacherous at best — would now be obscured by dense clouds. Besides, he insisted, we had to think about the *dahalo*.

"The *dahalo* . . . ?"

"The robbers," Benjamin said. He meant the robbers who terrorized this neck of the Malagasy woods, armed with Kalashnikov automatic rifles. They'd murdered seven tourists just the other day, along with a Malagasy driver. Didn't I know about that?

In fact, I didn't know about that. Nor did I particularly believe it. Besides, I was determined to get back to Fianarantsoa that evening, partly because every room at the sole hotel in Ranomafana had been booked for the night — an almost unheard-of occurrence. (For some reason, just about the entire staff of the embassy in Madagascar of the People's Republic of China was staying there.) Still, in my hurry to leave, I failed to consider another very good argument against our departing Ranomafana just now. The truth was that Benjamin, my driver, had rendered himself profoundly drunk.

I don't know why I overlooked his condition at first, but it became obvious about half an hour later, high on a dark and perilous mountain road, when Benjamin suddenly jerked the steering wheel to the right for the umpteenth time, narrowly averting a plunge over the edge of another invisible precipice. He pulled his head back in through the driver's window, and the car lurched to a halt. Thick waves of fog swirled around the headlights, and the only sound was the faint rumble of the car's engine, vibrating through the darkness. Finally, Benjamin — my guide, my driver, my only hope of getting safely back to Fianarantsoa — spoke to me. He had a question. There was something he wanted to know.

"Where are we?" he asked.

At first, I said nothing. Finally, I turned to look at Benjamin. I simply repeated his words. "Where *are* we . . . ?"

Benjamin nodded.

"*You*," I said, "are asking *me*?"

He nodded again.

"Where *are* we . . . ?"

Another nod.

"You mean, you *don't know?*"

He shrugged. After a moment, he shrugged again.

A long and rather trying conversation ensued, after which Benjamin put the car back in gear, and we crawled ahead through the darkness. After another considerable period of silence, Benjamin said that he was sorry. Then he said it again. And again. He would not stop saying it. "*Je suis desolé,*" he repeated. "Frankly," he added. "From the bottom of my heart," he said. "A thousand times," he insisted. "Sincerely." There was a long pause, then Benjamin peered at me through the inky darkness. "Are you still mad at me?"

I cleared my throat. I had nothing to say.

Benjamin drove on, creeping forward through the waves of fog that obscured the mountain road. For all either of us knew, we had completely lost our way, but there was no choice except to press ahead. Eventually, Benjamin forgot about being sorry and began to rail against government corruption. Each time he reached a new peak of rhetorical indignation, he forgot to drive — and the car stalled. "*Ça ne marche pas!*" he exclaimed at one point. "*Ça ne marche pas!*" He meant the government's abuses of its authority, but he might as well have been referring to the car. It wasn't going anywhere either.

"*You are drunk,*" I said. I drew out each word, as though sharpening a knife.

Benjamin nodded sadly in the darkness. "It's true," he said. "That's what bothers me most. That's the unhappiest part."

In the end, I decided to forgive him, and Benjamin promptly brightened — until he remembered the *dahalo*. The robbers. As he coaxed the Peugeot through the night, Benjamin embarked on a lurid chronicle of the *dahalo's* crimes and the sophistication of their arms. He spoke fearfully, as though he expected to see them leaping onto the road in front of the car at any moment — hundreds of them, in outlandish costumes, all barrels blazing. "We should never have left Ranomafana!" he swore. "*Jamais! Jamais!*"

In fact, I was starting to worry a little about the *dahalo* myself. Mostly, however, I was thinking about Chez Papillon. If we hurried, I thought, we might just make it back in time for dinner. I peered ahead into the impenetrable black fog, still as thick as ever, maybe thicker. "I think it's clearing up," I said. "Could we go just a little faster?"

Benjamin tightened his grip on the wheel and squinted into the gloom. He kept to a stately pace. A half hour crept past, and I was still thinking about Chez Papillon. Specifically, I was thinking about lobster. More specifically, grilled lobster. *Avec pommes allumettes.* And perhaps a small salad. But first — *les potages. La bisque d'écrevisses du chef au crouton, peut-être?* Well, that sounded good. *Et du vin?* Hmm. I'd say a half-bottle of dry white Lazan'i Betsileo . . .

I must have been dreaming, for it was still impossibly dark, and I was still in a car — but now it really did seem that the fog was clearing. Miraculously, Benjamin had found the paved two-lane *route nationale* that runs south from Antsirabe to Fianarantsoa. The *dahalo* hadn't bothered us yet, and it seemed — as we sailed through the night toward Fianarantsoa — that they had missed their chance. Still, there were other perils yet to be faced. I was thinking about lobster, but Benjamin didn't seem to be thinking about anything at all. Twice, he hit turns at extreme speed and almost sent us cartwheeling off into the dark, mysterious domain that is revered by the Malagasy as a place where wise spirits dwell, a realm celebrated in the elaborate and erotically carved monuments that crowd Madagascar's famous cemeteries.

I asked Benjamin to slow down, and he spent the rest of the drive back to town wallowing in an orgy of self-recrimination and remorse. Finally, we sputtered into Fianarantsoa. We pulled up outside l'Hôtel Moderne du Betsileo, which housed Louis Papillon's renowned restaurant. I paid Benjamin what I owed him. Still overflowing with apologies, he shifted into first gear, released the clutch of his father's quarter-century-old Peugeot, and rolled away into the deep Malagasy night, never to be seen or heard from again — or at least not by me.

I felt oddly saddened to watch him go, but Benjamin Hery was not why I had come to Madagascar. Muddy and matted, I stumbled into the hotel's brightly lit reception area and bar, where Emile the headwaiter greeted me in his burgundy jacket and blue rubber sandals. He told me I had time to shower before dinner and promised that he would have a table ready for me when I came down. And so he did.

Banket 6,
Harare 4

WHEN I LIVED IN AFRICA, I was based in Harare, the capital of Zimbabwe. At the time of my arrival there, early on a Saturday morning in 1987 towards the end of the gorgeous Zimbabwean winter, I didn't really know what to expect. I had never been to Africa before. In general, I thought I would find a small, independent, black-ruled southern African state, and that was what I did find. But I also found something else, something very different — an even smaller state-within-a-state that was almost exclusively white. And that was not what I had expected at all.

Zimbabwe in those days was the youngest of the independent countries of southern Africa. It had emerged in 1980 from the ashes of the renegade republic of Rhodesia, formerly a British colony and long a pariah state. In 1963, the colony's northern half had been granted independence from British rule and so became a black-governed country called Zambia. But the southern half rejected majority rule — or at least its white settlers did — and instead issued a Unilateral Declaration of Independence, or UDI. Thus was born the renegade republic of Rhodesia, an international outcast, where maybe 300,000 whites held sway over some eight million blacks.

For nearly two decades, the whites managed to hold out. Their illegal regime survived in spite of international economic sanctions, withering diplomatic pressure, and a brutal bush war waged by two black guerrilla armies. But that small defiant rump of Rhodesian whites could not hang on forever. Finally, in 1980, the old Rhodesia was buried beneath the dun and olive veld, and Zimbabwe was born from the ashes — an independent state under black majority rule.

A lot of the whites left, fled to South Africa or Britain or Australia. But a considerable number remained, and for the most part they made a good fist of their new circumstances. Granted, they had help from the country's black people, who resisted the temptation to embark on a campaign of reprisals or recrimination. Instead, by the late 1980s, Zimbabwe had become a small miracle of tolerance and civility, at least in the sense that people were no longer killing each other on grounds of their race. In this obstreperous world, that was no minor accomplishment.

But this spirit of tolerance did not mean that white people and black people actually had much to do with each other as human beings. It didn't mean that they lived in the same neighbourhoods, or patronized the same restaurants, or belonged to the same sports clubs, or followed the same sports, or went over to each other's houses for dinner, or had much to say to each other on the rare and stilted occasions when they did find themselves forced to converse as "equals". It didn't mean, on the whole, that whites and blacks even *liked* each other very much. Some did. A lot did not.

Those whites who opted to remain in Zimbabwe did so thanks in large measure to a speech — "The Speech", in white Zimbabwean parlance — delivered by the new black leader, Robert Mugabe, in March, 1980. Previously excoriated by whites as a murderer, a Communist, and a terrorist, Mugabe promised reconciliation and peace. And he kept his word. When the war ended, so did the killing.

"He was arch enemy number one a few weeks before," a man named John Brown once told me. He was a wealthy white farmer who had served as a major in the territorial army during the fighting. "We were out to kill him. If we could have pinned his ears to a plank, we would have. Thank God we didn't."

Thank God indeed, for it turned out that life in the new Zimbabwe was to unfold much as it had in the old Rhodesia, amid a perpetual *son et lumière* of flowering trees, birdsong, vaulting skies, and nearly relentless sunshine. Borne upon a faint breeze, the scent of wood smoke drifted through the broad, tree-walled avenues of Harare, accompanied by the occasional tremor of distant drums.

At least for whites, the country remained what it had long been — a sort of African scale model of heaven, a heaven carefully tailored to suit a particularly fastidious English sensibility. Newcomers to Harare are invariably struck by what a green and pleasant city it is. Things work, and when they break they are promptly fixed. Almost everyone obeys the traffic signals — called "robots" here — and that's a rarity in Africa, where the traffic signals almost never function. In Zimbabwe, they do.

City parks in Harare and elsewhere are kept scrupulously clean, each a symphony of flowers and flowering trees. When I lived there, mail was delivered six days a week, often the same day it was posted. Even the private couriers

— earnest-looking men mounted on bicycles or on putt-putting motor scooters — were dressed in jackets and ties. Like most people in Zimbabwe, they went about their business with a solemn and dignified air.

Could this be *Africa*, the most distressed and troubled continent on earth? It was indeed, but it was not the Africa I had expected to find when I arrived in Zimbabwe in 1987 to begin work as a newspaper correspondent. What I found, in a lot of ways, was *Rhodesia*.

At times, it seemed that almost nothing in the country had changed with the advent of majority rule. One Sunday afternoon, I headed out to a place called Thornpark Grounds just outside Harare. Typically, it was a gorgeous day, another brilliant afternoon on the highveld in winter. The sun beat down from a vivid blue sky, as it nearly always does in mile-high Mashonaland, and there was an edge of coolness to the sparkling air. Meanwhile, that same air was split by the thunder of galloping hoofbeats, as teams from the capital and nearby Banket joined in battle for the national polo title.

Occasionally, one of the players broke from the action and aimed his huffing, foam-flecked pony toward a grove of lemon trees at the perimeter of the field. "C'mon! C'mon, man!" he'd shout toward one of the black grooms waiting on the sidelines with spare mounts saddled, bandaged, and ready. The rider leapt from one spent pony, vaulted aboard a spare. Immediately, he dug his heels into a fresh pair of flanks and galloped back towards the fray.

With their mallets aloft, the players wheeled and raced their ponies back and forth all afternoon, chasing a small white ball across the hard-packed field and kicking up waves of reddish dust. The spectators sipped sundowners on the clubhouse stands or lounged in deckchairs by their cars. Each time a goal was scored, a cheer or a smattering of groans rose from the crowd — and a thin black man in white overalls snapped to attention. He trotted out from the end zone to thrust a bright red flag into the cool African air.

That idyllic imperial scene — the colonial elite at its leisure — might easily have dated from a half-century earlier, when Britain still ruled Rhodesia, and a close-knit compact of wealthy white Rhodesians did pretty much as they pleased. It was astonishing to think that this particular championship polo match — in which Banket finally prevailed, six to four — was played almost a decade after Zimbabwe was born, following its brutal independence war.

It was as if nothing, or almost nothing, had changed. Demographically, this new country called Zimbabwe was pretty much the same as Rhodesia had been. The vast majority of its people were black, divided into two main tribal groups, the Shona and the much less numerous Ndebele. The number of whites had fallen — from a high of about 300,000 to fewer than 100,000 — but they remained the economic elite.

A decade after independence, white and black Zimbabweans — or Zims, as they are known — still dwelled in almost completely separate worlds. In Harare, as in other Zimbabwean cities, whites reside for the most part in rambling suburbs that ring the commercial centre — lush, spacious neighourhoods with tall stucco walls, elegant white-washed bungalows, gleaming luxury sedans, sparkling swimming pools, and private tennis courts, all set amid spire-like cypresses, scarlet poinsettias, and groves of tulip trees, flamboyants, and purple jacarandas. Sprays of bougainvillea cascade almost everywhere, spilling over white-washed walls like iridescent waterfalls, the blossoms so brilliant you almost have to squint to look at them.

The white suburbs usually bear quaint names imported from England: Mount Pleasant or Avondale or Highlands; and each has its own shopping mall and usually a private sports club, where cricket, tennis, rugby, lawn bowling, field hockey, and especially golf are the pastimes of preference.

With their loss of direct political power at independence, and the abolition in 1987 of the twenty seats that had been reserved for their race in the House of Assembly, most white Zimbabweans retreated from active politics, attending instead to homes, businesses, and sports, where life remained much as it was. In some ways, life was even better, for there was no more war. And they enjoyed amenities you might not have expected, such as some decent domestic wines — each year, they flew the first bottles of Mukuyu Nouveau down to the capital in hot-air balloons. Of course, Zimbabwe is a former British colony, so its culinary accomplishments lag behind those of, let's say, a Madagascar or a Senegal, both former French possessions. But still, Harare has some intriguing restaurants — Greek, Indian, Italian, French. For fast food, there are several Wimpy's hamburger outlets and lots of fish-and-chips stalls. There's a Woolworth's store. It's a pretty good movie town too, with several modern cinemas that show first-run films on wide screens. There's even an annual film festival, and occasionally you could find a late-night special screening of *The Rocky Horror Picture Show.*

Plus, you got Africa. The people, the landscape, the wildlife, the weather. Almost every morning, a cool but vivid sun swelled above the bauhinea trees in my yard. All day, the hugest blue skies imaginable sprawled overhead, bigger skies than we ever have in central Canada. The vastness of the heavens above southern Africa may be an illusion — it probably has to do with the tendency of the clouds in that part of the world to form extremely high up in the atmosphere — but it works. By late afternoon, the landscape turned to patterns of emerald and bronze until, sharp at seven, the sun sank below the highveld. Darkness toppled like a weight, and the Milky Way shattered the sky — a dense archway of light plunging through the centre of the heavens. During the Harare winter, the nights got bloody cold. There'd be a fire inside, in the living room. I'd put Verdi or Puccini on the record player, stroll out onto the verandah, and just stand there, drinking in the winter air. The poinsettia in the garden would be in brilliant scarlet blossom — and yet I could see my breath! You could have fallen in love with Zimbabwe for the weather alone.

But there were troubles, too. After the war ended in 1980, Zimbabwe's two black groups stopped fighting against their common white-skinned enemy and followed the grim rule of post-colonial African politics. They started fighting against each other. That is, they went back to fighting against each other.

Conflict between the two groups — the Ndebele and the Shona — was actually nothing new. It dated all the way back to the 1830s, when the Ndebele people, an offshoot of the warlike Zulus to the south, invaded what is now southwestern Zimbabwe under a chief named Mzilikazi. They overthrew the agrarian Shona people of the region and set up their capital near what is now Bulawayo, Zimbabwe's

second-largest city. Currently a handsome town of flowering trees and broad avenues — broader even than Harare's
— Bulawayo did not have an auspicious beginning. Its name
means "place of slaughter" in Sindebele.

Sixty years after the Ndebele invasion, the British turned
up. In 1893, the Ndebele made a desperate stand against the
European advance. They were led by Lobengula, the son of
Mzilikazi, but they lost and were forced to surrender their
land. It was not until Zimbabwean independence almost
ninety years later that the Shona and the Ndebele regained
formal control of their lands, or the lands they had once
competed for.

But in Matabeleland, which is where the Ndebele mainly
dwell, the troubles did not stop with independence. The
race war was over, but the tribal conflict went on. No one
really knows how many people died in political violence in
Matabeleland after 1980. Certainly, there was nothing
remotely approaching the bloodbaths that have inundated
other African countries in recent years — the hundreds of
thousands murdered in Rwanda, Uganda, or Mozambique.
By comparison, the Zimbabwean death toll seems downright puny, almost benign. Maybe one thousand people
were killed in all, over about eight years. It may not seem
like much by some standards, but it got people's attention in
Matabeleland.

Most of these killings were the work of so-called "dissidents" — bands of marauding robbers and murderers who
roamed southwestern Zimbabwe after the war. The new
Zimbabwean government, dominated by the Shona,
charged that the "dissidents" were Ndebele warriors, tied to
PF-ZAPU, the one-time rebel army led by a septuagenarian

independence hero named Joshua Nkomo. But at least some
of the killings were the work of government troops — the
infamous Fifth Brigade of the Zimbabwean Army, trained
by North Korea and unleashed in Matabeleland in 1982 in a
ham-fisted effort to quell the troubles. In 1985, amid
mounting evidence of bloodshed and a wave of international protest, Mugabe withdrew the Fifth Brigade. The
North Korean trainers were sent packing, and the troops
were reschooled by British personnel.

But the "dissidents" remained. A good deal of what they
did — the mutilation of their victims, for example, or the
murder of more than seventy white commercial farmers in
only a few years — seemed calculated to wreak as much
political and economic havoc as possible. Of course, most of
the people who ended up dying were black but, as is usually
the case, it was the white victims who seemed to get most of
the attention. On the other hand, although they constituted
only a small fraction of the victims of Matabeleland's troubles,
whites were by no means incidental to the carnage. They
were targets, too. In fact, in proportion to their small population, the death rate among whites was six or seven times
higher than the corresponding figure among blacks.

Near the height of the troubles, I drove out to Bulawayo
to have a look. Just three months earlier, at a place called
Esigodini not far south of Bulawayo, sixteen white members
of a missionary farming community had been hacked to
death one night, a slaughter apparently committed by a
group of dissidents led by one Morgan Nsingo. It was by far
the worst spasm of inter-racial bloodshed since Zimbabwean
independence. Still, it would be a mistake to interpret the
killings at Esigodini — or the slaying of other whites in

Matabeleland — as simply a matter of blacks running amok and slaying their former colonial masters.

Underneath, the carnage was really a matter of economics. The killers at Esigodini, for example, were evidently recruited by a group of peasants who'd been squatting on land owned by the Christian mission. The peasants became incensed when the government stepped in and ordered them off. This was a fairly common occurrence, because squatting was a problem all over Zimbabwe. But in Matabeleland the government's response was seen as further confirmation of tribal injustice — Ndebele people being mistreated by the majority Shona. After all, the Shona controlled the government. Whites became a target for outrage because whites still owned the best land.

One weekday morning, I drove west towards the Botswana border, in order to visit a cattle farmer named Ted Kirby, whose name I'd got from some friends in Bulawayo. He lived about an hour's drive outside the city and turned out to be a stocky, articulate, and stubborn man, sixty-three years old, with pale blue eyes, a leathery tan, and a wiry brush of short-cropped grey hair. He told me he'd come out to Africa after the Second World War and had been farming in Matabeleland since 1950. He said he was determined to stick it out, never mind the dangers. Maybe there wasn't much choice. "Look at it," he said. "I don't want to move. What are our opportunities? If we got so we wanted to move, I shouldn't imagine that anyone else would want to come here."

No doubt he was right, but that hadn't stopped others from moving. In 1980 — the year of Zimbabwean independence — there were 730 commercial farming operations in

Matabeleland, almost all of them run by whites. By 1988, only 390 were left, and the number continued to fall. "We are losing farmers," said Kirby. "There is a steady drain."

Relaxing that morning in the modest sun room of his white stucco farmhouse, sipping a mid-morning coffee and gazing out at a Brazilian candle-nut tree in the garden, Kirby recited the litany of bloodshed and havoc that he and other farmers had weathered in only the previous eight months.

Not twenty kilometres away, he said, John Norval had been murdered. Soon after that, Brian Hubbard met the same fate. Then there was the case of Johann Kreidl and his wife Maria. Both were badly injured in an ambush; she took a bullet in the head; their guard was killed. Not far from Kirby's place, Andy Macdonald was murdered. Four other farmers were shot dead over at the Somabhula Club. Up north, Jay Dabbs went down in an ambush. Four black farmers were fatally shot at Bambezi. A militia guard was killed on the Plumtree Road, just about where Peter Grant lost both a guard and his foreman in another attack. David Conolly was ambushed on the Figtree Road but somehow got away. And then, of course, there were the sixteen dead at Esigodini.

"There've been plenty," Kirby mused. He stroked his chin and nodded with grim satisfaction at this bullet-riddled chronology. His manner seemed incongruous for only a moment, and then I understood. After all, he was alive to tell the tale.

Now, wherever he went, Kirby carried a firearm — either a West German G-3 automatic rifle or an Israeli Uzi submachine gun. If he travelled any real distance — say, on a tour of his two properties — he took along a pair of bodyguards, members of Zimbabwe's People's Militia, both armed with G-3s. "I think it would be stupid to take any risks, however slight."

Normally, the dissidents chose their targets with some care. They attacked farmers when they were at their most vulnerable — not in their homes, but along roads or at cattle-dips or watering holes. Another problem was the farmers' sheer physical isolation. Between Kirby's place and Bulawayo — sixty kilometres to the east — there was only one other farm and a Seventh Day Adventist mission. To the west, there was nothing but scrub forest most of the way to the border with Botswana. "That is our problem," Kirby said. "We are a very sparsely populated community."

Still, this was where Kirby had chosen to live out his days. His wife, Jean, had never really known much else. She was born in Matabeleland and had dwelled on its white-owned farmland all her life. "One does worry, obviously," she reflected as she went about her morning chores. "I suppose, in the back of your mind, it's always there."

That said, she left off what she was doing — pickling onions, in this case — and joined her husband and me as we strolled outside into the cascading sunshine for a look around. A bit later, she excused herself, saying she had some errands to run. Kirby and I watched her climb into an old Land Rover — that boxy and dented icon of imperial Africa. She looked positively jaunty at the wheel, in her print dress and her bright yellow sunhat. With a smile and a wave, she drove off into the Matabeleland sunshine, headed for town. Hunched in the seat behind her, she had a paramilitary guard, clad in khaki; he clutched a G-3 automatic rifle between his knees.

Then, almost like magic, peace came to Matabeleland.

The country's two feuding political parties — representing Zimbabwe's two main tribal groups — abruptly agreed to unite, and the troubles were over. True, for the minority Ndebele, the unity accord was more a hostile take-over than a love match. But if peace was to be the criterion for success, then it worked. The dissidents straggled in from the bush to accept a government amnesty, and the carnage ended. It turned out that there had been only 113 of them, which just goes to show that you don't need many men, and you don't need many guns, to cause a lot of trouble or to raise a flood tide of grief.

The end of the killing in Matabeleland did not mean that all of Zimbabwe's worries were over. Others were worsening. Efforts to extend public services to the black masses had inevitably strained the country's infrastructure and its finances. The economy was holding up better than those of most other newly independent African states — which isn't saying much — but it was barely growing, and the country was desperate for foreign currency.

Just as bad, or worse, tens of thousands of graduates were pouring out of the high schools each year, but there were no jobs to be had. Delinquency and crime were going up fast. The horror of AIDS was spreading down from central and east Africa. Corruption was stealing its way through the body politic. And, after almost a decade in power, the government of Robert Mugabe was becoming indolent and brittle — pretty much the normal pattern in post-colonial Africa, where *le gran chef* wins power, grows old, and refuses to budge.

For white Zimbabweans, the main impact of these difficulties was a curtailment of luxuries, and a dimming of confidence, rather than real hardship. A tall socio-economic barrier kept them insulated from most of their country's troubles, as well as from its 8.5 million blacks. Few people talked about that barrier, or at least not in plain language. Instead, they used a welter of almost comic euphemisms. For example, Harare's mainly white neighbourhoods are invariably referred to as the *low-density* suburbs. Meanwhile, the vast and crowded black settlements outside the city are called the *high-density* suburbs.

These antiseptic terms cannot really mask the vast economic, social, and especially racial differences that separate an Avondale or a Mount Pleasant from a Chitungwiza, the largest of the black communities that border Harare. In many ways, Chitungwiza bears the same relationship to Harare that Soweto — the most notorious of the black townships of South Africa — has to Johannesburg. It is a dormitory community, supplying cheap black labour that conveniently disappears when evening falls. It is mostly poor, with few services or recreational facilities. It generates very few jobs of its own.

On the other hand, it would be misleading to portray Chitungwiza as a place of unrelieved or even prevailing squalor. While modest, most of the houses are carefully maintained and sport some proud domestic flourishes — a pair of flower boxes or a set of fancy gates. The streets are mainly tidy, well-lit, and dotted with pedestrians going about their business with dignity and purpose.

Chitungwiza is a part of Africa, of course, and those who live there are Africans, but they are urbanized Africans, city-dwellers. They are among the minority of their people who have entered the modern world of wage-labour, rent payments, electrified appliances, TV sets, and bank loans. Such people typically dwell in two cultural realms at once, caught between the past and the future, with one foot in the city and another in the old Africa, the still mysterious continent that unfolds beyond the cities.

You don't have to drive far from either Chitungwiza or Mount Pleasant — a half-hour will do — to go back centuries in time, to something closer to traditional Africa, where the people continue to dwell in kraals of mud-and-wattle rondavels with roofs of thatched grass. These areas are known nowadays as "the communal lands", where the people scrabble for their keep. Those who live here may be poor, but their villages have an air of almost timeless order. The earthen yards around each house are swept scrupulously clean, and the afternoon silence is broken only by scattered birdsong, the bleating of goats, and the steady thump that women make as they grind corn into meal with great wooden mortars and pestles that seem themselves to be centuries old.

The world in which these women dwell is a very different country — a different territory of the mind and of the spirit — from the rambling green neighbourhoods occupied by Zimbabwe's whites. After nearly a decade of political independence, I found it astonishing to stand back and contemplate the huge rifts that divided whites and blacks in Zimbabwe still. They really were foreigners to each other, strangers in a common land.

'That's
Africa, Pal'

I NABBED A CAR THIEF in Zimbabwe once, and the experience taught me a sobering lesson about being white in a black country. The thing was, I managed to catch that thief — if catch is the word — for two reasons only. He was black. And I was white.

I was working in my office that morning, in the house where I lived. This was in the Avenues, an old Harare neighbourhood that is the only part of the city where whites and blacks live side-by-side in substantial numbers. My house was a small white-stucco bungalow that had handsome wooden floors and wooden-framed windows with copper fittings and a working fireplace — all but essential in wintertime on the highveld of Zimbabwe. The kitchen and dining area were brightly lit, open to each other, and had floors of dark polished stone. Early in the day, the cool morning and its vivid light poured inside, like watercolour paints. At night, the kitchen area made a superb starting place for parties.

An assortment of lichee, mango, avocado, and white-blossomed bauhinea trees flourished in the yard outside the house, not to mention a row of poinsettia shrubs and showers of iridescent bougainvillea that washed over the walls.

The house itself had been built in the early years of this century, in a style that some jokingly refer to as Rhodesian Gothic. It was my first house, and I ache now whenever I think of it.

That morning — the morning I caught a car thief — I noticed some movement out of the corner of my eye, something moving past my window through the front yard. I looked up and saw a man wandering around under the lichee tree. I got to my feet and called to him from the window. The fellow swung around, eyes wide. He wore a dark, ill-fitting jacket, baggy pants, an old fedora. He looked like any of the dozens of sombre unemployed men you'd see any day ambling around Harare's wide avenues, under the flowering trees. Just now, he was evidently both disoriented and afraid. I asked him what he was doing in my yard. He wouldn't say. He just kept repeating that he meant me no harm. If I would just let him go, he would be on his way. "Please, *baas*," he implored. "Please, *baas*."

"No," I told him. "You just stay right there. I'll be right out. I want to talk to you. Stay right there."

What is truly amazing is that the fellow actually *did what I said*. It must have taken me a full minute to walk to the back of the house, head outdoors, and then march around to the front again — and there he was. He hadn't run away. Before long, a pair of Zimbabwean police happened by. They looked through the gates and asked who this fellow was. One thing led to another, and the man was taken off in one of his country's small blue police cars. It turned out that he was a car thief. He was on the run from the law, and he'd jumped over the wall at the back of my place and raced around to the front.

Obviously, he should have kept on going. As soon as I called to him from the window, he should have been over that front wall and gone. Was he just slow-witted? I don't think so. This was a young black man, probably just up from the countryside, not sophisticated at all — and I was white. By definition, I had power. He probably thought I had powers that were beyond his comprehension. So he played it safe. He did what I told him to do, and I guess he ended up by going to jail.

Paul Theroux once wrote, "The realization that he is a white in a black country, and respected for it, is the turning-point in the expatriate's career. He can either forget it, or capitalize on it. Most choose the latter."

Respected for being white? That is only the half of it. If white people are assumed to be worth respecting simply because they are white, then where does that leave black people? It does not leave them in the low-density suburbs of Harare, for one thing. In neighbourhoods such as Mount Pleasant or Highlands, you almost never saw a black face that didn't belong to a servant or a labourer or a postman.

A black Zimbabwean woman I knew was one of the rare exceptions. She was the wife of a senior civil servant, and they lived in one of Harare's affluent, low-density communities. She once told me about what happened to her one morning when she went around to greet some new neighbours. They were whites and were just moving into a house up the street. Naturally, there was considerable commotion at their house that day, what with the movers wrestling furniture inside and gaggles of tradesmen doing odd jobs — workers hammering, men in overalls bustling about. Amid the dust and clamour, the new mistress of the house caught sight of my friend, a black woman, striding along the garden walkway and up onto the front terrace. The woman of the house promptly put up her hands and rushed forward. "No, no!" she cried out. "I've got no work for you. Go away!"

The woman who told me this story promptly broke into laughter. She didn't seem to harbour any grudge or, if she did, she managed to hide those feelings from me. She was a confident, exuberant woman — it was probably no easy matter to depress or discourage her. Besides, black Zimbabweans in those days could always console themselves with the thought that, whatever prejudices they faced in their own country, it was worse in South Africa.

Whenever I travelled to South Africa, I would encounter the harshest racial attitudes you can imagine. I didn't have to search for them. They were out there, on display. And it wasn't their harshness that I found surprising. Just the opposite. It was their almost endearing ingenuousness. It was the sincerity, the lack of guile, the air of gentility and grace, with which people would heap scorn upon their fellows. That, for me, was a surprise.

The first time I visited South Africa, I flew down to Johannesburg from Harare with only a twelve-hour visa stamped in my passport. That was all the time that the South African ministry of home affairs would allow me. In those twelve hours, I was supposed to take possession of a new car, which I had already purchased over the phone, and then drive the vehicle up to the Zimbabwean border at Beitbridge, high in the Transvaal. The border would close at six p.m., which meant that it would be quite impossible for me to get there in time to cross out of South Africa before my visa expired. I had already explained this problem over the phone to the nice woman at home affairs. "You're right," she said.

I asked if my visa could be extended to twenty-four hours.

"No," she said.

So, here I was — my first time in South Africa. I cleared immigration and caught a taxi that carried me from the Jan Smuts Airport straight around to Fosset's Garage in Kempton Park. I was greeted by the same sales agent I had dealt with on the phone from Montreal, several weeks earlier, when I had arranged to purchase the car, a Nissan Langley. Later that morning, the agent — a pinch-nosed Afrikaner with a some-what oily and ingratiating personality—would take me out to get my ownership papers stamped at a government office. He was a married man, he told me as he drove. "But . . . " He reached over and popped open the glove compartment. He produced several photographs of someone he identified as his new mistress, a frail white girl with stringy black hair and a dazed expression, who looked about seventeen. She was posed on a bed in a pink nightie, clutching a large teddy bear.

But that was later. Right now, the agent announced that the owner of the dealership wanted to meet me. Apparently, this was the first time that Fosset's Garage had sold an automobile over the telephone to a Canadian newspaper correspondent. So we climbed a flight of stairs and knocked at the door of the owner's office and announced our business. A voice called on us to enter, and we pushed open the door.

Immediately, I encountered a hearty Afrikaner gentleman of a venerable age. He had sleek white hair, a face like a rumpled sheet, and the croaking voice of a life-long investor in the tobacco industry. He strode around from his desk and took my hand in a firm grip. He looked me straight in the eye. "I'm a racialist," he announced. These were the first words he spoke. He paused for effect and then added, "*I love blacks.*"

I didn't know what to say. Was I supposed to clap? Cheer? *Kneel . . .*? I just looked at him.

The man smiled and told me I wasn't to believe all the terrible things I might have heard about his country. He took me by the arm and led me from his office, down the stairs, and out towards the service bay. "Come with me," he said. "I want to introduce you to some of my blacks."

The man's use of the possessive pronoun in this context — "*my* blacks" — had an immediate resonance for me. It reminded me of something I'd heard before. This was just the way that wealthy Salvadorans referred to the rural poor in their country. *Nuestro campesino*, they would say. *Our* peasantry.

As we walked out to the service area, the owner of Fosset's Garage enthused about what "wonderful people" blacks were and how I, too, might learn to love them if only I gave them a chance. "They're like my children," he said. "They treat me like a father."

We strolled around the service bay for a time, meeting sundry black people in grimy coveralls. Then the owner of Fosset's Garage in Kempton Park took me aside and lowered his voice for about the first time since I'd met him. "But there is one thing you must know about black people," he counselled me. "If you hire a black man to do a job for you, and you say you will pay him ten rand, then you must pay him the ten rand. If he does a bad job, and you pay him only eight rand, then you have broken your word. You have stolen his money. And he will kill you. So, you must pay him the ten rand." Here, the man shrugged and smiled. "Oh, you can give him a cuff," he allowed. "You can give him a hiding. But you must pay him the ten rand."

On subsequent visits to South Africa, I ran into other whites who spoke with the same absence of guile about their racial feelings. A white merchant in the Transvaal town of Carltonville — a man who undoubtedly would consider himself a progressive on the "native question" — once told me he was actually in favour of reforming his country's apartheid laws. Why was that, I asked him. He narrowed his eyes and peered at me. "We've got to civilize the buggers," he said.

Maybe these whites lived lives of such intellectual isolation that they didn't hear the clanging sound that their voices made when they spoke this way. And they *were* isolated. One thing you could say with confidence about white South Africans during the long, dark years of apartheid was that they didn't get out much. They were confined to their own cultural echo chambers, insulated from the intellectual cross-currents of the larger world both by their country's remote location and by its politics.

I found myself in the far south of South Africa once, in Cape Town, in the early winter. I planned to leave the country that morning, on a flight to Johannesburg and then a connection to Harare. The taxi driver on my trip out to the airport was a chatty, good-hearted white woman in her late thirties. She told me she'd never lived anywhere but South Africa. She'd never even been on an airplane. That morning, as is often the case in Cape Town in winter, it was cold and rainy. Dense low clouds sagged overhead, heavy as boulders. When we got to the airport, the woman turned to me and asked how I was going to manage to fly anywhere that day. With all these clouds, how was the pilot going to be able to see where he was going?

At first, I just looked at her. I couldn't make out what she was asking. Then I understood. I explained to her that the airplane was going to fly *above* the clouds, that it would be sunny up there and the pilot would be able to see a good long way.

The idea seemed to break upon her with the force of a revelation. Her face lit up. To fly *above* the clouds. To fly *above* the rain. Clearly, she had never contemplated such a thing before. Amazed, she just shook her head. It had never occurred to her until this very moment that there was a place up there where the weather was different — where maybe more than the weather was different — from this place down here.

Zimbabwe wasn't perfect, but it *was* different. Only once during my years in Zimbabwe did I encounter a white person who openly scorned blacks, who spoke of them with the sort of naive and unprovoked abandon that you so commonly heard in South Africa. I'm sure there are many white Zims, then and now, who speak this way in private, among themselves — I *know* there are — but Troy Williamson didn't seem to care who heard him. He was the guide on a canoe trip I once took down the Zambezi River through the Mana Pools National Park.

East of Lake Kariba, the Zambezi drifts through a yawning canyon, an extension of Africa's Great Rift Valley. The land teems with wildlife, including Zimbabwe's largest concentrations of lions and black rhinoceroses. The furrowed wall of the Zambia escarpment towers to the north beneath a soaring dome of blue. Great African elephants heave above the shore, atop low sandbank cliffs, their ears billowing like sails. For a blur of sun-soaked days, we drifted east with the current towards Mozambique, past shiny archipelagos of hippopotami. On the shore, we saw herds of scowling Cape buffalo, small bands of grazing zebra, cantering herds of antelope. We counted at least half a dozen lions, two of them patiently guarding the gutted carcass of a hippo sprawled beside a tributary stream.

At night, aggrieved hyenas skulked near our tents and howled at their gods before trotting away on silent paws. By day, we paddled beneath a soaring canopy of birds; like an endless squadron of kites and streamers, they darted and shimmered above us. This was the parched end of the dry season — not an especially good time for bird-watching — yet we counted ninety-eight species in only a few days. Or, I should say, Williamson did. He helped us identify an almost perpetual aerial circus of darters, skimmers, rollers, bee-eaters, cormorants, egrets, eagles, and huge marabou storks that wallowed overhead like feathered jumbo jets stacked in holding patterns above imaginary airports.

Williamson was an impressive figure in many ways. He was a young Zimbabwean with flowing blond locks, a deep resonant voice, and considerable self-assurance. He certainly possessed an impressive stock of bush-lore. One afternoon, we beached our canoes in order to have a picnic lunch on the shore. Presently, an elderly, curious, and no doubt hungry elephant thudded over and began to engage in obviously threatening behaviour, shaking his head, hurling his trunk, and stamping towards us in mock charges that became progressively more like the real thing. Williamson sent us down to the canoes and remained behind to deal with the elephant. He calmly removed his shoes, and chased the animal off by clapping the heels together. The sound drove the elephant crazy, and away he went, tail literally tucked between his legs.

There'd been another time — not on our trip, but a year or so earlier — when a lion had attacked a party of canoeists while they slept on the shore of the Zambezi one night. The beast was actually dragging one of the party off in her sleeping bag. Williamson was the guide on that occasion, too, and he somehow managed to rescue the woman and drive the lion away. I'd read an article about it at the time, in the Harare *Herald*.

This was a young man of considerable courage, a man who knew his way in the wilds. But he also harboured some shockingly brutish views about black Africans. When you totted them up, I don't suppose that his ideas were really all that unusual. You will find racists just about anywhere, of course. But I was struck by Williamson's willingness, even his eagerness, to vent his prejudices out loud and at large, among people he barely knew.

The problem came to a head one night after dinner as we gathered by our campfire under a vaulted ceiling of stars. Several of us had heard enough, and we told Williamson that he could keep his ideas on this particular subject to himself. We argued for a bit, and the disagreement grew pretty heated. But Williamson clammed up after that.

His repeated outbursts got me thinking — and not just because they were so unpleasant. What struck me about Williamson was the depth of his conviction. When we finally confronted him by the banks of the Zambezi River that night, he didn't really back down. He simply shook his thickly maned head and declared that we just didn't understand. We didn't live in his country, so we couldn't possibly understand how it was with blacks. I immediately said that I *did* live in his country. By that time, I'd lived in Zimbabwe for two years. It may have been an effective debating point, but Williamson was at least partly right. I really was just a visitor to Zimbabwe — and there *was* a difference between whites who had made their lives in the country and those who, like me, were just passing through. Most white Zimbabweans had come out to Africa following the Second World War, or their parents had. And they didn't journey all the way to Africa in order to enjoy an interesting cultural experience. They weren't tourists. They didn't come to learn about Shona stone sculpture or Ndebele tribal dances. They came, basically, because they couldn't find work in post-war Britain. They came to earn a living, to make money. It was no more romantic than that.

The point is, whites in Rhodesia didn't have much interest in Africa as they found it. They were far more interested in making the land over to suit themselves. It was a rough business, and they went about it in a rough way. They were a frontier people, deliberately pushing back the wilderness. The task didn't call for great intellectual subtlety, or huge reserves of compassion, or soaring flights of sympathetic imagination. What it required was hard work and a tough spirit, and that was what they gave. When something got in their way, they moved it or overcame it or killed it. That was how they treated the land, and it was how they treated the people who lived on it.

A decade after Rhodesia became Zimbabwe, most of the country's remaining whites still dwelled in a kind of social biosphere, a planet of the mind that intersected only incidentally with this place called Africa. They walked many of the same streets as their black compatriots, but they did not often connect. I suppose the same could be said of whites in Canada, for example, who mostly don't have much to do with people of other races. But this was Zimbabwe, a black country under black rule on a black continent. Why were the races still so separate here? For a time, I found it all a bit depressing, but then I spoke to a man named Masipula Sithole.

Late one afternoon, he and I were sipping tea on the terrace of the Mount Pleasant Sports Club, in the heart of one of Harare's posher neighbourhoods. The oblique rays of a low sun splayed through the cypress trees, and the air had an edge of Harare's wintertime coolness. At our feet, beyond the banks of trimmed shrubbery, a garden of earthly delights unfolded into the distance, including rows of *en-tous-cas* tennis courts and the sprawling green fairways of an eighteen-hole golf course. Players occasionally strolled past, their golf clubs knocking in their bags. All of them were white.

My companion gazed out at his surroundings, this paradise for wealthy whites, and he shrugged. "Don't expect us to be lovey-dovey," he said. "We are like people everywhere — black, white. There is the basic difference of colour."

Masipula Sithole (his surname is pronounced Si-TOE-lay) was black. He was a professor of political and administrative studies at the University of Zimbabwe. When I'd called him up and asked to see him, so that we could talk about race relations in his country, this was the meeting place that he had proposed, this clubby bastion of white privilege. I imagine that this was deliberate on his part, a mild provocation. It turned out that he was now a member here.

"It's not unusual that blacks golf here," he told me. "I haven't seen blacks lawn-bowling, but I play tennis on Saturdays. Some blacks are in the league. Big deal . . . ?" He turned to me, pausing for rhetorical effect, then shrugged again. "That *is* a big deal. It used not to happen, eight years ago."

He was right. In many ways, Zimbabwe *had* changed since independence. Blacks held direct political power now. They dominated the public service; they were free to dine in any restaurant, dwell in any neighbourhood, attend any school, and join any club. Things were permitted to blacks that had never been permitted before. True, the changes were often more theoretical than real. In most Harare restaurants, the seated patrons were almost invariably white, while those serving them were black. Blacks were still little more than a token presence at the city's expensive sports clubs. You didn't find them living in the low-density suburbs, or only rarely.

This de-facto segregation may make Harare today sound not greatly different from many North American cities, where black people are also woefully under-represented on the membership rolls at affluent country clubs or as patrons at pricey restaurants. No doubt some of the same social dynamics are at work in North America as in Africa. But in Zimbabwe, whites represent only about one per cent of the population: they are not merely a demographic minority; they're a demographic sliver. Besides, Zimbabwe is now a black-ruled state. The president is black. With only rare and occasional exceptions, all his ministers are black and all members of parliament are black. Yet the economic elite remains resolutely white.

There's something about a fair complexion that loads the dice in your favour, not just in Zimbabwe but all over the map. In Mexico, for example, the best-selling beer has long been a brand called Superior. Its advertising symbol is a very white, very blonde woman who looks like a leading contestant in the Miss Sweden beauty pageant. The brand's slogan is *La rubia que todos quieren*. The blonde everyone wants. A lot of Mexican products are advertised this way, by people who don't look the slightest bit like most Mexicans. They look instead like the cast of Dynasty. I asked a Mexican government official why his people were doing this to each other, glorifying a physical image that had so little do do with themselves. It was apparent from his reply that he didn't get the point of my question. He told me that, surely, this was exactly what advertising was for — to hold out the promise of something better.

In a book of hers about Zimbabwe, Doris Lessing writes of an Arab poet "who was praising the pearl-white skin, the milk-white skin, of his girl, for, he said, Europeans did not know what they were talking about, when they were proud of their 'white' skins. For real poetic whiteness, you needed a girl who had been shut up in a shady room all her life, and never allowed near strong light." Lessing wound up asking the same question that has often occurred to me. "What is this thing about whiteness?"

In Zimbabwe, white privilege seemed to stand out in such high relief because this was a black country and there were so very few whites. Still, the separation of Zimbabweans into two worlds, white and black, probably wasn't solely a result of racism, narrowly defined. That afternoon at the Mount Pleasant Sports Club, Masipula Sithole rubbed his middle finger against his thumb to make a familiar and probably universal sign. He said, "No money." Even the few blacks who could afford to join a swank white sports club probably wouldn't be inclined to do so, he said, because hardly any of them knew how to play golf or tennis. "These are not the typical social skills that have been open to black people."

Most social gatherings in Zimbabwe also tended to be monochromatic, either all-black or all-white. But that, said Sithole, wasn't the direct result of racial tension either, or not of current racial tension. First, you had to consider the sheer momentum of the past. The thing was, blacks and whites had always socialized separately. This was the way things had always been. Such patterns do not change quickly and not just because some people want them to.

Sithole himself was one of the very rare exceptions. A black man, he lived in Mount Pleasant, a white suburb. He admitted that he wasn't entirely at home there, but this was not solely because of his skin colour, either. It was more complicated than that. "I have invited whites, you know, to some of my parties," he said. "They're usually on time — and they're the first to leave. They stay only for a drink or two and only to make their presence known to me. I attribute that to having little in common to talk about."

What *did* white and black Zimbabweans have in common to discuss over drinks? Even sports — that dependable ice-breaker — made for uneasy small talk. For Zimbabwean blacks, soccer is a nearly religious passion, but white Zimbabweans don't much care for soccer. They prefer rugby or cricket. The problem in Zimbabwe is not so much that whites and blacks dislike each other, though that is sometimes the case. The problem is that they truly do not dwell in the same world — they have *never* dwelled in the same world — and this is not an easy thing to change.

Sometimes, of course, their feelings ran to genuine hostility. But at least Zimbabweans were not denouncing each other on public streets any longer. At least they were not at war. Instead, they were keeping a decent and more or less respectful distance. When you thought of everything they'd been through and of all they'd done to each other — including an inter-racial war that claimed roughly thirty-thousand lives — it began to seem that a little mutual respect was no small thing.

"The whites lost a lot, a lot," said Sithole. "Property? That goes without saying. But, to me, 'a lot' conjures up a style of life, authority, servants who obeyed at a flick of a finger. I think it is wrong to expect whites to accept this change with a smile. I think they are doing better than expected."

And so the new tennis-playing member of the Mount Pleasant Sports Club shrugged his shoulders one last time and peered down at the swimming pool, the sprawling fairways, and the groves of cypress trees, all now transfixed by the slanting light of a late winter's afternoon. He shook his head. "I don't care for this lovey-dovey thing," he repeated. "The minimum I care for is being civil to each other. The minimum I require from you is the minimum you require from me. I think we have gone a long way in eight years in Zimbabwe in treating each other civilly."

And there was more. At least some Zimbabwean whites finally seemed to be coming to terms with another basic fact of their existence — that their country was located *in Africa*. They were *Africans* themselves.

Take Robin and Kathie McIntosh, a couple of white Zims I got to know. She was born and raised in South Africa, while he was born in Rhodesia to British parents. They were married in 1979, the year before Zimbabwean independence, and they came to live on Robin's farm, sprawling over 1,200 hectares in the rolling Enterprise Valley northeast of Harare.

For years, they grew Virginia tobacco and ran a herd of pedigree Simmental cattle, and they were happy. They made out just fine. But lately they'd found that their interests were shifting in an odd direction — towards Africa, of all places. They began to care about African things. Before long, in addition to cattle, their farm was home to: several elephants, two four-metre pythons, thirty zebra, a considerable community of wart-hogs, a small herd of Cape buffalo, a smattering of guinea fowl, two ostriches, and a dozen species of antelope.

Late one morning in the brilliant austral winter, I dropped by for a visit. Kathie poured out two cups of tea from a silver service and settled back into her chair beside a wrought-iron table, painted white. All around her, bauhinea trees spread their branches against a cobalt sky and threw dark pools of shade onto a clipped green lawn. Meanwhile, only a few metres away, the highveld of southern Africa sprawled towards the horizon — a midwinter sun beating down upon rock-covered *kopjes* and scattered *msasa* trees. As if projected upon a giant outdoor movie screen, small herds of zebra, kudu, eland, and impala foraged through the dry, khaki-coloured scrub. "We've got nice crocodiles in our garden and elephants on our front lawn," Kathie boasted.

She and her husband owned all this land and, now, they owned all these animals, too. After living all of their lives in Africa, they had at last lost their hearts to the place, and that was a switch. After all, since the turn of the century, European settlers had flocked to this African hinterland, essentially bent on destroying it first, and then making it into something else. Elephants were gunned down because they broke through cattle fences. Antelope were exterminated because they competed with domestic stock for forage. Crocodiles were killed because they sometimes attacked humans. On and on it went. The white man came to Africa, not to celebrate the place, but to subdue it, to overcome it.

And now here were Robin and Kathie McIntosh, and they were turning their cattle farm into a wildlife preserve. Either they were at last coming to terms with Africa, or Africa was coming to terms with them — and why not? Watered by the Domvorgwe River, their property really was a kind of Eden, a graceful maze of granite *kopjes*, coral trees, orange groves, and thickets of scrubby *msasa* and mahobo-hobo trees, where around each bend there unfurled another prospect of a seemingly infinite variety of antelope, heads down to graze or raised high to browse through the trees—daikers, stenbok, reebok, tsessebe, kudu, eland, and impala.

One evening, as dusk crept through the Enterprise Valley, Robin and Kathie took me up to Eland Lodge, a thatch-roofed A-frame cottage they had recently built on a hillside in a remote corner of their property. The cottage had an airy loft with four beds and was handsomely appointed with wicker furniture, plush pillows, and African crafts. The McIntoshes hoped to rent it out to foreign visitors, part of their plan to make a living out of letting Africa be Africa.

It was certainly a seductive idea. But I had to wonder, was it already too late? Maybe the McIntoshes were living in a dream world, grasping at an idealized continent that white Zimbabweans had never much valued before and that was fast disappearing now. Besides, it was one thing to discover a proprietary affection for African fauna or landscape and quite another to live as equals with the country's black majority — a far more complicated task. Still, on that one hillside, on that one evening, I found it no great challenge for once to put all these thorny inter-racial questions aside.

As a red African sun smouldered across the valley through a haze of wood smoke, Robin McIntosh busied himself mixing sundowners from a cooler in the truckbed. Soon, a trio of kudu ambled up the hillside to poke amid the nearby scrub. A pair of emerald-spotted doves swooped through the rusty light, and the croaking of bullfrogs rumbled across the still highland air from the distant rushes of the slender Domvorgwe.

Kathie McIntosh sank back into a wicker chair and sipped her brandy and water — a white woman in a black country. "T.A.P," she announced in a wistful voice. She nodded at the sepia view that unfolded before her. "T.A.P.," she repeated, as though this were an incantation or a prayer. She raised her glass to the fading light and then smiled at me. "That's Africa, pal."

5

FROM CUBA TO ANGOLA

Welcome
to the
Tropicana

I T WAS IN HAVANA that I met my first Salvadoran
guerrilla. This was not the likeliest of places for such an
encounter. Officially, there were no Salvadoran guerrillas anywhere in Cuba. But here I was, one day in early
1982, reading a book while having lunch in the ground-
floor coffee shop of the Habana Libre, formerly the Hilton.
The book I was reading just happened to be about El
Salvador. On its cover the book bore the words "El
Salvador" emblazoned in red. They might as well have been
a flag.

Before long, the diner beside me at the lunch counter
turned to me and struck up a conversation. He wanted to
know if I had ever been to El Salvador myself, and I replied
that, yes, I had. This seemed to please him immensely. He
announced that he was a Salvadoran. He was a young man,
just twenty-one, of medium height with a dark, slightly reddish complexion and a thick wedge of jet-black hair. He was
also, it turned out, a guerrilla. He'd been brought to Cuba
on a leadership training programme, along with about two
dozen of his *compañeros*.

Well, this was certainly a surprise. The Cubans always vehemently denied providing assistance of any kind to the Salvadoran rebels. And no wonder. The US government would surely have seized upon any such link to bolster its charge that Havana was fomenting subversion in neighbouring lands. This, in turn, would further justify Washington's own support for the military-backed government in El Salvador and no doubt fuel an escalation of US sanctions against Cuba.

So the Cubans always insisted that there were no Salvadoran rebels in their country. Yet it seemed that there was at least one, for here was a Salvadoran rebel seated next to me at the lunch counter in the coffee shop at the Habana Libre, formerly the Hilton. In due course, he told me where he was staying — a small residential hotel in Miramar — and I took a taxi out there several days later to see him. I found him relaxing in the lobby, waiting for me, just has he'd promised to do. We each carried a glass of papaya juice out onto the patio, and we chatted for an hour or so in the late-morning sunshine. To protect the man's identity, I agreed to give him an invented name — Jaime.

Despite his young age, Jaime said he had been a rebel already for seven years and now held the rank of lieutenant commander in a provincial front of the FARN — the Armed Forces of National Resistance, one of five Salvadoran guerrilla armies that were fighting in common cause against the government in El Salvador. He told me that this was his second visit to Cuba. He was now halfway through a four-month training programme in leadership skills.

Jaime told me quite a lot about the professional aspects of his activities in Cuba. But we also spoke of more personal things, including his own reaction to Cuba, socialist beacon to the Americas. He allowed that he wasn't much impressed with the country. The people lacked what he considered a proper collective spirit. They were too materialistic, he said — especially the women, whom he had found to be interested only in men who had a nice house, a car, and money. He shrugged. "I am just a *campesino*," he said. "My family was poor. I am poor."

Jaime and I chatted on a while longer, and eventually I left him to head back downtown. Several days later, I wrote a story about the encounter that would appear on the front page of my newspaper. Not surprisingly, the article eventually showed up in briefing materials distributed by the US State Department for the purpose of further demonizing Cuba. (That wasn't my purpose, but there you go.) What struck me most about the whole incident, however, was the simple fact that it took place. You'd have thought that Havana would want to keep any such activity as this — Salvadoran rebels being trained on Cuban soil — as secret as possible. Certainly, a little state secrecy did not seem entirely beyond Havana's capabilities. Cuba was a police state, after all.

The absence of security precautions in this case was astonishing. Salvadorans tend to be physically distinct from Cubans. They are mostly *mestizos* — that is, of mixed European and Amerindian blood — while Cubans are white or black or mulatto. If you saw a Salvadoran strolling along La Rampa in Havana in 1982, you would quite likely notice him, and you would wonder what he was doing there. So what did the Cubans do? Did they hide the Salvadorans away in some top-secret facility where no one would ever see them? Did they mount any kind of security effort at all, some attempt to keep the presence of the Salvadorans from becoming too conspicuous? Well, no, they didn't. The Cubans simply instructed the Salvadorans that, if anyone asked them where they were from, they were to reply, "Nicaragua."

That was it, as far as the security precautions went. It seemed to me that there was no logic here at all. On the other hand, this was revolutionary Cuba, where logic has never been what you would call the organizing principle of the state. Instead, the island has long been a sort of tropical breeding ground for contradictions, and so it remains. Of all the countries I got to know during a decade of living abroad as a newspaper reporter, none bewildered me as thoroughly as Cuba did. My reactions to the place turned somersaults on a more or less constant basis. One moment, I'd be delighted. The next moment, appalled.

One afternoon, back in the early 1980s, I flagged down an unofficial taxi near the Havana waterfront and climbed inside. The driver was an elderly man with a crooked nose and twin muffs of stiff white hair. He slumped behind the wheel of his 1953 Buick — a pair of pre-revolutionary antiques, both still rumbling along, against all odds. "I am not a Communist," the man told me at one point. He shrugged and tapped both hands against the wheel. "But," he added, "these ones are better than the ones before."

He meant that Fidel Castro and his colleagues were an improvement on dictator Fulgencio Batista, whom they'd overthrown nearly a quarter-century earlier. The driver of the Buick listed the advances made by the revolution — education, health care, employment — and, as he spoke, I felt myself feeling increasingly positive about Cuba — a country where even elderly men in '53 Buicks could count the revolution's accomplishments.

Shortly after that conversation, I was strolling at dusk along the San Rafael pedestrian mall in downtown Havana. Off to the side, some minor commotion caught my eye, and I turned to look. Three women — all middle-aged and primly dressed — had seated themselves upon a low metal barricade erected near the entrance to a small ice-cream parlour, and two policemen had approached them. Two of the women were white, I noticed. The third was black. One of the policemen ushered the two white women back into the flow of pedestrians, while his partner stayed behind to examine the identification papers of the remaining woman. I have no idea whether the colour of her skin was a significant factor here. Pretty soon, the policeman initiated a procedure familiar to motorists everywhere. He pulled out a pad of some kind and began to scribble in it. It looked, for all the world, as if he was writing out a ticket.

Sure enough, the policeman tore a slip of paper from the pad and handed it to the woman. I waited until he sauntered off. Then I walked up to the woman to ask her what had just happened.

"*Tengo que pagar una multa*," she said, a bit flustered. She had to pay a fine.

I asked why.

She shrugged. "I was tired," she said, "so I sat down. Now I have to pay a fine."

By this time, a group of passersby had gathered around to listen. The woman explained what the policeman had told her: that someone from the neighbourhood Poder Popular

("People's Power", the local administrative bodies in Cuba) would soon be visiting her to collect payment of the fine. The woman said she didn't know how much the penalty would be, as this was the first time she had ever been fined for sitting down. The people in the crowd clicked their tongues and shook their heads in quiet disapproval of the policeman's action. Suddenly I felt pretty negative about Cuba, a country where respectably dressed, middle-aged women received fines for sitting on low metal barricades in front of ice-cream parlours.

Not long after after that, I switched on the television one evening in my room at the Habana Libre, formerly the Hilton, to watch the news. The item being broadcast concerned a group of young pioneers — Cuba's revolutionary mass organization for children — who had decided, no doubt spontaneously and without prompting, to send an open letter to the children of the world denouncing the evils of *imperialismo*, a Cuban code word for just about anything associated with the United States.

The letter was read aloud by a girl of about twelve. She had curly hair, a bright open face, a button nose and was dressed in her young pioneer uniform of kerchief, blouse, and skirt. With one fist clenched aloft, she punched the air defiantly and spluttered the letter's contents into the microphone, like some pre-pubescent caricature of all the screeching, bug-eyed student revolutionaries I have ever known. It was not an inspiring sight.

The next morning, at breakfast in my hotel, I struck up a conversation with a Swedish scientist who was in Cuba to attend a medical conference. He told me a story about a Cuban acquaintance of his, a man who was born dirt-poor, the son of an illiterate sugar-cane cutter. The man was now a world-renowned authority on recombinant DNA.

That evening, I went out for a stroll near the Malecón — the broad avenue that curves along the Havana waterfront. I saw a familiar neon sign depicting a rifle-toting Cuban militia member shaking his fist angrily out towards the sea, in the direction of the United States. Illuminated beside him were the words: "¡*Señor Imperialista, no tenemos absolutamente ningun miedo de usted*!" Mr. Imperialist, we have absolutely no fear of you! I looked at that slogan, and I thought, not for the first time, how much I hated slogans. Meanwhile, just a block or so away, at the House of Czechoslovakian Culture, a recording of that well-known anti-imperialist anthem — "Hello, Dolly," by Louis Armstrong — was being blasted into the warm evening air that wafted along La Rampa.

So this was Cuba — something for everyone. Here was a country depicted by the US government as having the most elaborate system of social control in all the Americas. On almost every streetcorner, there was a Revolutionary Defence Committee, whose many responsibilities included round-the-clock surveillance of local residents. Here was a country supposedly crawling with domestic spies, a country where police handed out tickets to prim, middle-aged women for the offence of sitting on metal barricades outside ice-cream parlours. Yet all they bothered to do to protect the anonymity of foreign revolutionaries seeking the over-throw of a US-backed government in Central America was to tell them, "Say that you're from Nicaragua."

When it comes to state security, I suppose you have to remember that Cuba is a long, long way from the Gulags of the former Soviet bloc, both geographically and culturally.

Here it is, plunked down smack-dab in the Caribbean Sea, where it sways to the same humid air that shifts the palm fronds, syncopates the music, and puts an easy lilt in the stride of people on neighbouring islands.

When I think of Cuba, I think immediately of the Tropicana, the famous Havana nightclub perched for decades on the brow of a low hill in Marianao. I know that the place is touristy. If it reflects Cuba's Afro-Latin culture at all — and it does — then the reflection is a bit distorted, a version of Cuban reality tarted up for foreign consumption. Still, whatever else you say about it, the place *has* survived. Come right-wing dictator, come civil war, come revolution, come Communism, come God knows what, the Tropicana has stayed open, the patrons have kept showing up, the musicians have kept playing, and the dancers have kept right on dancing. Any time I travelled to Cuba during the 1980s, I always made a pilgrimage to the Tropicana and always found myself both exhilarated and reassured by the rollicking spirit of the place. Somehow, it never seems to change.

It begins with the peppermint voice of Nat King Cole crooning through the royal palms and out into the stillness of the tropical night. "Autumn Leaves", "Love is a Many-Splendoured Thing", "Brazilian Lovebirds". One mellow classic follows another. Then, at about nine-thirty, there are signs of movement among the massive haguey trees. The burning ends of cigarettes dart back and forth as stage-hands hurry out of the way. You catch a glimpse or two of women gliding into place. They wear elaborate costumes and have extremely long legs.

Suddenly, the recorded voice of Nat King Cole falls

silent. A woman's voice bellows out in Spanish, her Rs stuttering like long machine-gun bursts. *"¡Señoras y señores! ¡Bienvenido a la Tr-r-r-ropicana! ¡Un paraíso bajo de las estr-r-r-rellas!"*

Spotlights ricochet through the waxy foliage. Clouds of smoke roll across the stage, over the audience, through the trees — and, all at once, dozens of very tall, very slender Cuban women seem to explode out of the night. They stride through the smoke and the glare of the footlights, descend from the branches of the trees, march up from among the audience itself, converge from all sides to parade around a huge circular stage. Apart from their massive headpieces — galaxies of tin foil tottering on high — the women seem to consist in equal parts of never-drooping smiles, always-moving bustles, and never-ending legs.

The orchestra strikes up a Latin show tune, heavy on the brass. A choir appears, singing in the branches overhead. The women remove and toss away their bustles. And now, like human bumble-bees, a hive of men swarms onto the stage, in sparkling gold boots, flared white pants, and little gold-lamé bolero jackets. Everyone starts to dance. For the next two hours, it's legs, legs, and more legs.

And that's the Tropicana—either the Americas' longest-running salute to great gams, good music, and dubious taste, or a splendid Latin snub to Communist orthodoxy.

Even now, three decades after Fidel Castro and his guerrilla army marched down from the Sierra Maestra and into Havana to take power, the Tropicana remains a kind of Cuban legend, a glorious hold-over from Havana in its pre-revolutionary heyday, when the city was a Caribbean promised land of graft, intrigue, and sin. Somehow, the place has managed to survive the revolution and has flourished even during the slow dreary years when the Soviet imperium extended even unto the heart of the Caribbean, a long, long way from Petrograd and just a short lap south of the Florida keys.

The place is now a bit musty and maybe could use a dab or two of paint, not to mention some new tables and chairs, but maybe its somewhat seedy quality is among its charms. The Tropicana celebrates some slightly garish and intensely erotic rhythm that resonates in just about every Cuban chest or pelvis or stride. The place works on you like a large glass of Havana Club rum, with a sprig of mint and a dash of angostura bitters. It reminds you that some things in life don't change and never should change — precisely because nobody in his right mind could ever want them to.

Okay — the Tropicana *has* changed in some marginal ways. Back in the 1950s, when Havana was wide open to Americans of a certain, let us say, criminal bent, the clientele at the place was more or less dominated by fast-talking US gangsters and their local *amores*. After the revolution intervened, the terraced al fresco dining area at the Tropicana bulged with group tours from eastern Europe — on the whole a rather dour lot, I always felt, poker-faced, crusty, and pale.

There were exceptions to that Slavic stereotype, both in the audience and even on the stage. On one visit to the Tropicana in the early 1980s, I stayed on for the second show, usually a steamy and particularly sensuous celebration of Afro-Latin themes. This time, however, it also included an extended performance by a lanky Bulgarian pop star aided by three smashing Bulgarian back-up singers clad in dresses that were luminous and all but evanescent. One of the vocalists also wore a cast on her right leg that climbed almost up to her hip, but she didn't let it slow her down.

They were great. And brave. As an encore, they sang a funky Euro-pop version of "Guantanamera" that could have caused an international incident if the Cubans in the building had taken a dislike to it — wanton abuse of "Guantanamera" being more or less the Cuban version of sacrilege. Instead, everyone rocked. The song sounded wonderful.

I don't want to gloss over the more onerous aspects of life in Fidel Castro's Cuba in the years before the collapse of the Soviet Union. Still, if this was Communism, then it was Communism of a peculiarly Caribbean kind — Communism a la Tropicana, where even the president of the republic would mix you a tropical drink. Hell, he mixed me mine.

I recall a sunny Friday afternoon in the winter of 1982. The Cuban president and national hero was in his office at the Palace of the Revolution. He was preparing *mojitos*, Cuba's national drink, working from a drinks trolley that had been rolled in by a waiter in a crisp white jacket. I have recorded the recipe for posterity. A spoonful of refined sugar at the bottom of a tall glass. A splash of lime juice. A generous sprig of fresh mint. Stir these ingredients vigorously — mash them up a bit, in fact — to get the minty taste going. Pour in some three-year-old Havana Club rum. Top the glass up with ice and soda water, and administer a dash of angostura bitters. Maybe a tad more rum. Stir again. Serve.

When the drinks were prepared, Fidel Castro handed the glasses out to a small group of visiting Canadian parliamentarians and a handful of journalists. He stood back, in his olive-green fatigues and that crinkly grey beard. He raised his own glass.

"¡*Viva la Revolución!*"

The following evening, Canada's ambassador to Havana at the time, James Bartleman, hosted a reception for the visiting Canadians at his residence in Miramar. Lots of influential Cubans were invited, and they came. It was known that Fidel himself had received an invitation, but, for security reasons, it was not certain whether he would show up. The word in Mr. Bartleman's living room was that the Cuban president would almost definitely be a no-show. He'd already met the Canadians once, after all. It wasn't likely he'd make another appearance. The guests shrugged, freshened their drinks, and went back to grazing from the circulating trays of canapés. Some days you got a Cuban president over cocktails. Some days you did not.

Then, all at once, an uproar rent the dense Caribbean air. Sirens wailed on the street outside, headlights flared, men shouted, shadows criss-crossed the night. And, a minute or so later, Fidel Castro himself materialized in the living room — as splendid and unreal as a revolutionary Santa Claus. His olive-green uniform seemed to glow, his beard to crackle, his voice to vibrate, as though he were driven by some powerful electrical charge. He transformed the emotional current in the room and drew the other guests towards him, like iron filings around a magnet.

Someone brought him a drink, and Fidel lit a cigar and held forth on subjects ranging from martial law in Poland to Cuba's mottled human-rights record. He dominated the gathering for upwards of an hour. When it came time for him to depart, he bid farewell to each of the parliamentarians in turn and prepared to set off. Just then he hesitated. He turned back to face the room. In a loud voice, almost a bellow, he called out, "*¡Me faltan dos! ¡Me faltan dos!*" Fidel realized that he had indeed missed two members of the Canadian delegation. The hold-outs were Liberal MPs Stanley Hudecki and James Schroder who, it turned out, were still in the garden. The cry went up for them to make their presence felt inside, and quickly they did.

"Stanley!" cried Fidel. "James!" He threw out his arms and strode toward the two Canadian backbenchers. He grasped them in succession, in a pair of fraternal *abrazos*. He practically lifted them from the floor, and held them for several heartbeats longer than was strictly necessary, before setting them gently down. Now, his farewells complete, Fidel Castro turned on his heels and was gone, in a bewilderment of screeching tires, flashing headlights, and screaming sirens. The heat of the Caribbean night rolled back into the silence of that suddenly gaping room.

Who would have predicted on that dense and memorable night that (a) the international Communist empire would collapse in only a few short years, or that (b) one of the final Marxist outposts in the known universe would still be bobbing above the Caribbean blue — a very long way from Moscow but just 160 kilometres from Key West, Florida? Nobody I knew. And yet, so it was. Soon, the lights would be blinking off in almost all the Communist capitals of the world, but the old revolutionary juice would still be flickering through the crumbling colonial warrens of Old Havana. But only just. Meanwhile, the rumba rhythms of the Cuban night would be pounding out their three-two beat, loud and long and clear.

Havana
Club

I T WAS 1990, and I was back in Havana for the first time in several years. As usual, the first chance I got, I headed straight for the Tropicana. I sat on my own during the first scintillating show, sipping a *mojito*. At least on stage, everything was much as it had ever been — the brisk ensemble jazz, the clouds of dry ice, the racing spotlights, the crooning baritones. From their platform in a huge haguey tree that towered above the stage, the choir still harmonized into the inky Caribbean night. And the legions of rangy, grinning Cuban women still danced up a tropical storm on legs that seemed to stretch from Havana to Cape Horn.

Granted, the audience had changed. Gone were the pale-faced armies of East Bloc tourists. Like so many scattered fragments of the Berlin Wall, they had vanished, to be replaced by a more raucous crew — Mexicans, Venezuelans, Italians, Spaniards, even Canadians. That night, it just so happened that a group of Mexicans had taken over the table next to mine. After the first show, they invited me over to join them.

They were working on several bottles of Havana Club and had already made admirable progress. We did a round of introductions, raised our glasses, and settled in for the finale.

As usual, the cast was smaller than for the flamboyant first show — and the performance was choreographed on a more modest scale — but the result was bluesier, sweatier, and sexier. This time, however, there was no Bulgarian pop act wailing out *Guantanamera*. That era was truly past. For some time to come, the Cubans would be singing *Guantanamera* alone.

After the show, our group dispersed. I headed out with two of the Mexican women and the baritone soloist from the Tropicana to a cast party at a nearby address. There, in a room swimming with soulful Latin pop music and marijuana fumes, several singers from the Tropicana took turns in the middle of the floor to belt out versions of recent hits by José José, Emanuel, or Juan Luis Guerra. One of the Mexican women got up and sang a truly appalling rendition of a *ranchera* called "Cariño Nuevo", but nobody threw anything at her.

Rather than throw things, what these people really wanted to do was dance. Soon, everybody was out on the floor, spinning to a recorded tumult of rock, salsa, reggae, and rumba. Bottles of Havana Club made the rounds among the dancers, and the party rolled on until four a.m. — for the heartbeat of the Tropicana will never die.

On the other hand, the heartbeat of Karl Marx was sounding a trifle unsteady. The Soviet Union had already collapsed beneath its own weight. The Berlin Wall was gone. Eastern Europe was charting a new course beyond Moscow's control. And Cuba, distant Cuba, had been suddenly cast adrift. Already, the effects were being felt accross the island, from Havana to Santiago de Cuba — fuel shortages, scarcities of food and consumer goods, increases in

graft and other crime, an exodus of refugees, and much fren-
zied speculation about the fate of Fidel Castro's revolution.

Over on La Rampa in the Vedado section of town, for
example, the building that used to house the Czechoslovakian Cultural Centre had already been turned over to
the Cuban information ministry for use as a press centre.
The Czechs, of course, weren't much interested in Cuba
any more. Marxism either.

It was amazing how quickly things had changed. Now,
when I bumped into people on the street, they were eager
to talk — and not just about the weather. They wanted to
talk politics. They seemed to have no reservations about
denouncing their government to a complete stranger, someone they might well have shunned only a few years earlier,
for fear that he could be an agent of *imperialismo* or that some
local spy would witness the contact and report it.

One evening, I found myself in Guanabo, a coastal town
east of Havana, when a street party erupted, spontaneously it
seemed. Suddenly, dozens of young people were out dancing in the semi-darkness to loud recorded music, and the
song they kept playing, over and over again, was a new salsa
number by an exiled Cuban musician. It was called "Ya
Vienen Llegando", sung by an exiled Cuban mambo star
called Willy Chirino. It was about Cuban exiles in the
United States, who would soon return to reclaim their
country. The song began with a tortured lampoon of that
Communist anthem, the "Internationale", and the ensuing
lyrics celebrated the downfall of Communism in eastern
Europe and predicted that Cuba would be next.

This was the tune that young Cubans were playing, out
in a public street, at full volume, over and over again, as they

danced into the night. As far as I knew, no one was reported, or detained, or put under surveillance. No one seemed even slightly concerned about the political implications of the act. And maybe there were none. This was a party after all, not a political convention.

Almost everywhere I went, the story was the same. Things had definitely loosened up. Out on La Rampa at night, the once almost dreary street life of Havana had caught fire. The main reason was probably not so much ideological as economic. Hungry for foreign currency, Cuba had embraced foreign tourism with new fervour during the late 1980s. Now, you found Spaniards, Italians, Mexicans, and Canadians poking around almost everywhere. Their presence — a corrupting phenomenon in many ways — had also obliged the Cuban authorities to back off a bit in certain areas of social control. What choice was there? A ham-fisted crackdown on *parásitos antisociales* — a.k.a. Cubans fraternizing with foreigners — would have tidied things up all right, but it would also scare the tourists away, not to mention their dollars.

So things had become pretty *flojo*. Sex, gambling, drugs, black-market money trading — all were easy to find. Hundreds partied along the Malecón, down by the waterfront, until late into the night, every night. But there was an edge of sadness out there too, a heavy musk of frustration and longing that sagged on the salty tropical air.

One evening, I had dinner on my own in la Habana Vieja — the old city — at a place made famous by Ernest Hemingway when he lived in Cuba before the revolution. It's called la Bodeguita del Medio and is a Cuban museum piece, loud and busy and rough-edged. The place is famous for its pork dishes and for the superb quality of its *mojitos*.

After dinner, I decided I would walk back to my hotel in Vedado, a fair distance across town.

I strolled past the colonial Cathedral and out onto the Malecón. As was usual nowadays, at least by night, the high concrete breakwater on the seaward side of the avenue was jammed most of the way with *habañeros* of modest means — people who had nowhere else to go and no money to spend there anyhow. You heard music and laughter, but if you listened closely you could sense a very different mood beneath the surface, a relentless undertow of longing. I strolled over and struck up a conversation with one young couple — Manuel and Gina — who were huddled together on the seawall, on their own.

Manuel was twenty. He had slicked-back hair, a handsome, regular face, and was wearing blue jeans and a T-shirt. He told me that he worked in a Cuban cigar factory as a foreman. Right now, he wanted to talk. Once he started talking, he couldn't seem to stop. "My brain is never still," he said. "It's spinning and spinning. I don't feel well. I feel depressed." He shook his head, as if to clear it. "Ham?" he said. "*Ham* . . . ? You could put some ham in front of me, and I wouldn't recognize it. I could taste it and I wouldn't know what it was. Ham? I think about it all the time. I can't remember what it's like." He shook his head. "*Clothes* . . . ? Let's not even talk about it."

Gina listened quietly, stroking his arms and back. She was in jeans, too. She had long frizzy hair, a throaty voice, a simple, open-faced beauty. It seemed that they were tired of their lives already, these two — tired of a slow existence eked out in cramped quarters, on a monthly ration card, with little prospect of change. Manuel said he realized that the Cuban revolution had brought considerable benefits to most people here — in health care, housing, education. But he dismissed them all with a wave of his hand.

"Yes, yes, I know," he said. He shook his head again. "But when you're healthy, you just don't . . . it just doesn't . . . " He gave up. He couldn't put it into words. It wouldn't compute. Manuel said he couldn't predict the future — whether this government would stand or fall. "If something happens, you don't hear about it," he said. "They don't publish it. There are police everywhere. At every corner, they're watching . . . "

His voice trailed off, and Gina broke in. "There's going to be an explosion," she announced softly. "The people will explode."

The night seemed suddenly ominous. For a moment, forboding seemed to bristle through the dark — until a woman's voice suddenly shrieked with laughter somewhere nearby, and the air pressure suddenly seemed to change, quick as the mood swings of youth. Manuel pushed his hands back through his hair. He looked over at me. He said, "Have you ever been to Havana Club . . . ?"

In fact, I never had. But I'd certainly heard of the place. It was a nightclub — the newest and swankiest in town. Just about all the young *habañeros* I ran into soon turned the conversation around to Havana Club. They could each rattle off the unimaginable prices at the place, like an incantation or a prayer. Ah, Havana Club — where they hit you up at the door for a $10 US cover; where Coca-Cola (the real thing, not the Cuban imitation) could be had for $5 US a glass; and where a man could pick up a woman on his way in. Any woman. All he had to do was choose among the dozens impatiently shifting their weight from one patent-leather shoe to the other in the parking lot. He'd need dollars, of course.

If there was a temple to materialism in contemporary Cuba, than that temple was a discotheque, and Havana Club was its name. And so, a couple of nights later, I decided to head out to Miramar, a western suburb of Havana, to see for myself what the buzz was about.

Karelia, a young Cuban woman I'd met at the après-Tropicana party several nights earlier, had agreed to come along. She was a dark-skinned woman with a fine oval face and an expressive girlish beauty — thick, dark eyebrows above flashing, almost Asian eyes, a compact nose, and a large smile. She wore a green cotton dress for the occasion and had tied a dark green ribbon in her hair. I picked her up at the apartment building out in Alamar, east of Havana, where she lived with her mother, her two younger brothers, and her younger sister. She worked as a dancing instructor at a place near the Plaza de Armas. This would be her first visit to Havana Club.

The car carried us west along the Malecón — jammed this night as on most nights with revellers, layabouts, and young lovers locked in aching embraces. The car descended into the tunnel beneath the Almendares River and surfaced on Séptima Avenida, Havana's Embassy Row. Presently, we turned right and rode up to the bright shining expanse of the Hotel Comodoro, recently refurbished by Spanish investors.

Havana Club had its own entrance, at the western end of the hotel. At ten p.m., the scene outside was probably not exactly what Karl Marx and Friedrich Engels had in mind when they urged the workers of the world to unite. Women were what I saw. Dozens of young, smashing women. Mostly mulatto, with *café-con-leche* skin. They were mainly dressed in tight Spandex dresses, and they all sported shiny new patent-leather pumps and had small purses slung from their shoulders on long straps. They were waiting for foreign men to stroll by and take them inside. Foreign men with dollars.

Karelia and I walked toward the pillared portals of Havana Club, overlooking the black-satin expanse of the sea. I paid $10 for me and another $10 for her, and we stepped into the hallowed, air-conditioned interior of Havana Club, where a terraced network of rust-brown banquettes descended to the dance floor. It was crowded and noisy, with strobe lights and spotlights and mirrors and smoke effects. We found our way to the bar, ordered a couple of $5 Cokes — the rum was practically free — and looked around.

Some place.

The music was great, mostly Latin rhythms — rumba, mambo, cha-cha, samba, and salsa — spiked with American rap and disco nouveau. Out on the dance floor, two worlds embraced — or collided. Like so many slender satellite states, so many leggy island colonies, dozens of Cuban women danced with their foreign patrons, sipped their $5 Cokes, giggled, and waved to their friends.

The women were young, and they were wonderful dancers, all. The men tended to be older and heavier, and their footwork on the dance floor seemed doggedly wrong — but never mind. Someone had to pay for these shimmering Spandex dresses, these polished dancing shoes, this swirl of perfume, intoxication, and sin. I watched the dancers and listened to the music, and found myself thinking back to a very different sea-side scene.

Oriente Province. December 2, 1956. When Fidel Castro

and Ché Guevara landed on the Cuban coast aboard the yacht *Granma* that day — to begin their campaign against the US-backed dictator Fulgencio Batista — they had a force of eighty-one men under their command. Before long, that little force was reduced even further, to a rump of just twelve ragged men. But Fidel did not despair. He continued to fight and to attract followers. Two years later, in January, 1959 — after an absurdly heroic struggle — Fidel and Ché and their troops marched down from the Sierra Maestra to take power. Batista had fled the country, and the course of Latin American history had changed.

And here I was, sipping a *Cuba Libre* in Havana Club, and what I wondered was this — if Fidel could recover from his setbacks in the Sierra Maestra in those glorious if long-ago days, could he not make a comeback now? Could he not turn this crumbling revolution around? The odds looked pretty grim. After all, Ché Guevara had long been dead; and, as I surveyed the crowd of celebrants at Havana Club, it seemed to me that even a Ché Guevara and a Fidel Castro, reunited, would have a tough slog winning new recruits to the revolutionary cause among this party-minded crew.

Later, after we'd hit the dance floor for a time, Karelia and I found ourselves a banquette in a dark corner of the club. Here we chatted, sipped our drinks, and watched a hulking foreigner who was slouched on a sofa just a few feet away. He was profoundly drunk, it seemed, barely conscious. Beside him, a slim handsome fellow — evidently a Cuban from his appearance — was hard at work. By slow deft degrees, the Cuban was trying to pick the foreigner's pocket.

So this, I thought, was what the Cuban revolution had come to — young men robbing drunken foreigners in

Yankee-style discos where they accepted only US cash. It seemed an impossibly long way from the battle cries of Comandante Fidel and his men up in the Sierra Maestra during the years of rebellion against Batista. You had to wonder how much longer this revolution could hold on.

A few days later, I happened to be in the office of Felipe Carneado. He was a member of the Communist Party Central Committee and was also the senior government official responsible for church-state relations. He was in his sixties and an articulate man — urbane, intelligent, avuncular. But, like a lot of Communist Party officials, he had a tendency to lapse into that numbing patois I thought of as Revolutionese. I asked him what he thought about this new generation of Cuban youth. Were they worthy flag-bearers in the socialist cause?

He raised his sombre grey head. "The majority of Cuban youths," he said, "are currently a force of joy in favour of the Revolution. The self-denial of the immense majority of Cuban youths is a marvel."

Hold on, I said. What about the black-market currency trading? Or all the Cuban women for sale? Or the resurgence of gambling and drugs? What about all those kids out along the Malecón every night?

Señor Carneado nodded. Yes, yes. He'd noticed these things, too. Like others, he blamed Havana's increasing incidence of graft and sin on the pernicious effects of foreign tourism. "Eight years ago, there weren't these tourists, this dependence on the dollar," he said. He shrugged. "In any country, you'll find black-market trading for dollars. In any country, you'll find prostitutes."

He was right. In any country, you will. But this wasn't

any country, this was revolutionary Cuba. If you looked at
the situation in a certain, idealistic light, it all seemed a bit
disheartening. Was there no hope at all for the grand egali-
tarian ideal? But then I thought of something that Karelia
had told me. We'd been having dinner one evening at a
place along the Malecón, a restaurant called 1830. She'd
been telling me about her years at school in Havana.

Like all urban youngsters in Cuba, she and her fellow
students had been dispatched to the countryside for a month
or so each year, to aid in the harvest. In the past, I had sometimes imagined the scene, usually through a haze of arm-
chair idealism — all those earnest uniformed youths, their
faces fixed in socialist concentration, all hacking away at tall
stalks of sugar cane with their machetes, or heaving their
crates of tropical produce up onto rows of flatbed trucks,
always beneath a cloud cover of proletarian grey.

"It wasn't like that at all," said Karelia. "We didn't do any
work at all. We just threw tomatoes at each other."

And I realized now that I really did prefer her earthy real-
ism to the sort of antiseptic illusion conveyed by Felipe
Carneado's Revolutionese. Who would even want to get to
know these phony young Cubans of his, these forces of joy
in favour of the Revolution? Much better a bunch of kids
out in a darkened street at night, all dancing to a counter-
revolutionary tune. Much better a group of students dispatched to the countryside, running and ducking through a
sun-bathed field, lobbing tomatoes at each other. I could
almost hear their voices now, singing at the top of their
lungs to a sweaty rumba rhythm or laughing above the
ocean's roar. It was hard to say for sure, but it sounded a lot
like the heartbeat of the Tropicana to me.

Uncle
With a
Basket

I HAD INSTALLED MYSELF at the polished wooden bar of the Grand Hotel Oloffson in Port-au-Prince and was exploring the intriguing mysteries of another rum punch while tinkering with the typed version of an article I had just written for my newspaper. Shaded electric lamps made a small pool of light against the inky tropical darkness that loomed beyond the verandah. Ceiling fans whirled overhead, above the oriental rugs, the wicker furniture, the luminous folk art, and the patrons gathering in twos and threes. On the verandah, a barefoot trio wailed out one fervent *merengue* after another, and the lights went on among the palms. There was only one other person seated at the bar, a young woman. She was perhaps three empty spaces away from my private corner of the Haitian night.

"Excuse me," she murmured. She leaned on the bar with one hand buried in her long ash-blond hair and the other balanced delicately on her left hip. Out of nowhere, she asked me, "Do you have a dream?"

"A dream?" I said. "I . . . well, I have lots of dreams."

"I have a dream," she declared. She nodded to herself

and returned at least a portion of her attention to her drink. She swallowed and surrendered herself to what was evidently a shiver of pleasure. "My dream is that I shall one day open a small hotel in Jacmel," she said. She meant a small colonial city on Haiti's southern peninsula. "I shall have a patron in Port-au-Prince to finance me, and I shall run my hotel as a private place for my friends — all artists and intellectuals. And . . . I shall take a lover." Here, she paused for another sip of her drink. "But," she added. "I would only ever take a writer for my lover." She stopped. She turned to me. She tilted her head gravely. She lowered her voice. She said, "Are you a writer . . . ?"

That was the Grand Hotel Oloffson. Tottering on a hillside above the miserable harbourfront slums of Port-au-Prince, the hotel had had a chequered history. Once described as "a nightmare of nineteenth-century design," the building is an outrageous folly of balconies, cupolas, spires, gables, and turrets, almost choking itself with overwrought gingerbread. It was built more than one hundred years ago as a mansion for Haitian president S.D. Sam. Later, when US Marines occupied Haiti in 1915, they converted the building into a hospital and added a small surgery and a maternity ward.

In 1935, more than 130 years after Toussaint L'Ouverture led a slave revolt to gain Haitian independence, the Oloffson was finally established as the republic's first international hotel when it was purchased by a Norwegian sea captain named Oloffson; he kept crocodiles in the swimming pool. Perhaps the Oloffson's chief claim to notoriety, however, comes courtesy of a writer. (Writers seem to be popular at the Oloffson.) In this case, the writer was Graham

Greene. The Oloffson served as the model for the Hotel Trianon, site of most of the furtive action in *The Comedians*, Greene's novel about faith and faithlessness in Haiti under François (Papa Doc) Duvalier. In fact, Greene lived at the Oloffson while writing the book. He was not the first illustrious visitor, however. When the hotel was purchased from Captain Oloffson in 1954 — and the crocodiles were removed, carefully, from the swimming pool — the new owner, a Frenchman named Roger Coster, adopted the practice of naming the hotel's rambling suites and cottages after their more famous guests: the James Jones Cottage, for example, or the Lady Antonia Fraser Studio, or the John Gielgud Suite, where Greene lived while writing *The Comedians*.

The twenty-four-room hotel was purchased in 1960 by Al Seitz, a cigar-chomping Connecticut Yankee, who died in 1982. His widow, Sue Seitz, kept the hotel going for a time after that. She installed a new garden and improved plumbing, and the Oloffson continued to bill itself as "the darling of theatre people and the literary set." (Once, the Oloffson brochures had also mentioned "newsmen" as a special category of celebrity, but that reference was later dropped — a careless oversight, no doubt.) Either way, this was the kind of chichi boast that might well constitute the kiss of death just about anywhere else but seemed rather winsome when considered over a fine rum punch — quite possibly the finest in the Caribbean — beneath the silent whirl of the ceiling fans in the Oloffson bar.

Gradually, the wicker furniture fills with a mystifying assortment of Haitians and expatriates. Bathed in a halo of electric light on the verandah steps, the ragtag trio flings itself into another *merengue*. The wretched slums of Port-au-Prince are swallowed by darkness, and the lights go on among the palms.

I always liked to arrive at the Oloffson by night. The steep drive up to the entrance of the hotel was lined with palm trees and flourishes of bougainvillea, illuminated by ground lights. The building itself unfolded ahead, glowing through dark waves of tropical foliage — a rambling and indecipherable array of architectural excess. A porter would heave my bag onto his shoulder and guide me past the swimming pool, home to the ghosts of countless unsung crocodiles and the very place where the secretary of social welfare in *The Comedians* slit his throat in despair. We climbed up the stone staircase and entered the hotel bar, where clusters of stylish patrons colluded in whispers and scattered laughter beneath trails of cigarette smoke and the slowly whirling fans. On my first visit to the place, I settled on the Irving Stone Suite, overlooking the bobbing lights of Port-au-Prince harbour. A dusty black-and-white mongrel noisily nursed her puppies beneath the floorboards.

In the morning, breakfast was served on the long verandah that bordered the Oloffson bar. At about eight o'clock, a dapper little man in a grey suit and an ascot would flounce up onto the deck, carrying a polished black walking stick. He set about greeting just about any familiar face he encountered or, come to that, any *unfamiliar* face. He was Aubelin Jolicoeur, an art dealer who wrote a gossip column for a Port-au-Prince newspaper. He had also served as the model for Petit Pierre, the garrulous and not overly courageous Haitian journalist in *The Comedians*, a point of historical and literary interest that M. Jolicoeur took careful pains to mention during all conversations.

In the evenings, the Oloffson bar attracted an otherwordly assortment of Haitians and expatriates. Among them: a Haitian economist who lectured me on the weaknesses of the Canadian school system and the strengths of the Canadian soccer team, both of which he knew far more intimately than I; a Canadian expatriate who had recently opened two North-American-style doughnut shops in Haiti, poorest country in the Americas; an American writer living at the Oloffson while researching a book on Haitian cemeteries; an American businessmen who said he had lived in Haiti for more than two decades and who listed for my benefit the five good things about Haiti that the foreign press never writes about. Number three was the fact that Haitians do not desecrate their cemeteries.

The alleged deficiencies of the coverage of Haiti in the foreign press was a theme that came up repeatedly whenever I found myself in Port-au-Prince. One night, for example, the Canadian doughnut-shop owner joined me for dinner at an excellent restaurant in Petionville, enclave of the Haitian rich, perched high above Port-au-Prince. Presently, he began to rail against a series of articles he had read about Haiti in some foreign newspaper. They'd been published a year or so earlier, he said. He was a bit vague about the name of the publication, but he was dead certain what he thought of the writer. "I wish he were here now," he told me. "I'd break his neck. Lies. Just lies and ignorance."

As he ranted on, it began to seem that the newspaper articles in question had a certain *familiarity*. It seemed that I knew these articles rather well. Had I not, in fact, even *written* them? In fact, it seemed that I had, and so I felt protectively for my neck and bought my dinner companion another beer.

As far as this man was concerned — and it was a view he shared with other privileged residents of the country — foreign journalists visiting Haiti write only about poverty, or political repression, or secret police, or desperate people fleeing in leaky wooden boats, or more poverty. In truth, his criticism probably wasn't far off the mark. There could be no denying that the country has had a lousy reputation abroad or that much of that reputation rests on the reporting done by foreign journalists. But does that make the reporting *wrong*?

First of all, Haiti really *is* alarmingly poor. It is also desperately over-crowded, disastrously deforested, and almost bereft of natural resources. Take away a smattering of coffee, a dash of sugar, a pinch of bauxite, and what you have left are foreign remittances, foreign aid, and handicrafts.

Second, until very recently, Haiti really *was* ruled by a dictatorial and tragi-comic crew. In the 1980s, the tyrant was Jean-Claude "Baby Doc" Duvalier — a tubby young playboy whose official title was President for Life. He was the son of the infamous Papa Doc and held power along with his svelte mulatto wife (the First Lady for Life) and his embittered mother (reportedly in a deep funk after having been demoted from First Lady herself to the position of Guardian of the Haitian Revolution, whatever that was). Ministers spent an average of about six months in office and then, having enriched themselves to a suitable extent, were replaced.

Finally, the whole country really *was* a dangerous place for most of its people. It was roamed by corrupt and vicious government thugs known far and wide as *tons-tons macoute* — a *créole* phrase that means "uncle with a basket." The term refers to a sinister figure in Haitian folklore. In his terrible basket, this grim uncle would carry off your head. No wonder ordinary Haitians were trying to escape the place. In those days, they were fleeing by the hundreds, bound for Florida in makeshift vessels that often broke up at sea even before they hit the Bahamas, leaving all their erstwhile passengers to drown in the ocean swells.

On the whole, it would have taken a remarkably ingenious and imaginative journalist to paint a portrait of Haiti that did not lean a little towards the negative side. If the rich didn't like the coverage, then this was just another cross they would have to bear. It was hard for me to feel very sorry for them. After all, when it comes to crosses in Haiti, it is the poor who do most of the heavy lifting.

One morning in Port-au-Prince, I climbed into a car I'd rented and headed up through the Artibonite Valley to the northern coastal city of Cap-Haïtien. I wanted to talk to some of these people who were determined to risk their lives on the dangerous and costly run across the Atlantic and the Strait of Florida in search of what was not exactly a comfortable or even safe haven in the United States. I didn't have much trouble finding them. In the coastal villages outside Cap Haïtien, I spoke to dozens of poor Haitians, all of them caught up in one way or another with the dream of flight across the sea.

It was a dream that more often became a nightmare. Just three weeks earlier, a small wooden boat had sunk off the south Florida coast. It had been carrying sixty-three Haitians, all of whom had slapped down their life's savings in exchange for the slim hope of a better life as illegal immigrants in a country that did not want them. Only thirty of the passengers survived the sinking. Nineteen men drowned, and fourteen women. Their bodies eventually washed up on a Florida beach. They included the corpse of a twenty-four-year-old Haitian named Joseph Metelus.

In a village called Acul du Nord, I spoke to his mother, Irene Metelus. She told me that a total of three families had saved for five years in order to amass the $1,600 US it had cost them to send her son to his death off the south Florida coast. The plan had been for Joseph to find work in the United States and then wire money back to them.

In and around Cap-Haïtien, I found an endless stream of people who either had pinned their hopes on a risky sea passage to the United States, or, like Irene Metelus, had been forced by catastrophe to abandon those hopes.

Mountainous, crowded, and shaped like a claw, Haiti huddles on the western third of the Caribbean island of Hispaniola, stitched by geography to the Spanish-speaking Dominican Republic, but forced by history, culture and circumstance into a haunted world of its own. At the end of the eighteenth century, the slaves, maroons and mulattoes of what was then the French possession of St-Domingue rose up and defeated a substantial French military force commanded by General Charles Leclerc, brother-in-law of Napoleon Bonaparte. In 1804, the victorious former slaves called their new land Haiti, its original Arawak name.

Even with independence, life in the second-oldest republic in the New World never ceased to be a struggle — desperately impoverished, blotted by bouts of folly and greed, hounded by tyranny. And yet, that stark picture doesn't tell the whole tale, either. In the midst of this brute struggle to survive, there is another side to life here that isn't brutal at all. And to that extent, I suppose, my Canadian acquaintance — the owner of those two doughnut shops in Port-au-Prince — was probably right. It was possible for a journalist to be too negative about Haiti.

One Saturday afternoon, for example, I strolled around the Place des Armes in a town called St-Marc — halfway up the coast between Port-au-Prince and Cap-Haïtien — and watched the local families out promenading around the square, all in their finest clothing, with their children done up in bows and ribbons, like figures on some elaborate birthday cake. Everybody nodded to each other, smiled, and chatted. I saw a pride and a dignity here that often got lost or overlooked in the standard, heart-rending portraits of Haiti as a country of helplessness and despair. Mind you, these people had enough weekend finery to go around. Not all Haitians do. And yet, even those without sufficient clothing somehow manage to find a way.

Late one weekday morning, in a village on the northern coast, I once spent some time talking to a local woman and then rashly asked her if I might snap some photographs of her family. My request was entirely selfish — I wanted the pictures to illustrate an article I was working on. But the woman misunderstood, as did a group of villagers who had gathered around. They thought I wanted to take portraits for their benefit. I quickly explained that my camera was not an instant model — it didn't provide pictures right away. That was all right, someone said. I could send the printed photos back.

And then the bedlam began. The woman's family — and it was by no means a *small* family — promptly retreated into their cramped, mud-walled house with its corrugated zinc roof. Of course, they had to change into their best clothes — that was taken for granted. But the transformation was no easy matter. Like the other villagers, they were poor rural Haitians, people who supported themselves mainly through subsistence farming — planting yams or plantain — or by growing coffee for sale. The sandy track that ran through the village was littered with wicker mats, spread with drying coffee beans. These people were industrious, but they were extremely poor. It seemed that nobody in this village even *owned* a complete set of best clothes.

The other villagers crowded outside the house, and an elaborate shuttle system was set up, as if by telepathy. Soon, small boys and girls were darting off to neighbouring houses to fill a flurry of orders for various articles of dress. They then scampered back, each clutching aloft some required piece of clothing — a brassière, a pair of shoes, a belt, a white blouse, a tie. Finally this woman and her family were groomed and garbed and ready for what was obviously, to them, an extremely important occasion. They paraded from their house and assembled out in front to pose for a series of photographs, while their neighbours gazed intently on.

As I snapped the shutter on my camera, first from this angle, then from another, it occurred to me what an injustice we do when we think of people only as victims, when we treat them as helpless creatures of an unkind fate, or when we think of them as being somehow less human, simply because they are poor. Maybe these people didn't have enough good clothes to go around, but they had found a way to dress as though they did.

That image of pride and of ingenuity was almost a kind

of metaphor for the entire country. Haiti brims with a richness of spirit — of rhythm, music, faith, colour, beauty, and magic — that matches any in the Americas. I could see the evidence almost everywhere. In Port-au-Prince, for example, I watched the never-ending carnival of commerce that unfurls beneath the long porticos lining the Boulevard J. J. Dessalines, cluttered by day with small-time merchants called *Mesdames Sarah*, after a chattering yellow tropical bird. Meanwhile, the pocked pavement of the street itself is jammed almost constantly with *tap-taps*, Haiti's brilliantly painted passenger trucks, each swelling with an excess of human cargo and swept along by the pious hopes or saintly virtues emblazoned on its hood in hand-lettered script: *Endurance*, *Patience*, *Gloire à Jésus*, *Miraculeuse*, *Imaculée*, *L'esprit saint*. Back and forth, the *tap-taps* jolt and lurch all day, like an eternal traffic jam on the road to heaven.

Or, down on the country's southern peninsula, I'd stood atop the heights of the Massif de la Selle and seen an almost edenic land. In the green distance, processions of slender, sure-footed women glided down to morning market, through mingling streams of sunlight and foliage, each balancing a basket of golden mangoes or emerald bananas atop her head. It was almost as if they were all preparing to step directly onto the canvases painted by Haiti's famous folk artists.

Haitians were poor, all right. But they were anything except dull or defeated. It really was wrong to write about them only in terms of their poverty. There was much else to say. And so, when I returned to the country several years later, I was determined to look beyond Haiti's glaring economic woes, to write about something other than misery and distress.

Bonsoi,
Dam Mrin

T HERE I WAS, all alone, late at night, in a place I did not know, with less than half a tank of gas in my rented car and the name of a total stranger scribbled in my notebook — the story of my life. I began to ask around.

But asking around was not as easy as it might sound, for my modest French barely dented the percussive Haitian *créole* disgorged by the peering faces that loomed up out of the night in Gonaïves, a rambling dusty city in central Haiti, now plunged into a darkness so profound it seemed to have shape and substance and weight. I pulled up beside another group of shadows clustered by the road. I asked them if they knew where Herard Simon lived. He was an *houngan*, a *voudou* priest whose name had been given to me by someone I knew in Port-au-Prince. These good people knew exactly where he lived, it seemed, and promptly began to pile into the car.

I set a limit of two, both of whom landed heavily in the passenger seat at my side — a young man and his father. They guided me along the main road, then off on a dirt lane that disappeared into the night. We drove away, fanning dust through a tangled archway of trees, until we reached an even narrower spur road striking off to the right. We turned onto that. I found myself wondering if there were not some place I would really rather be, and my foot eased back on the gas. Each time I slowed down, my passengers began clapping me on the shoulders, shouting, *"Allez! Allez!"* and pointing off into the gloom.

Finally, my companions motioned for me to slow down, and we turned right again, this time onto a gravel ribbon lined by coco palms. We broke into a forest clearing, and a large box-shaped building materialized in the headlights straight ahead. I hit the brakes, and the car lurched to a halt. The structure that stood before us was open in front, with concrete-block walls at the sides and back. It had a slanted roof made of corrugated metal. Inside, by the glow of the car headlights, I could make out rows of crude wooden benches and a pile of what looked like African drums. The outer walls of the building were inscribed with weird devices — concentric circles pierced by swords and arrows, stylized flames and horses. Dominating all else, was a slogan boldly painted in red:

*Pèp ayisyen chaché retounen nan rasin nou
Rasin nou sé voudou.*

I did not have to be fluent in *créole* to decipher this message. "The Haitian people seek to return to our roots," the slogan declared. "Our roots are voudou."

It was 1987, more than a year after the fall of Baby Doc Duvalier. Known now as le *dechoukage* — a *créole* word meaning "the uprooting" — Baby Doc's ouster had brought an end to the stifling thirty-year dictatorship of the Duvalier clan, and it briefly seemed that Haiti's long tradition of tyranny, misrule, and fear might at last take a happier turn.

Already, the country had gained a new constitution that held out the shaky promise of democracy, social equality, and respect for civil rights. The document also specifically repealed a long-standing prohibition on *voudou*. It had taken a long time, but nearly two-hundred years after Haiti's independence, legitimacy was at last being granted to the religion that some eighty per cent of Haitians considered their one true faith — *voudou*.

We clambered out of the car. There was no sound but the cric-crac of crickets, ebbing and flowing through the heavy darkness. I realized that my two guides had brought me straight to a *hounfour*, a *voudou* temple — presumably the temple belonging to Herard Simon. I wandered around the building, calling out Simon's name, but the temple was deserted. In the distance, a dog barked. Another howled in reply. I returned to the car and explained to my companions that I wanted to go to Simon's *house*, not his temple. They nodded, and we climbed into the car and set off the way we had come. Eventually, we pulled up outside a drab concrete-block wall I hadn't noticed before. The headlights illuminated a battered metal gate.

"*Klaxonez! Klaxonez!*" my two friends shouted, and I blared the car horn until the gates finally shuddered and scraped open.

A young woman appeared. She carried a flashlight and wore a white kerchief around her forehead. Her name, it turned out, was Mamoune Corvil, and she was Herard Simon's nineteen-year-old niece. Mamoune led the three of us on foot, past the gates, across a dirt yard, and then through a narrow passageway that opened onto a small dirt court, lined by wooden verandahs and lit dimly by a *tête gri-dap* — a kerosene lantern.

An imposing woman approached us from the darkness, barefoot in a loose brown dress, smoking a cigarette. This was Hélène Simon, Herard's wife and a great *mambo*, or *voudou* priestess, herself. She spoke French haltingly, with a husky voice and a thudding *créole* accent. Mme. Simon informed me that her husband was in Port-au-Prince and would not return for a couple of days. "Would you like to stay here for the night?" she asked.

"Are you certain?" I said.

"*Bien sûr!*" she exclaimed.

And so I accepted. I stayed up until well past midnight that night, sweltering in the dense lowland heat, talking to Mamoune about *voudou*. In deliberate but excellent French, Mamoune explained a little about Dahomey, Banda and Congo, three of the *voudou* traditions that flourish in the Artibonite Valley. A forthright young woman with power-fully defined features and flashing eyes, Mamoune spoke quickly, in a tone that discouraged contradiction. "My uncle is a great, great priest of *voudou!*" she boasted.

The following morning, Mamoune greeted me in the yard behind the house with a tin mug of sticky, sweet coffee. After breakfast, I presented a bottle of Jane Barbancourt rum to Mme. Simon as a gift of thanks. Before setting off, I said that I would return in several days to meet her husband. I climbed into my rented car and set off through the ponder-ous heat, winding up over the gorgeous, green *Chaîne du Bonnet* mountains and then north along the banks of the *Rivière Lumbé*, bound for Cap-Haïtien, a place I'd visited on previous trips to Haiti and wanted to see again.

Known locally as le Cap, the city is congregated on la Plaine du Nord between the foot of Morne Rouge and the sea — a stately assembly of colonial row-houses with pastel-stucco walls, filigree balconies, and tall, arched french doors, arrayed shoulder to shoulder, like wooden soldiers on parade.

Le Cap has its share of Haiti's urban squalor, but it is an infinitely more settled and subdued place than Port-au-Prince, something *les capois* are fond of pointing out to visitors. The city is a sort of *petit patrie* — a little fatherland — an enclosed world, psychologically sufficient unto itself.

It had long been so. Shortly after independence, a freed slave named Henri Cristophe, an inn-keeper by trade, claimed the northern half of Haiti as his domain, named it *le Royaume du Nord* and crowned himself king. He took a European-born woman as his queen, Marie-Louise Coidavid, and built her an opulent palace called *Sans Souci*. For himself, he erected a mountain-top fortress at the summit of *Bonnet à l'Evêque* — the infamous *Citadelle Laferrière*. Some twenty-thousand lives were lost in the construction of that stupendous folly, which was never to be attacked. In 1820, beset by insurrection, le Roi Cristophe took his own life — by firing a single gold bullet through his heart, it is said.

Now, his memory lives on in a multitude of ways — in the name, for example, of a splendid old hotel down in le Cap, the Roi Cristophe. Built in 1723 as a private mansion, the hotel is a maze of courtyards and corridors with burnt-clay walls and polished wooden furnishings, set in a walled garden amid a tangle of almond trees, banana plants, coco palms, hibiscus and bougainvillea. I splurged on a large room, with lofty ceilings, an antique desk and wardrobe, and rough french doors that opened onto a sprawling tiled balcony overlooking a grove of lemon trees. In the distance, the lower slopes of Morne Rouge began their long march to the summit.

One evening in le Cap, I strolled alone through the darkened city, past a slim young woman in a black dress and kerchief who was shaking out a brazier into the street so that the orange coals wobbled and scattered in the breeze; past a tiny workshop where a pair of carpenters diligently sawed through a long bowed plank; past a gingerbread balcony where children leaned over the railing, singing a song to the street below.

Later, back at the Roi Cristophe, I stood on the balcony outside my room, cradling a glass of Barbancourt rum, as a torrential rain thundered into the garden, like a vast dropcurtain of water. The downpour eased, and I peered up at the darkened sky just in time to watch five luminous discs sweep through the clouds overhead and then suddenly fly apart an instant before they disappeared from view. I swear I saw them, but I have no idea what they were. I couldn't say then, and I can't say now.

The following morning, I left Cap-Haïtien and drove back down to Gonaïves and eventually found my way to the house of Herard Simon. Mme. Simon was out in the yard when I showed up. I hadn't told her what time I would return, but it seemed she was waiting for me anyway. She got into the car, and we drove off together, heading toward her husband's *hounfour*. On our arrival, Mme. Simon promptly stalked off into the surrounding banana fields, carrying a *machète*. I waited in the shade of a grove of almond trees as Simon himself held court against the wall of the *hounfour*. A gaggle of younger men were gathered at his feet, shuffling papers and exchanging glances and nods as Simon conferred with them.

Finally, his business completed, Simon approached me. "*Je suis à votre disposition*," he announced. He turned and ambled off toward the cool interior of the *hounfour*. I followed.

Despite his startling bulk, Simon moved with something like grace. He was clad only in jean shorts and a brightly patterned cotton shirt that hung open to reveal his balloon-like belly. His chin bore several days' growth of salted stubble, and he had mismatched eyes. He settled himself at a rough wooden table and began to speak.

A priest of three different *voudou* traditions — Nago, Congo and Dahomey — Simon spent much of that afternoon patiently leading me through some of the concepts underlying *voudou*. He spoke of the loas, or spirits, of the four basic elements — Shango, Ogoun, Obatala, and Ochu. He described the two expressions of the human soul: the astral soul, that may become manifest in any living thing; and the *ti bonne ange*, that may present itself only in another human. He spoke of Olorun, the presiding god of the *voudou* pantheon, and Legba, his son.

Simon told me there was nothing sinister about *voudou*, despite its eerie reputation in the North American mind. For most North Americans, the word *voudou* conjures up images of sorcerers gathered by firelight to plunge pins into wax dolls — a practice that has nothing to do with *voudou* and is unknown in Haiti. Most of our notions of *voudou* are similarly distorted. *Voudou* is a religion, no more diabolical at heart than any other. It seeks to do what other religions do — provide a way of living in this world and a means of apprehending the next.

Yet, since its origin in Africa and its almost desperate burgeoning in Haiti during the years of *le maroonage* — when escaped slaves, called maroons, fought bitter guerrilla wars against their French colonial masters — *voudou* has lived a clandestine life, celebrated furtively, by moonlight. There have been attempts — especially by François "Papa Doc" Duvalier — to exploit the religion for political purposes. Such efforts only served to make *voudou* seem more grim or malevolent than it really is. In fact, *voudou* has much more to do with celebration than mourning. It is more about life than death.

Gradually, however, the religion became entangled with the *ton-tons macoute*, Papa Doc's pervasive security network of thugs and bullies, which did nothing to brighten the religion's already shady image. But Papa Doc was long dead now, and his son Baby Doc had at last been uprooted. Maybe *voudou* was at last going to emerge into the open.

At the end of our conversation in his *hounfour* that day, Simon invited me to return to Gonaïves the following Saturday to attend a *grande-prière*, a *voudou* ceremony held in homage to the souls of the ancient dead. I thanked him and accepted. Then I climbed into my car and set off beneath the blistering sun, wending my way back through the Artibonite Valley towards Port-au-Prince.

I spent several days that week in Jacmel, on Haiti's southern peninsula. It's a small and enchanting city of wrought-iron balconies, twisting alleys, and baked-clay colours, terraced among balustrades of royal palms and groves of portly cashew trees. The town overlooks a broad, green-walled bay that sweeps out to the blue Antillean sea. In the distance, tiny wooden *voiliers* totter back and forth across the goose-pimpled waters, sprouting patched and mottled sails — like geriatric dragon-flies.

I was staying at a remarkable little hotel, la Jacmélienne, balanced at the edge of the sea upon a narrow arc of smooth stones and black sand. On the morning of my arrival, I changed into my swimming trunks and made my way down past the gazebo and beyond the palms, hopped off the low breakwater to the stony beach, darted several steps to plunge into the ocean.

I surfaced into the dazzling sunshine and bobbed on my back for a time amid the gentle swells. A fine mist drifted through the spindly palm shafts by the beach, where the waves stumbled against the sandy bottom and toppled onto the shore. The twin promontories of Jacmel stretched out to the distance on either side, their green summits dabbed with the delicate red flourishes of *flamboyante* trees, like smudges of lipstick on a giant's collar. Both ridges stooped down to meet the sea. The lines they made, as they intersected with the ocean horizon, suddenly seemed to form the edges of the knowable world.

That afternoon, I hiked up to the town's central plaza, perched upon a rounded hill amid groves of cashew trees. Along the street, clumps of men huddled over rickety wooden tables, playing dominoes in the shade of makeshift awnings. I turned a final corner towards the square and was beset by a flock of schoolgirls bouncing homeward, all in navy frocks and white socks with their hair done up in beribboned plaits. Some twirled parasols, and most clutched earnest-looking leather satchels. They giggled and jostled past, making me think of miniature barristers streaming out of court. Every last one of them had just won her first big case.

Below the square, a doddering old mansion hugged the hillside, with a red tin roof, green shutters and two broad, lopsided balconies. This was the Manoir Alexandra, owned by a woman of advanced years named Alexandre Vital, who had converted her home into a hotel when her husband died in 1945. Now, she had five large rooms to let, and an all-embracing view of the city below. Her manager, Françine Marquin, took me upstairs to have a look. From the balcony, I gazed out upon an intricate panorama of aging cream- and clay-colored houses linked by terraced alleys, all bathed in brilliant foams of bougainvillea, like wads of orange cotton batten, punctured by the spiky foliage of palm and *véritables* trees. Beyond — the deep blue mirror of the sea.

I even debated moving up to Mme. Vital's hotel right then and there, but in the end I remained down by the sea at la Jacmelienne, with its white-stucco walls, clay-tiled floors, and wooden jalousies. That evening in the dining room, overlooking a palisade of shifting moonlit palms, about half a dozen women in white cotton dresses officiously arranged dinner for the hotel's only guest, who happened to be me. A warm onshore breeze wandered through the palms and across the railings, and the women gathered off to the side, speaking among themselves in whispers, casting occasional glances my way.

After my solitary meal, I retired to the bar where several members of the local American expatriate community stopped by for a drink. A Haitian trio played moody *créole* folk songs on a guitar, maracas, and a *manniba*, a resonant, steel-tongued bass instrument, and I wound up talking about *voudou* to a laughing, crystal-voiced woman from Aspen, Colorado.

I left Jacmel shortly after that, to keep my appointment in Gonaïves. I drove north beyond Port-au-Prince, up through the Artibonite Valley until I got to Herard Simon's place. It was almost dark when I arrived, but Mamoune was waiting for me. She told me the *grande-prière* was to be held at the house of a woman named Titi Lefrançois. She took my hand and guided me through the neighbouring fields and the semi-darkness. A gibbous moon dangled overhead. Presently, we reached Mme. Lefrançois' home, where a palm canopy had been erected in the yard and where the earth was already marked by the drying blood of a goat, now sacrificed to the souls of the ancient dead. Dozens of people jammed the edges of the yard, illuminated by tallow candles and a *tête gridap*.

Several drummers huddled in one corner beneath the canopy, where they were under the instructions of an elderly woman — the *hounsis* — who wore a white kerchief and rattled a *maraca*. Soon the drummers began to play, hesitantly at first, until they established a rhythm — then pell-mell. Sensing the beat, the crowd set up a powerful repetitive chant, voices rising and swooping in complex harmony.

An old man shuffled around the clearing and occasionally removed his straw hat in order to point at individuals in the crowd. He was selecting the dancers and then pairing them off. The chosen couples took their places beneath the palm fronds and proceeded to sway back and forth, moving from one end of the clearing to the other, in the slow, deliberate steps of the *Baron Samedi*.

Suddenly, the old man hovered before me, with his hat pointed directly at my chest. Mamoune gave me a shove, and before I could dig in my heels I found myself on my own in the centre of the clearing. I was soon paired with a willowy, grim-faced woman, barefoot in a pale-blue dress. Again, the drummers began to pound their leather *tambours*. Sweat sluiced down their muscle-knotted arms like rivulets streaming over rocks. I followed my partner, dipped and twisted, as she led me back and forth beneath the palm shelter, her skirt raised to her thighs. The crowd's chanting turned to a roar, and all the women began to wave their arms overhead to the rhythm of the drums. My partner's expression remained perfectly still, utterly intent, as she played the folds of her skirt back and forth and ground her way through the clearing from end to end.

The drumming grew thunderous, pervasive, hypnotic. It seemed to penetrate skin, flesh, bones. The crowd became a blur of flailing arms, the voices so loud that the throbbing chant seemed to reverberate inside my head, endlessly repeating itself. Several times, on a sudden impulse, I twisted around in a spin, and the crowd practically shrieked. This was evidently hilarious — a white boy dancing the *Baron Samedi*! When the dance ended at last, I was trembling, dizzy, drenched in sweat. Instinctively, I leaned over and planted a kiss on my partner's cheek, raising howls of apparently delighted laughter from the crowd. From nowhere, Mme. Simon rushed over to congratulate me. "*Bonne forme!*" she shouted. "*Bonne forme!*"

Then, before I knew what was going on, I found myself

being guided back to the centre of the clearing where I was surrounded by five women. The drumming resumed, and the women began to dance around me. They pulled off their kerchiefs and waved them like fans. They set to mopping the perspiration from my face, neck and arms. Several of the women played their hands through my hair, then down my neck and my back. Before long, I had been subjected to what was either an extremely warm welcome — or among the most detailed physical examinations of my life. The *guedes* — *créole* spirits of the lecherous dead — were evidently hard at work.

Before long, there was a break in the music. Most of the men went off somewhere to deal with men's affairs. Meanwhile, a tall woman strolled through the remaining crowd of women. She carried a large enamel coffee pot and a tray of plastic cups. Here and there, she stopped to pour out a cloying, syrupy cane liqueur. The women stood about, taking dainty sips. They tossed their heads this way and that, shot bemused glances from one to another. Laughing in the semi-darkness, with their free hands resting easily at their hips, they made me think of young socialites at a cocktail party.

Well past midnight, the drumming and the dancing still rollicked in the yard by Titi Lefrançois' house, but Mamoune and I walked back through the fields to her uncle's place, where I had again been invited to stay. I had also agreed to return a week later, to attend a *voudou* congress at Simon's *hounfour* — a sacred occasion, when the deities would be manifest, and the loas would descend to mount and to possess the faithful.

A week later, I did return. Mamoune guided me out

through the coco palms and almond trees near the *hounfour*. In the darkness, young men crouched over huge leather drums, and a hundred *voudouisaints* writhed in the grip of the Petro spirits. The dancers spun like tops, smashed into each other, knocked over chairs, crashed helplessly to the earth. Men suddenly burst from the crowd, twisted in circles, collapsed to the ground, grovelled and bucked. A woman plunged to her knees, flopped onto her back, writhed in the earth until her dress fell away. She leapt upright, caked with sweat and dirt, shook herself, turned, and fled, naked, through the trees. Men squatted down and addressed each other with weird hand-clasps, bizarre gestures, and spasms. Women swooped back and forth through the firelight, like birds on the wind, and a silver three-quarter moon peered down from the dark Haitian sky.

The drumming and the dancing, the mounting of the spirits and the quivering of bodies, would continue until nearly sunrise. But I had to return to Port-au-Prince the next morning — I planned to leave Haiti the day after. So I headed back to Herard Simon's house well before dawn. That night, as I drifted off to sleep in the sweltering darkness of the Artibonite Valley, I found myself thinking, not about *loas*, but about flesh-and-blood people — the Haitians I had met — and I remembered a traditional *créole* farewell I had learned. *Bonsoi, dam mrin. Pralé dodo.*

Goodnight, pretty women. I will sleep.

The
Price
of Beer

O N MY FIRST TRIP to revolutionary Angola, I was driving one morning along the rubble-strewn streets of the capital, heading back to my hotel. I swung around a corner to my right, and I was promptly waved over to the side of the road by an Angolan police-woman in a brown beret.

She marched up to my side of the car, asked for my papers, and proceeded to flip through them, just taking her time. She was evidently looking for something out of order. She found nothing that qualified, however, and so she reluctantly handed the documents back. Still, she did not let me drive on. I guessed that I was about to be pressed for a bribe, and I was prepared for that, or thought I was. But I was not ready for what this policewoman actually said. Instead of insinuating something to me about cash, she came out with what seemed to be a complete *non sequitur*.

"You don't," she wondered, "happen to have any beer in tins?"

I just looked at her. "Beer?" I repeated.

She nodded. "In tins."

I was not in the habit of carrying tinned beer in my car, and I didn't have any now. I told her so, and she grimaced and hemmed and hawed but finally let me continue on my way.

Still, the encounter got me thinking — why would a traffic policewoman in Luanda try to shake down a foreign motorist for a tin or two of beer? Did all Angolans carry tinned beer in their cars as a matter of course, or for the express purpose of quenching the thirst of corrupt traffic officials? Was this some arcane Angolan custom that seemed unreasonable only to the uninitiated?

It turned out that what I'd encountered in the person of that traffic policewoman was the *real* Angolan economy at work, as opposed to the formal economy, which basically did not exist. In Angola, in the late 1980s, everybody had a little something going on the side, and monetary stability — such as it was — came packed under pressure in a can.

In Angola, beer *was* money — literally. Individual tins of imported beer served as the equivalent of a monetary system. They were used as cash, but they also provided the basis for determining the value of most other commodities. When Angolans bartered among themselves — a quantity of grain, say, for a pair of shoes — they calculated the relative value of their goods in terms of beer. Everything was related back to that. An Angolan family could live, albeit frugally, on two cases of twenty-four tins per month, bartering or reselling the brew one tin at a time. As I discovered, even the police were in on it; beer was the currency in which they sought bribes from foreign motorists.

The main reason that Angolans resorted to using beer as a substitute for cash was simple: they had to use *something*. In

Angola, paper money was a joke. The official currency was called the *kwanza*, and it was valued at about twenty-three to the US dollar, but that rate was absurdly out of touch with the world in which Angolans really dwelled, where the real rate of exchange was calculated in terms of beer. In Angola, the street value of a case of twenty-four tins of imported beer was a cool twenty-eight-thousand kwanzas. At the official rate of exchange, this worked out to $1,225 US — for a case of beer! Here was one good reason that no one in his right mind ever used the official rate of exchange.

There were others. A dozen years after Portugal's African empire collapsed in a heap, here was poor revolutionary Angola, stumbling along with its national currency still pegged to the value of the Portuguese *escudo*, circa 1975. That static rate remained the basis for the formal economy — except that, in Angola, there *was* no formal economy. There was only the pretence of one.

Let's assume that you were a foreign visitor to Angola in the late 1980s and were foolish enough to change your money at the official rate, something that nobody with a discernible brainwave pattern would conceivably ever do. (Okay — I did it once. But *only* once.) Let's assume further that you had managed to borrow someone's ration card and wished to purchase a kilogram of beans at a government store. The official price for a kilogram of beans was forty-five kwanzas and so, at the official exchange rate, your purchase of beans would cost you the equivalent of less than $2. Not bad for a kilo of beans — until you considered that, in Angola, *you could not buy beans at a government store.* Oh, in theory, you could. But, in practice, no.

In practice, if you wanted to buy beans — or just about

anything else — you would have had to venture out to one of Luanda's sprawling circus-like black markets, known as *candonguas*, the largest of which was called Roque Santeiro, after the title of a Brazilian soap opera. Here, you could obtain all the beans you could afford, but you would have had to pay in real money. Out here, a kilogram of beans would set you back, not forty-five kwanzas, but *three thousand*. At the official rate of exchange, this worked out to exactly $128.65 US — for a kilo of beans. That's pretty steep. But, in fact, nobody bought beans at the official rate. Instead, they used beer, imported, in tins.

"Everything is more or less related to that," said an Argentine acquaintance of mine, a woman who'd lived and worked in Angola for many years. "For the past year, beer has stayed at about the same price."

The price of beer served to determine the value of almost everything else. That was certainly true at Roque Santeiro, where Angolan shoppers could wander through row upon row of makeshift stalls, all burgeoning upon a broad slope of red earth, with a panoramic view of a huge unofficial garbage dump. Beyond, the sparkling blue waters of Luanda Bay. Here, they could obtain consumer goods ranging from the most humble — beans, say, or a cassava porridge called *fungi*, the staple of the Angolan diet — to scotch whisky, French champagne, and knock-offs of US blue jeans. If they wished, they could pay ten thousand kwanzas — or about six tins of beer — for a litre of vegetable oil boldly stamped with the information that it was "furnished by the people of the United States of America," who presumably did not expect their gift of food to be sold for profit.

But this was Angola, and goods shipped as international

aid not uncommonly ended up being sold for cash — or beer. In fact, most of the merchandise on sale at Angola's *candonguas* had probably been pilfered from somewhere, from the port in Luanda, for example, or from government warehouses or factories. Angolans referred to such theft as *fazer desvio* — making detours — and it was the most common means by which people supplemented their low official incomes, enabling them to live on the beer economy.

Beer got into Angola by several different routes. For example, European and US petroleum firms with operations in the country all ran company stores where their employees could purchase imported goods — including beer — for hard currency. The Angolan government itself operated a vast duty-free retail emporium for diplomats and others with access to foreign currency. Known as the Jumbo, the store squatted near the inland edge of Luanda. It was a huge monument to Mammon, jammed with imported foods and consumer goods, including ten different brands of scotch whisky and seven kinds of imported beer.

It was the beer that caught your eye, for the stacked cases of German, Danish, and Belgian ales and lagers seemed to stretch until forever. But you had to have hard currency to buy them. A case of twenty-four tins of beer cost about $17 US, and the lineups at the Jumbo's fifteen cash registers were perpetually crowded with diplomats or foreign-aid officers, all pushing shopping carts piled high with six, seven, or even eight tottering cases.

Outside the store, the parking lot was usually buzzing with local women in kerchiefs and bright wraparound skirts, whose job it was to buy the beer — Angola's equivalent of the gold standard — and lug it away. They paid a stable price of twenty-eight thousand kwanzas a case, representing the black-market (or true) rate of exchange. The cases would then be broken up and the beer bartered or resold at fifteen hundred kwanzas a tin, which made a tidy profit for these women.

All this heady but unofficial economic activity was quietly tolerated by the Angolan government, which probably explains why the state-run Jumbo was never out of beer. "They run out of tea," my Argentine friend told me. "They run out of coffee. They run out of milk. But beer?" She shook her head. "They *never* run out of beer."

It was true — they never did. What I found most astonishing about the beer economy in Angola was how efficiently it seemed to be working. That was a rare thing in Angola where, at least at first glance, almost everything else seemed to be falling apart. Luanda, for example — once the pearl of Portugal's overseas possessions — was now an urban disaster zone, swollen by refugees and crumbling from neglect. Once, the city must have been a wonderful place to live, at least if you happened to be wealthy and white. During colonial times, it had been home to roughly 300,000 Portuguese settlers who divided their time between hilltop mansions and offices in the tiled, medium-rise buildings that traced the palm-lined arc of the Avenida Marginal.

On weekends, they ferried themselves out across the sky-blue waters of Luanda Bay to the finger-shaped Ilha de Luanda or to a sandy chain of low coastal islets that dot the Atlantic coast of Portuguese Africa. There, they sipped ample quantities of beer or *vinho verde* and whiled away another slow colonial afternoon — plump, bronze, and happy in a way that maybe only white expatriates with a lockgrip on power in a black country can ever manage to be. For that small European minority, Luanda must have been a kind of heaven.

But it was not to last. A liberation war broke out, Angola won its independence, the Portuguese fled, and before very long the place was a mess — crumbling, peeling, boarded-up, and filthy. Twelve years after the Portuguese withdrew, the skyline of Luanda was still punctured here and there by the bones of pre-independence apartment towers, still half-finished and long abandoned, with their rusted construction cranes still tottering at their sides. There was almost no legitimate commerce any longer, and only the black market thrived.

Almost everywhere I looked, in the capital and beyond, I saw disrepair and decay, all set against the clamour and din of war. Angola had once been the world's third-largest coffee producer, self-sufficient in beef and grain, with an impressive industrial infrastructure. But now, apart from a godsend of oil platforms bobbing off the coast of the northern Cabinda enclave, the economy had gone up in smoke, rust, and gelignite.

Angola's precipitous decline was not really surprising in retrospect. For one thing, the country was at war. Besides, when the Portuguese fled in 1975, they took with them their monopoly on modern technical and managerial skills, the very skills that had kept *their* Angola going. There was certainly no ready supply of African technocrats waiting in the wings to take over.

This was a fate that Angola shared with many other newly independent African states. In Mozambique, for example — another former Portuguese colony in southern

Africa — there are said to have been a total of just twelve black Mozambicans with university degrees at the time the Portuguese withdrew. This was in a society of about fourteen *million* people. Hard to believe? Perhaps. So let's say that the number is wrong. Let's say it wasn't twelve blacks with university degrees. Let's say it was 120. Or 1,200. It doesn't matter. It wouldn't have made any difference. Even if there'd been three *thousand* black Mozambicans with university degrees, there still would not have been remotely enough people with the kind of technical and managerial skills needed to keep the country's European institutions and facilities intact. Of course they fell apart. What else could they do? This was true in Mozambique, and it was true in Angola.

When the post-independence government assumed power in Luanda, under a poet-turned-politician named Agostinho Neto, it sought to impose Marxist-Leninist economic policies. The government nationalized just about everything in sight, right down to the smallest of barbershops, and it did this in large measure because socialism was a principle to which the new Angolan leaders subscribed. But a provincial governor told me years later that, even had Neto and his colleagues been inveterate capitalists, they probably would have felt compelled to take over everything anyway, including the barbershops. The plain fact was, no black person in Angola knew how to make a living by cutting hair. So what was the new government to do?

Besides, no sooner had the Portuguese withdrawn than the various nationalist factions fell to fighting among themselves, each with its foreign patrons. The MPLA — Portuguese abbreviation for the People's Movement for the

Liberation of Angola — seized power under Neto and with the backing of thousands of Cuban troops. Pitted against it was UNITA — the National Union for the Total Independence of Angola — under Jonas Savimbi, who was supported by South Africa and the United States. A smaller third force had backing from Zaïre, but did not last long. Twenty years later, however, the MPLA and UNITA were still at war.

Independent Angola was born in blood and has never known peace. In its first ten years, the war claimed at least a 100,000 lives as direct casualties. God knows how many more died as indirect victims, killed by hunger maybe, or inadequate health care. Child mortality reached almost unimaginable levels. In some parts of the country, nearly five hundred children out of every one thousand died in their first five years. In only a decade, according to a UN estimate, the direct cost of the fighting had reached $17 billion US. And still the conflict raged on.

At first glance — and second glance, and maybe third glance too — Angola was a mess. You had only to walk into any state-run store in Luanda to see that much. These were the places ordinary Angolans went, in theory, to purchase their monthly rations. In practice, however, the state-run stores were nearly always empty, for the shelves were nearly always bare. Not *almost* bare. *Completely* bare.

One afternoon in Luanda, I strolled into a typical government store to see how things were going. The lights were off, because the electricity wasn't working, and a dozen or so staff members loitered about, doing nothing and looking glum. The shelves were vacant. Of ten basic rationed commodities supposedly provided by this store, only two — beans and sugar — had *ever* been in stock during the previous month.

This was socialism, Angolan-style, and it was a disaster. Maybe a centrally-planned economy is a workable thing, capable of providing goods and services in an orderly fashion, but such a system would require one thing before all others: it would require a large and highly trained corps of technocrats — all those people charged with making the thousands of central decisions required every day in order to keep a command economy ticking over. That would be an ornery business in the best of circumstances. Even European socialists weren't able to manage it very well, and they had access to a lot of highly skilled people.

In Luanda, there were no traffic lights, and almost nothing worked. The electricity was sporadic or non-existent. Water mains burst and were left to gush for days. No shops were open, except the official government stores, and they were almost always empty because enterprising Angolans were making a living by diverting all or most of the merchandise to the sprawling illegal markets. Lots of people got by that way. And since the official monetary system didn't work, they invented another; they used beer as currency.

Almost everyone in Angola had some kind of *esquema* for survival. Whoever had access to a government vehicle, for example, would "borrow" it for a couple of hours a day, to provide an unofficial taxi service at black-market rates. Whoever received part of his wages in consumer goods — a fairly common practice — would immediately barter or sell them on the black market. Someone with a friend who worked for one of the foreign petroleum companies — Angola's principal source of wealth — would thereby have access to the considerable stocks of imported consumer goods on sale at the company stores, which he could then barter away.

Almost anybody in a position to steal, stole. And, never mind the official prohibition on private enterprise, almost anybody with anything to sell, sold. The grubby downtown heart of Luanda was kept alive by enterprising women known as *kitandeiras*, who squatted on old powdered-milk tins and hawked their meagre stocks of beans or cigarettes, surrounded by empty buildings and crumbling façades.

Angola's official economy was almost entirely a sham, and government services were mostly mirages, but "arrangements" could be made. If you had a car that needed fixing, or a passport that needed renewing, or a telephone that had to be connected, there was always a way. You merely had to find a *cunha* — that special individual who could be found lurking in just about any institution and who would be willing, for an appropriate fee, to ensure that the machinery of state grumbled briefly into motion in order to produce the required good or service.

From the outside, Angola looked like a place that didn't work at all. But that impression was wrong, an illusion. In fact, Angola did work, in its way. Somehow people came up with the arrangements they needed for getting things done, and they got on with their lives.

Enough
Land for
the Walking

E VEN THE MOST INTRACTABLE of this planet's wars
have a way of winding down in time. In 1988, after
decades of bloodshed, it at last began to seem that
the war in Angola was starting to dwindle. And then, with
astonishing speed, a ceasefire was negotiated and signed by
Angola, Cuba, and South Africa, all of which had troops
fighting in the country. Suddenly, Angolans faced a prospect
they had scarcely imagined for much of their lives — they
could start to think about peace.

Unfortunately, a parallel conflict continued to grind on,
pitting government forces against UNITA rebels under Jonas
Savimbi, and *that* war would persist for years to come. Even
so, you could already sense a faint euphoria in the air.
Already, people seemed to be emerging from the ruins.

Shortly after the ceasefire went into effect, I and several
other foreign journalists made a trek down into the far south
of Angola, where the war had been waged most bitterly. We
rode in the backs of army trucks, past ruined bridges, abandoned villages, and whole towns demolished by the long
years of fighting. Along a ninety-kilometre route that ran

southeast from Kahama to Xangongo — a vital supply corridor — our truck bounced across a high plateau dotted by cattle kraals, mud-and-wattle villages, and tall rickety baobab trees. This was Africa as it had been for centuries, maybe millenia. At times, our surroundings seemed so peaceful, so apparently timeless, that I could almost pretend that people hadn't been dying here in shocking numbers or that these plains hadn't been overrun by the machines of war.

At other times, though, we drove past Angolan and Cuban military installations — intricate networks of trenches, foxholes, and bunkers bristling with tanks, cannons, and batteries of anti-aircraft rockets, all partly hidden by copses of trees or covered by camouflage netting. And one morning, a pair of Soviet-built MiG-23 fighter-bombers streaked overhead, slicing through the African sky like a pair of supersonic arrowheads. In close formation, they rolled onto their sides, roaring above the thatched huts and scrub growth of the southern plateaux. Suddenly, they rocketed away, their afterburners leaving two pale orange traces in the faint morning haze. So much, I thought, for the silent timelessness of the sprawling African veld.

Few civilians were out hiking along the roads in those days, and there was almost no civilian traffic, apart from an occasional nearly derelict truck bumping along on wonky axles through a private cloud of dense brown smoke. But, here and there, we did see the flesh-and-blood signs of ordinary life returning to the land — small clusters of people going about their business, striding along footpaths that criss-crossed the dun-coloured earth. Mostly, they were members of the Mamuila clan, a subgroup of the Ovambo people who predominate in southern Angola, just as they do across the border in northern Namibia.

When we got to Xangongo, we found a town battered almost to oblivion — a charred and jagged ruin of rubble and gutted houses where only a single church remained intact. And yet, people were returning to the place already, to try to recover their former lives. Outside the town, we drove across a long low bridge that spanned the Kunene River. It had been blown up and rebuilt God knew how many times and was now a roller-coaster of crumpled concrete and mangled reinforcement bars. It could still be crossed though — very slowly, one vehicle at a time.

There were about half a dozen of us on this trip, all foreign reporters based in different parts of Africa — Abidjan, Harare, Johannesburg. I already knew most of the others passably well, from previous assignments in other lands. One morning, the Angolans flew us by Russian-built helicopter from Kahama down to the border with Namibia. The South Africans and the Angolans — sworn enemies only a month earlier — were now preparing to institute joint patrols along the frontier, aimed at monitoring compliance with the terms of the ceasefire. We were to observe the process as it was getting underway.

We arrived at about noon, escorted by an Angolan officer named Major Osvaldo Van Dunem. He was thirty-eight years old and was a handsome, informal, and gregarious man. He wore a thick moustache, and his freckled brown face had a polished glow, like varnished teak or mahogany. We'd got to know him pretty well during the trip so far, thanks mainly to his appetite for kibbitzing with the press. Even on the roughest roads — and all the roads were rough

— he liked to ride in the back of the truck with us, telling war stories. The women journalists were all pretty taken with him, and he hadn't exactly made enemies of the men.

When our helicopter set down near the Namibian frontier, there was a vehicle on hand to drive us to the border post at Wacana. Here, we were greeted by about a dozen military officers gathered in the sparse shade of a grove of scrubby mopane trees. Half the officers were Angolan, half South African. For almost fifteen years, they'd been trying to blow each other up. Now, here they were, about to give a joint al fresco news conference for a gaggle of foreign hacks. At least the setting was appropriate for the occasion — we were surrounded by ruins. Once, there had been some buildings here; now, just rubble and the scattered, crumbling remnants of walls.

But the war was apparently over now, and so there was at last something to celebrate. The South African Defence Force had set up a refectory table under the trees and laid out a quantity of beverages — bottles of Paarl wine and tins of Lion lager, Coca-Cola, and orange soda. They insisted that there be drinks and small talk first, formal questions later — a remarkably civilized notion in the circumstances.

One by one, the South African officers introduced themselves by their first names and then raised their drinks to the glaring midday sun. We all stood about in the remains of a battle zone, sipping beer, wine, or orange soda, three very disparate groups trying to mingle. The conversation kept being interrupted by the smack and boom of exploding bombs, courtesy of a team of Angolan sappers who, with the aid of a South African engineer, were detonating the slews of landmines that had been sown around us over the years.

When the formal news conference began, the South Africans promptly insisted that they truly were determined to end this war, despite considerable skepticism from the outside world. "People are not giving folks a fair chance," protested Colonel David Moore of the SADF — or "David" as he had urged us to call him. "We are very optimistic."

At the time, I wasn't so sure that optimism was really the most realistic sentiment. And yet it turned out that Colonel Moore was exactly right. The ceasefire held. A lasting peace was eventually signed. In due course, both the South Africans and the Cubans withdrew for good from Angola. And, at least in its international dimension, the war was at an end. On the other hand, the local fighting dragged on, as Jonas Savimbi and his UNITA rebels continued to battle government forces, just as they have been doing since independence in 1975. For Angola, one war was finally over, but another war ground on.

Not long after that memorable afternoon — libations under the mopane trees with the officer corps of two African armies — I departed Angola for the last time. It was a frustrating thing to leave a country that remained in such an unresolved state, at once at war and not at war. Still, there was a coda to my experience of Angola, and it made me hope that this country, like the rest of Africa, would survive and maybe even flourish, despite its troubles, war or no war.

I was in Namibia at the time, the mostly arid region that sprawls south of Angola. This was one of several trips I would make there, to cover the territory's uneasy progress towards independence after decades of illegal South African rule. One weekday afternoon, I set off alone from Windhoek, the Namibian capital, to drive north to the

Angolan border. There had long been war in Namibia too, and it was in the north that the fighting had been heaviest. Recently, it had broken out again.

Namibia covers a vast terrain, balanced between two deserts — the Kalahari to the east and the Namib to the west — and the land has a monumental quality to it, at once beautiful and severe. I travelled through desert or semi-desert all the way, across sprawling basins, past abrupt and treeless ridges, through vast groves of scrubby acacia trees — pale green cottonballs scattered across the sand-paper earth.

I made the trip in two stages. The first took me from Windhoek up to a town called Tsumeb. As I drove, the afternoon sunshine slanted over the scrub bush to the west and splayed across the shallow treeless valleys ahead. Dusk sailed down from the north, where a huge storm was building. Before long, immense black clouds covered the entire horizon. They billowed across the sky like some great black nemesis, its surface shattered every few seconds by sudden bolts of lightning that made me think of cosmic exclamation points. The lightning rattled and exploded in the distance, and the dense African night seemed to swallow the earth.

Not far south of Tsumeb, I drove through a range of low rounded hills and suddenly plummeted into the bowels of what was the most violent electrical storm I've ever encountered. Little rain fell, but those great shafts of lightning ripped through the night all around me. On the nearby hills, small mopane trees exploded, and bushes only a few feet from the road burst into flames, as if strings of landmines were being detonated by some celestial tap-dancer. I tightened my grip on the wheel, tried not to touch anything metallic in the car, and drove on to Tsumeb through this unnerving spectacle of fire, this battle of earth and sky.

The following morning, it was over. Sunshine returned, and I drove north past the town of Oshakati and up toward Ruacana on the border with Angola. That long road barely wavered, as if it had been built on the edge of a straight rule through what South Africa had long referred to euphemistically as its Northern Operational Area — in fact, its northern war zone. There was very little traffic, apart from SADF vehicles roaring back and forth in impressive convoys, like giant mud-green bugs.

The only other hazards along the way were strictly pastoral. Now and again, small herds of cattle or goats made poky road-crossings, followed by barefoot boys with crooked staffs. Here and there, dozing donkeys sunned themselves along the median. There wasn't much vegetation apart from the scattered steel-wool clumps of mopane trees or spindly palms that jutted above the clay soil, like pinwheels.

Although Namibia is among the most sparsely populated areas in Africa, Ovamboland is an exception. Roughly half of the country's 1.3 million inhabitants dwell here in the traditional homeland of the Wambo people, who migrated to southern Angola and northern Namibia during the fourteenth century, after roaming down from the great lakes of east Africa. Even in Ovamboland, however, there is no sense of human congestion. The major towns are really something of an illusion. Ruacana, for example, is a pinprick on the map where the Kunene River nudges the Angolan border before heading west to plunge toward the coastal Namib desert and the sea.

I drove on, north of Ruacana, to a fault line where northern Namibia suddenly drops off the broad wall of the coastal escarpment. In the northern distance, a range of blunt sawtooth peaks gnawed at the sky, flanked by a vast African plain. This was the border, and what lay beyond it was Angola. I drove right up to the border post, which didn't amount to much — basically a couple of security checkpoints and a gap in a low wire fence. I parked my car in the long dry grass and got out for a closer look.

It was late morning by now, and the sun beat down onto a series of low hills lightly forested with mopane trees. Everything here seemed oddly familiar; yet it took a few moments before I realized where I was. Finally, it came to me: this was the exact same spot on the very same border that I had visited seven months earlier, when I'd flown down in a Russian-built helicopter with Major Osvaldo Van Dunem of the Angolan armed forces. I recalled those drinks beneath the mopane trees, and the shuddering smack of exploding landmines. But now I was coming to the place from the opposite direction, from Namibia.

At the border post on the Namibian side, about a half-dozen SADF conscripts in brown drab were lounging beneath a corrugated metal shelter. Meanwhile, about ten paces to the north, two Angolan soldiers in camouflage fatigues stood duty at a pocked concrete sentry box. The two groups seemed to be paying little attention to one another. They were separated by a steel control bar, painted yellow and black, to which a red Stop sign had been attached. Two flags flew overhead — one, the orange and black banner of the People's Republic of Angola; the other, the white-on-blue emblem of the United Nations, for the

UN was overseeing Namibia's transition to political independence, in the aftermath of a clutch of southern African wars.

Right now, however, all was quiet. It was just another morning at the tail end of the rainy season, and the soldiers on both sides of the border looked pretty bored. For years, this very spot had been Ground Zero for three seemingly intractable conflicts, but the fighting was mostly over now, and there didn't seem to be much here to write home about.

So I started back to my car — and it was then that something caught my eye. I turned back towards Angola and saw a small herd of cattle rounding a bend in the road, visible through a break in a thicket of mopane trees. Moments later, I could make out some humans — a dozen Himma people, nomadic pastoralists, striding down from Angola. As they marched across the dry borderlands, they seemed like some flesh-and-blood vision of an ancient forgotten Africa. The men were straight-backed and bare-chested, in short black skirts. They carried long wooden staffs and gazed straight ahead.

The women were breathtaking — powerfully built, bare-breasted, with loops of leather strung like martingales over their shoulders and attached to short, red leather loincloths. The women held their heads preternaturally high, supported by stacks of thick silver necklaces. They thrust their shoulders back as they walked, their long arms swinging freely at their sides. On their wrists, they wore bracelets intricately woven in leather. Large bands of silver encircled their ankles. From their foreheads to their toes, the women's bodies were a reddish hue, rubbed with fine ochre clay. They balanced baskets of animal skins atop their heads.

The Himma people approached the border as if it wasn't there. They didn't slow their pace by a fraction or betray any hint that they were going to seek anyone's permission to cross some arbitrary line on the ground, a border that had nothing whatever to do with them. They walked up to the post with their cattle, and nobody said a word. The Angolan soldiers merely stepped back a few paces. The South Africans raised the steel barrier. Without a gesture or a break in their stride, the Himma people passed from Angola into Namibia, as if there were no such thing as separate countries, no war, no guns, no cripples, and no silent legions of the dead. The soldiers said nothing; they just hung back and watched these strange ambassadors go.

I did the same. I kept looking at the party of Himma people until they dwindled south into what the world calls Namibia. Before long, they vanished from my view. And, in the stillness of their absence, I could have sworn that the only things in life worth bothering about were these — enough land for the walking, some friends to share the walking with, the promise of rain.

Before long, I got back into the car and began the return leg of my trip, but I didn't pass the Himma people on my way. I suppose they had turned off on some road of their own, and it was a different road from mine. My road led down to Windhoek, to a hotel room, a portable computer, another story to file. Through the windshield of my car, the view consisted of roughly one part earth and three parts heaven. I felt as though I were weightless, as though nothing could hold me down. I picked up speed and soon had my foot pressed almost to the floor. I flew south across Ovamboland, through the crackling blue vault of an African sky.